The new interventionism, 1991–1994

WITHDRÁWN

At the end of the Cold War the hope was that it would be possible to reform international society. With the Security Council of the United Nations no longer immobilised by the constant threat of the veto, and the success of Operation Desert Storm in the Gulf War, there was widespread enthusiasm for the idea of a 'new world order'. Its central feature would be international intervention, not merely to deter or repel aggression across frontiers, but to protect the victims of civil conflicts within states. These hopes remain largely unfulfilled.

This book contributes to our understanding of this failure by examining the three major post-Cold War operations in which the UN has been involved. Each presented the international community with a different challenge: in Cambodia it was to implement a previously negotiated political agreement; in former Yugoslavia to devise a credible 2003 division of labour and authority between the UN and the European Union; and in Somalia to mount a humanitarian mission in a country without a government. In each case the authors focus on the problem of drafting and implementing appropriate mandates. The introduction explores the common themes as well as the major contrasts in the three operations and raises important questions about the possibilities for and limits of international reform. In addition, each chapter is accompanied by a chronology of events and a selection of relevant UN documents.

# The new interventionism 1991–1994

*United Nations experience in Cambodia, former Yugoslavia and Somalia*

*Edited by*
James Mayall
*London School of Economics and Political Science*

CAMBRIDGE
UNIVERSITY PRESS

Published by the Press Syndicate of the University of Cambridge
The Pitt Building, Trumpington Street, Cambridge CB2 1RP
40 West 20th Street, New York, NY 10011–4211, USA
10 Stamford Road, Oakleigh, Melbourne 3166, Australia

First published 1996

Printed in Great Britain at the University Press, Cambridge

*A catalogue record for this book is available from the British Library*

*Library of Congress cataloguing in publication data*

The new interventionism 1991–1994 : United Nations experience in
  Cambodia, former Yugoslavia and Somalia / edited by James Mayall.
    p.    cm. – (LSE monographs in international studies)
  ISBN 0 521 55197 8 (hc) – ISBN 0 521 55856 5 (pb)
    1. Cambodia – Politics and government – 1975–  2. United Nations –
Cambodia.   3. Yugoslavia – Politics and government – 1992–  4. United
Nations – Yugoslavia.   5. Somalia – Politics and government – 1960–
6. United Nations – Somalia.   I. Mayall, James.   II. Series.
DS554.8.N48   1996
341.5'84 – dc20   95–38498 CIP

ISBN 0 521 55197 8 hardback
ISBN 0 521 55856 5 paperback

# Contents

# Maps

# Contributors

DR MATS BERDAL, Research Fellow, International Institute of Strategic Studies

DR SPYROS ECONOMIDES, Lecturer in International Relations and European Politics, London School of Economics and Political Science

PROFESSOR MICHAEL LEIFER, Professor of International Relations and Pro-Director, London School of Economics and Political Science

PROFESSOR I. M. LEWIS, Emeritus Professor of Anthropology, London School of Economics and Political Science

PROFESSOR JAMES MAYALL, Professor of International Relations and Chairman of the Steering Committee, Centre for International Studies, London School of Economics and Political Science

DR PAUL TAYLOR, Reader in International Relations, London School of Economics and Political Science

# Acknowledgements

The authors are much indebted to Mrs Judy Weeden and Ms Elaine Childs for generous secretarial assistance in the preparation of this book; to Ms Molly Cochran and Dr Karin von Hippel for help in preparing the chronologies and appendixes; and to the stimulation provided by all those who attended the seminars and workshops held at the LSE on International Society Since the End of the Cold War where some of our ideas were explored and refined. We are also grateful to the Ford Foundation which funded this latter project. None of these people can be held responsible for our views.

# 1  Introduction

*James Mayall*

> The nations and peoples of the United Nations are fortunate in a way
> that those of the League of Nations were not. We have been given a
> second chance to create the world of our Charter that they were
> denied. With the cold war ended we have drawn back from the brink
> of a confrontation that threatened the world, and, too often, paralysed
> our organisation.[1]                                    Boutros Boutros-Ghali

What are the chances that international society will be able to respond
positively to the second chance identified by the United Nations
Secretary-General? The scale of UN activity since the end of the Cold
War might be offered as evidence that we are entering an era when
international obligations will at last rank alongside the defence of
national interests, even if they will not necessarily take precedence over
them. Of the twenty-nine 'peacekeeping' operations established by the
UN since 1945, sixteen have been created since 1987.[2] At the same
time, few of these operations have been unqualified successes, and the
demands placed on the UN system can equally be interpreted as evidence of spreading chaos and widespread threats to stability and international order in the wake of the collapse of familiar Cold War structures. Moreover, the potential demand for UN intervention around the
world is clearly greater than the Organisation's ability to respond, given
the resources currently available to it, or which seem likely to be made
available in the foreseeable future. Indeed, by the end of 1993 there
were clear signs that the governments of the major powers were more
interested in limiting than extending their international commitments.
These signs were most marked in the United States where anti-
peacekeeping sentiment was fuelled by the fact that the United States

---

[1] Boutros Boutros-Ghali, *Agenda for Peace: Preventive Diplomacy, Peacemaking and Peace-keeping. Report of the Secretary-General Pursuant to the Statement Adopted by the Summit Meeting of the Security Council on 31 January 1992* (New York: United Nations, 1992), para. 75.

[2] Sally Morphet, 'UN Peace Keeping and Election-Monitoring', in Adam Roberts and Benedict Kingsbury (eds.), *United Nations, Divided World*, 2nd edn (Oxford: Clarendon Press, 1993), p. 183 and Appendix E.

currently pays 31.7 per cent of the overall peacekeeping budget; there is also strong congressional opposition to placing American troops under foreign command.[3] But, judging by the speed with which many troop-supplying countries followed the American lead in announcing their withdrawal from Somalia in 1994,[4] United States' reluctance to see UN operations expand further is widely shared.

Whether the major powers will be able to reverse the trend of internationally coordinated efforts at crisis management, even should they wish to do so, is unclear. The trend was started during the closing stages of the Iran–Iraq war, when Mikhail Gorbachev's rise to power in the Soviet Union ended the paralysis of the UN Security Council. With the threat of the veto removed, a period of close cooperation among the five permanent members (P5) was inaugurated. The world is now so interdependent, and western governments in particular so vulnerable to public opinion mobilised through the media, that there can be no guarantee that they will not repeatedly be drawn into international crises, even where their own instincts and the balance of professional advice are in favour of non-intervention. The Secretary-General's challenge should not, therefore, be lightly dismissed. His *Agenda for Peace* may have been a product of the natural but unrealistic optimism that followed the end of the Cold War, but it raised the central political questions of our time – what is to be the basis of international order and how is it to be upheld?

The book is intended as a modest contribution to the debate about how these questions should be answered. Our aim is to see what an examination of three major interventions that have been carried out by the United Nations since 1991 – in Cambodia, former Yugoslavia and Somalia – can tell us about the prospects for international cooperation and the constraints that must be overcome if the UN Charter is to act as a constitution for international society, as the Secretary-General implies it should.

The crucial issue in this respect is the drafting and implementation of appropriate and authoritative mandates. Each of these operations illustrated a different aspect of the mandate problem that provides the main focus of each chapter: in Cambodia the primary problem was one of implementation following the Paris peace accords; in Somalia of the appropriateness of using Chapter VII in a situation in which the govern-

---

[3] 'The Clinton Administration's Policy on Reforming Multilateral Peace Operations' (Presidential Decision Directive (PDD) 25), issued on 5 May 1994. For the Executive Summary of this report, see *US Department of State Despatch*, 16 May 1994, vol. 5, no. 20.

[4] See chapter 4, pp. 117–8.

ment had admittedly collapsed but when there was not obviously any clear threat to international peace and security; and in former Yugoslavia the problem was one of a constantly shifting and evolving mandate together with a much more complex relationship between the regional organisation and the United Nations than in either of the other two cases. The purpose of this introduction is first to sketch the historical background out of which the 'new interventionism' emerged, and second to identify common issues that have been raised by the three crises and lessons that can be derived from the experience of the UN in its attempt to facilitate an appropriate international response.

The problem of intervention – or rather whether it can ever be justified, and if so, under what circumstances – lies at the heart of all debates about international order. Before turning to the immediate historical background of the rapid expansion of United Nations Organisation activity in the security field, it may be helpful therefore to outline the contending positions.[5] Apart from those un-reconstructed realists who deny the possibility of international society, there is a broad consensus that it exists, but primarily as a society of sovereign states, not peoples. On this view, while states are primarily concerned with defending their own interests, as defined by governments, they also combine to uphold the institutions of international society: international law, diplomacy and, more contentiously, the balance of power and the special responsibility of the great powers for international order. However, the consensus breaks down at this point. On one side stand the pluralists, those who maintain that sovereignty demands minimal rules of coexistence, above all that of non-interference in the domestic affairs of other states. The one exception to the ethic of self-help that underlines the pluralist position is to allow for alliances to deter or resist aggression. Against them are ranged the solidarists: those who hold that sovereignty is conditional and that the existence of an international society requires us to determine both the ends to which, in principle, all states, nations and

---

[5] There have been a number of attempts to classify international thought according to the positions adopted by theorists and statesmen on such issues as sovereignty, the use of force, intervention and international cooperation. The most influential are Martin Wight, *International Theory: The Three Traditions*, Gabrielle Wight and Brian Porter (eds.) (Leicester: Leicester University Press, for the Royal Institute of International Affairs, 1992); Hedley Bull, *The Anarchical Society* (London: Macmillan, 1977); and Michael Donelan, *Elements of International Theory* (Oxford: Oxford University Press, 1991). Wight and Bull offer a triad of positions – realist, rationalist and revolutionist – while Donelan identifies five – realist, rationalist, historicist, fideist and natural law. In this introduction I have reduced the positions to two – pluralist or solidarist – on the grounds that it was the compromise between these two positions, and the various combinations of rationalist and realist assumptions on which they rest, that shaped the UN Charter, and hence frames the current debate on UN intervention.

*Ideological stance*

peoples should be committed, and the means by which international society should be upheld.

Those who hold to the pluralist position – i.e. of an international society defined by the law of coexistence – do not deny that intervention occurs. On occasion, they may even consider it justified, for example, to maintain the balance of power, or to counter an intervention by a hostile state. But they would be unlikely to accept the notion of a disinterested collective intervention to uphold an abstract conception of international order. This is because they believe that coexistence between sovereign powers rules out the possibility of developing a genuine community of mankind. Pluralists might concede, to quote a recent American formulation, that intervention is justified where 'there is an international community of *interest* for dealing with [a] problem on a multilateral basis',[6] but they would reject any suggestion that it could ever be justified merely in defence of a common humanity, or by reference to an organic theory of society under which a surgical intervention might be deemed necessary to cut out a cancerous growth before it spread. It is probably fair to say that, left to themselves, the governments of the major powers would have continued to favour a pluralist interpretation of international society over more solidarist conceptions, under which state sovereignty is qualified by a wider set of obligations. But they have not been left alone. The experiences of the twentieth century, two world wars, the ideological confrontation between capitalism and communism, the relentless pressures of an expanding world market and, above all, the repeated experience of genocide from the Holocaust in the 1930s and 1940s, through Pol Pot's regime in Kampuchea during the 1970s, to the Rwandan tragedy of 1994–5, have led them to flirt with various forms of internationalism and/or cosmopolitanism, without ever carrying through the fundamental restructuring that would be required to put them into practice. Thus, after both World War I and World War II, it was the victorious great powers that were the primary architects of the League of Nations and the United Nations, organisations that faithfully reflected the confusion on the pluralist/solidarist divide which reigned in their own societies.

The Charter of the United Nations represents an attempt to bridge the two conceptions of international society. Under Chapter VII, the Charter countenances collective action to deter manifest threats to international peace and security. This commitment is arguably consistent with pluralist beliefs, since it can be represented as a global extension

---

[6] PDD 25, my italics.

of the right to form alliances, with the same objective. Indeed, from this point of view, collective security is in effect an alliance of the whole, under the responsible leadership of the Security Council. But the Charter also binds its signatories to respect certain fundamental human rights, including the right of all peoples to self-determination. These latter commitments rest on unambiguously solidarist assumptions. They therefore beg the question: how should international society respond when peoples' allegedly fundamental rights are systematically abused not by other states but by their own governments?

Since the end of the Cold War, the United Nations has been struggling with this question. It is our contention that, while the new interventionism raises important conceptual, even philosophical questions about the basis and extent of international obligation, answers cannot usefully be constructed a priori. We shall only know whether a measure of 'progress' is possible in international affairs by examining on the one hand the experience of the UN in responding to individual crises, and on the other the impact of this experience on member states themselves.

## The impact of the Cold War and its aftermath

The Cold War silenced the debate between pluralists and solidarists. The use of the veto, primarily but not solely by the Soviet Union, also ensured that even pluralist conceptions of legitimate intervention were seldom put to the test. By the same token, the stand-off between the two superpowers ensured that there was little room for contesting the political vocabulary of international affairs. Thus, state sovereignty was the principle that not only took priority over all others – except of course when it stood in the way of state or alliance interests – but was also regarded as self-evident: either you had it or you did not. By entrenching sovereignty on either side of the ideological divide, other awkward questions were put safely out of reach. While eventually virtually all states signed the Universal Declaration of Human Rights, and the majority also ratified the two supporting conventions,[7] it was governments alone which decided how they should implement their commitments. With the exception of South Africa, whose apartheid policy was singled out for international criticism from 1960 onward, governments were not accountable for their human rights record. And even South Africa, which fell prey to an alliance between the ex-colonial states and the

---

[7] The International Covenant on Civil and Political Rights and the International Covenant on Economic and Social Rights.

Soviet bloc, and which made the mistake of violating the professed values of the western democracies, was none the less protected by them from effective international sanctions.

Respect for sovereignty not only prevented humanitarian intervention but entailed respect for the territorial integrity of existing states. The merits of claims for national self-determination were never considered. Despite the right of all peoples to self-determination contained in the Charter, the exercise of this right came to be identified only with European de-colonisation. Subsequent secessions and/or irredentist enlargements were ruled out. This meant that the criteria for state creation and recognition, other than in the context of de-colonisation, were never examined. The west European colonial powers generally transferred power after a test of local opinion, but in many cases the independence election was the last to be held during the Cold War period. Authoritarian regimes replaced democratically elected ones, without it affecting in any way their membership of international society. Article 2 (7) of the Charter did not discriminate in the protection it provided to regimes from interference in their domestic affairs.

Finally, the combination of paralysis in the Security Council, caused by the virtually automatic use of the veto by one or other side, and the conventional, static and unreflective interpretation given to the principle of state sovereignty marginalised the United Nations in what had been intended as its central role – the provision of a credible system of international peace and security. It is, of course, by no means certain that the outcome would have been any different in the absence of the Cold War. Indeed, a counterfactual analysis reinforces some of the negative evidence reviewed in this book. On this view, it is the ungoverned nature of the state system and the deep attachment to the principle of state sovereignty, however chimerical it may prove to be, that explain the resistance of international society to improvement (i.e. to any progressive evolution towards a solidarist community of mankind), rather than any particular configuration of power. However, what seems likely is that, without the Cold War, the issue would have been settled one way or the other long before now.

The Cold War left two other legacies which cast a long and ambiguous shadow over subsequent attempts to re-construct international society. The first was the introduction of a distinction between, on the one hand, the humanitarian and, on the other, the political and security dimensions of international society. Since there was little prospect of forcing states to honour their obligations with respect to human rights, non-governmental organisations became adept at working to relieve suffering, with the tacit consent of state authorities and without confronting, let alone challenging, their sovereignty. So did UN agencies such as UNHCR and UNICEF, although formally the latter does not require explicit governmental consent in order to operate. This practice, while hardly ideal, worked well enough so long as the states in question were propped up by one or other side in the Cold War, or indeed by their own efforts. But the idea that there could be an international humanitarian order, somehow divorced from strategic considerations, was an illusion, as became abundantly clear when the state collapsed in Yugoslavia and Somalia.

The second legacy of the Cold War to international society was the theory and practice of peacekeeping. The Charter had envisioned international action to repel or deter aggression under Chapter VII and measures, falling short of enforcement, to facilitate the pacific settlement of disputes under Chapter VI. It has generally been assumed that peacekeeping falls under Chapter VI, although it was an improvisation, largely developed by the second Secretary-General, Dag Hammerskjöld, as a way of insulating areas of conflict from the Cold War. Peacekeeping operations depended on a mandate from the Security Council, and could therefore be mounted only where there was no objection from one or other of the superpowers. They also depended on the consent of the conflicting parties – thus reinforcing state sovereignty as the legal linchpin of international society – and circumstances where a ceasefire had been agreed, and there was therefore a peace to keep.

Since the ceasefire agreements that the UN was called upon to police were generally precarious, success depended on the peacekeeping forces being trusted by both sides. This in turn required strict impartiality. The expertise developed by the UN during the Cold War stands as one of the Organisation's major achievements. The legacy is ambiguous only to the extent that peacekeeping techniques were developed within the constraints imposed by the Cold War, thus making a virtue out of necessity. Once it was over, the Organisation found itself drawn into conflicts with different characteristics and for different reasons. For a time it became fashionable to talk of peace enforcement by the UN in situations which, it was claimed, fell halfway between Chapter VI and Chapter VII. As we shall see, in entertaining the possibility of a Chapter Six-and-a-half solution, the UN ran serious risks of becoming part of the problem, rather part than of the solution. Much the same conclusion seems now to have been reached by the Secretary-General himself.[8]

---

[8] See *Supplement to an Agenda for Peace: Position Paper of the Secretary-General on the Occasion of the Fiftieth Anniversary of the United Nations*, A/50/60, S/1995/1, 3 January 1995, paras. 33–46.

The three UN interventions examined in this book all bear the imprint of the Cold War and the structure it imposed on international relations. The Vietnamese invasion of Cambodia in 1978 was never accepted by the majority of UN member states, despite the fact that the government installed by Vietnam replaced the genocidal Khmer Rouge. Throughout the second phase of the Cold War, Vietnam was protected by the Soviet Union largely for power political reasons stemming from its rivalry with China and the United States. When after 1985 the Soviets progressively withdrew their support, possibilities for a political resolution of the conflict gradually emerged. Even then, so strong was the regional interest in favour of sovereignty and against the recognition of regimes imposed from outside by force that it was possible to involve the Vietnamese-imposed government only by creating a Supreme National Council, on which all Cambodian factions including the Khmer Rouge were represented. It was this council that was held to embody national sovereignty and which occupied the Cambodian seat at the UN.[9] Simultaneously, the United Nations Transitional Authority in Cambodia (UNTAC) was established with the unenviable, and ultimately impossible, task of creating a neutral political environment.

If the Cambodian intervention drew the UN into a complicated internal conflict concerning the legitimacy of the incumbent regime and its right to international recognition, its involvement in former Yugoslavia arose from the failure of international society to address two other issues: legitimate secession and the protection of minority rights. Although it was a communist state, during the Cold War Yugoslavia occupied a kind of ideological no-man's land. Indeed, after its expulsion from the Comintern in 1948, Tito was able to exploit this status to extract tacit guarantees of the country's independence. After his death the structure he had created gradually disintegrated; and since economically Yugoslavia had little to offer, with the end of the Cold War the outside world lost interest.

Certainly the major powers appear to have given little thought to secession and the problems of recognition that it might pose. The working definition of self-determination as de-colonisation had been tested several times during the Cold War, but only Bangladesh had fought itself successfully to independence, and then only after the decisive intervention of the Indian army and in geopolitical circumstances which were unlikely to occur elsewhere. When the Yugoslav federation fell apart, the western powers supported the restoration of democracy in the national republics, but paid little attention to the

[9] See chapter 2, pp. 33–5.

fears of minorities that would predictably arise. The Charter does not recognise minorities as having rights, vesting these entirely with the sovereign state on the one hand and the individual on the other. The collapse of communism led to an exaggerated optimism about the possibility of basing the international order on democratic foundations and about the utility of elections as a technique for conflict resolution. When, in multi-cultural societies such as Yugoslavia, they had the opposite effect, the UN was called upon to relieve the ensuing humanitarian catastrophe, without any clear understanding of what it could or should do.

Humanitarian disaster was the sole reason for the UN's third major post-Cold War intervention in Somalia. In this case there was no unresolved international problem deriving from the Cold War, since Somali irredentism had been finally abandoned after the country's defeat in the battle for the Ogaden in 1978. None the less, the Cold War had largely shaped the crisis that led to eventual UN intervention in 1992. Somalia, a desperately poor country at the best of times, had one saleable asset, namely its strategic coastline on the Red Sea. Under its dictatorial president, Siyad Barre, this asset was traded first to the Soviet Union and then to the Americans, primarily in return for military hardware. This was in turn used to fuel inter-clan competition – the traditional pattern of politics in a society where the state was an exotic import – and to establish a dangerously unstable clan hegemony, unprecedented in Somali history.[10] The end of the Cold War left Siyad Barre without any international cards to play, and exposed him to attack by rival clan alliances, themselves as unstable as his own, that had been put together to break his hegemonic control of the state. The aftermath of the battle left Somalia without a state of any kind, and so confronted the UN with an unfamiliar problem: how to deal with a country without a government.

In a variety of ways, the Cold War thus bequeathed to the UN the three major crises in which the capacity of its members to forge a new order would be tested. Even then, it is by no means certain that the Security Council would have mounted these operations – or at least those in former Yugoslavia and Somalia where military intervention preceded rather than followed the implementation of a serious ceasefire – had it not been for the dramatic success of Operation Desert Storm in driving Iraq out of Kuwait in February 1991. With hindsight, it is clear that the Gulf War was atypical of the crises that the UN would be called upon to deal with in the post-Cold War world. It arose out of a straight-

10 See chapter 4, pp. 102–7.

forward attack by one member of the UN on another. Iraq not only violated an internationally recognised political boundary, ostensibly in pursuit of an irredentist claim, but then proceeded to annex Kuwait. As a result, it proved relatively easy to put together a wide-ranging alliance, including the majority of states in the immediate region, and, on the basis of unanimity among the P5, to repel the invasion. It was, more or less, the Charter working as originally intended.

The subsequent involvement in Iraq's internal affairs – to impose from the air safe havens for the Kurds in the north and Shiites in the south – was far more controversial,[11] even though they were apparently accepted by Saddam Hussein in a series of memoranda of understanding. The circumstances that made it possible – and indeed morally necessary – arose directly out of Iraq's defeat in the war and the proximity of Turkish airfields to northern Iraq. They were not likely to be repeated elsewhere; yet it was this aspect of the operation that led those who favoured a more active UN role in international security to see it as a precedent for a new doctrine of humanitarian intervention. This enthusiasm even communicated itself to governments. As Anthony Parsons, a former British permanent representative to the UN, observed:

When the Security Council met at the level of heads of government in January 1992, all speakers expressed confidence regarding the peace-making and peace-keeping capability of the Organisation in the post cold war climate, and many undertook to strengthen its capacity to act preemptively before disputes degenerated into conflict. There was no hint from any delegation that the UN was anything but a major asset in terms of national interest, let alone global peace – a far cry from the equivocations of the mid-1980s.[12]

It was against this background of hope tinged with euphoria that the UN embarked on three operations of a scale and complexity never previously attempted. The countries involved were on three different continents and the conflicts in which they were caught up had widely different origins. None the less, we shall be able to assess how the Organisation coped with the challenge only if we can identify common themes which united the operations, despite these contrasts.

[11] This was because the legal rather than the moral basis on which these actions were taken was questionable. While some writers have seen it as the first move in the evolution of a new doctrine of humanitarian intervention, it was greeted with suspicion by several members of the Security Council who saw it as evidence of weakening western resolve to uphold Article 2 (7). See Adam Roberts and Benedict Kingsbury, 'The UN's Role in International Society', in Roberts and Kingsbury, United Nations, Divided World, pp. 35–6.
[12] Anthony Parsons, 'The UN and the National Interests of States', in Roberts and Kingsbury, United Nations, Divided World, p. 117.

## Peacekeeping and peacemaking in the post-Cold War climate

It is necessary at the outset to make a preliminary and familiar point. Every UN operation rests on two supports, the objects pursued by the member states, and in the final analysis authorised by the Security Council, and their implementation by the Secretariat and/or the various UN agencies to whom responsibility is delegated in the field. Any serious critique of the new interventionism must address both aspects, and in our three case studies we have tried to show how they interact. At the same time, if the UN is to expand its prerogatives, the ultimate responsibility must fall on governments, not the Secretariat. As Simon Jenkins has pointed out, blaming the UN – i.e. the Organisation – when things go wrong is very often an easy way of deflecting attention away from those who are really responsible – i.e. the permanent members of the Security Council.[13] What, then, are the lessons that can be derived from their handling of the Cambodian, former Yugoslavia and Somali interventions?

### The bases for UN intervention

Before the UN can intervene, the Security Council must draw up a mandate specifying the objectives of the operation and the means to be employed. Except in cases of unambiguous aggression, such as Saddam Hussein's attack on Kuwait in August 1990, the construction of a mandate presents formidable problems at the best of times. On the one hand it must be sufficiently flexible to allow for inevitable changes in the situation on the ground; on the other it must be sufficiently precise to prevent the UN from becoming embroiled in the conflict and hence unable to fulfil its role as an impartial umpire. The penalties for not getting the mandate right can be high, as the UN discovered during the Congo crisis between 1960 and 1964. On that occasion, the interpretation of the mandate – was the UN required to stand between the warring factions or to support the government on whose invitation the operation had been mounted? – soon divided the permanent members of the Security Council, who had drawn it up. As a result, both the Soviet Union and France withdrew their support and refused to pay their assessed contributions, thus saddling the UN with a financial debt which took years to pay off.

The major powers might have been better advised to have taken the

---

[13] Simon Jenkins, 'Out of the Valley of Death', *The Times*, 20 April 1994.

Congo operation as their model – and warning – than to have allowed public opinion to lure them into the belief that the success of Desert Storm, and enforcement action under Chapter VII, could be repeated in quite different circumstances. The three operations under review, as well as most of the others in which the UN has recently been engaged, involved the Organisation in attempting to broker political settlements to civil conflicts in societies deeply divided along ethnic as well as ideological or religious lines.[14] The conflicts thus had more in common with post-colonial struggles over state succession than traditional inter-state conflicts over territory. In circumstances where the line between the international and the domestic is blurred, three issues complicate the task of devising a workable mandate. The first is sovereignty: who holds it, and on what grounds is it to be either upheld or superseded? The second is the strategic objective the mandate is designed to serve: i.e. what is the intervention intended to accomplish? The third is resources: assuming the first two issues can be satisfactorily resolved, are the requisite manpower, money and material likely to be available?

### Sovereign constraints on UN mandates

It is perhaps significant that of the three operations, the one which, when all qualifications have been entered, can be judged the most successful was also the one in which there was no attempt to challenge the prevailing norms of international society. As we note at the beginning of chapter 2, the UN operation in Cambodia had no bearing on the international status of the country, which had been a fact of international political life since its admission to the UN in 1955.[15] Sovereignty was not, therefore, an issue, even though the disputed legitimacy of the government in Phnom Penh was at the heart of the political problem to which the UN sought a solution. This distinction may seem academic, but it is not. The fact that Cambodian statehood was not in question ensured that any UN intervention would have to be framed under Chapter VI – the pacific settlement of disputes – and would have to follow, not precede, a negotiated ceasefire and settlement plan. The fact that all parties broke the Paris Agreement, that prior to the elections Cambodian sovereignty was largely symbolic and that UNTAC was unable to fulfil many parts of its mandate does not detract from the fact

---

[14] 'Of the five peace-keeping operations that existed in early 1988, four related to inter-state wars . . . Of the 21 operations established since then, only 8 have related to inter-state wars . . . Of the 11 operations established since January 1992, all but 2 (82 per cent) related to intra-state conflicts': *Supplement to an Agenda for Peace*, para. 11.
[15] See chapter 2, p. 26.

that the UN is better placed as a peacemaker when it is acting under the authority of the conflicting parties than when it is trying to impose its will from outside.

The Yugoslav and Somali operations lacked these advantages from the start. The former arose out of the failure of the then European Community to accompany its recognition of Croatia and Bosnia-Herzegovina with credible conditions that would have reassured the minorities and deterred the various groups of Serbs from pressing their claim for a united Serbia. The distinguished international lawyer, Rosalyn Higgins, has argued that the rights and wrongs of the recognition policy are beside the point, that once the secessionist Yugoslav republics had been recognised they were entitled to the full protection of the UN Charter, i.e. including measures under Chapter VII, if they were subjected to aggression. Instead, she noted of the UN in Bosnia 'we have chosen to respond to major unlawful violence, not by stopping that violence, but by trying to provide relief to the suffering. But our choice of policy allows the suffering to continue.'[16]

The difficulty with this approach, however, is that it assumes that, providing juridical sovereignty has been conferred from outside, it need not have any empirical content at all. It is true – as Robert Jackson has demonstrated – that many Third World states are essentially wards of international society and thus heavily dependent on international recognition.[17] But it is one thing to prop up former colonies once power has been transferred, and quite another to confer sovereignty from outside in the middle of a war over state succession and when the legality and moral authority of the new boundaries are repudiated by many who will have to live within them.[18]

Much of the confusion surrounding the UN's role in former Yugoslavia arose from the fact that the Organisation was drawn into a series of overlapping civil wars, in which none of the antagonists was prepared to abandon the hope that they could either win militarily or at least improve their position before agreeing to a political settlement. This meant that their consent to the UN's presence was strictly conditional. None of the ceasefires or settlement plans, negotiated first by the European Community and then by the UN and European Union in harness, bore fruit, although this did not mean that they might not one day do so. Meanwhile, the UN peacekeepers, whose presence was intended

[16] Rosalyn Higgins, 'The New United Nations and Former Yugoslavia', *International Affairs*, vol. 69 (1993), p. 469.

[17] Robert Jackson, *Quasi-States: Sovereignty, International Relations and the Third World* (Cambridge: Cambridge University Press, 1991).

[18] See chapter 3, pp. 59–63.

initially to protect relief convoys to besieged minorities from being highjacked by the warring factions, had their mandate changed from Chapter VI to Chapter VII, to allow them to 'take all necessary measures' in discharging it. As we shall see, without a commensurate commitment of resources, and will, this change was largely symbolic.

Both the American-led Unified Task Force (UNITAF) which landed in Mogadishu in December 1992 and the United Nations Operation in Somalia (UNOSOM II) which took over in May 1993 operated from the start with a peace-enforcement mandate drawn up under Chapter VII. Since the motive for UN intervention was humanitarian, rather than to deter or repel a threat to international peace and security, in a sense, these mandates demonstrated that where the Security Council is so minded sovereignty need not present an obstacle to action, and that the Charter will allow them to do pretty much what they want. In this case the crisis which the UN attempted to address was a humanitarian catastrophe caused by the collapse of all authority – Somalia had in effect forfeited both its juridical and its empirical sovereignty. Yet empowering the UN to take all necessary measures to provide a secure environment in which Somalis themselves could re-construct their polity was at best problematic, and at worst deeply flawed. The state had collapsed because Somalis had elevated their clan and sub-clan loyalties above even a minimal commitment to public order. Against whom then was the mandate to be enforced?

### Goals and resources

If the issue of sovereignty imposed constraints upon the UN's ability to act decisively, the absence of a peace to which the conflicting parties were seriously committed undermined the Organisation's ability to achieve its stated objectives. This held true in all three cases. Even in Cambodia, the ceasefire did not hold; the Khmer Rouge repudiated the agreement it had signed in Paris, and several of the leading factions engaged in violence prior to the elections.[19] But at least in this case the UN had been given the clear task of holding the political ring and preparing the country for 'free and fair' elections, which it would both organise and oversee. Its control of all administrative agencies in the fields of foreign affairs, defence, public security and information was considered necessary to ensure strict neutrality. This it singularly failed to achieve for reasons examined in chapter 2, but it promoted sufficient order, none the less, to preside over an election in which, despite intimi-

[19] See chapter 2, pp. 54–5.

dation, over 89 per cent of those on the electoral roll cast their ballot.

In neither former Yugoslavia nor Somalia has the UN been able to extricate itself with anything like so much credit. Indeed, in the first case, the UN was still deeply embroiled in mid-1995 with very little chance of being able to implement the stated objectives of its mandates, which in any case did not extend to the organisation of elections. In the second, UNOSOM II was finally withdrawn at the end of 1994, leaving the country still without a government and as divided as when it had arrived. For those who wanted to craft a new order on the basis of cooperation amongst the major powers, it was unfortunate that the major part of the UN's initial test should have been in two such unpromising environments. Cosmopolitan solidarity had little value in either society. The break-up of Yugoslavia challenged the most basic rule of post-1945 international society – that boundaries should not be changed by force – for which, ostensibly, the Gulf War had so recently been fought. The total collapse of the Somali state, and the brutalisation of much of Somali society to which it led, was partly caused by the failure of repeated Somali efforts to challenge this same rule, which they had held in contempt since the creation of their independent republic in 1960. Yet the Security Council could not command either the resources or the will to frustrate the challenge in the first case or repair the damage in the second.

From the time of their original involvement in 1991 in former Yugoslavia, both the European Community and the United Nations had focused their peacemaking efforts on trying to find a political settlement within existing and internationally recognised boundaries. Meanwhile – apart from the posting of small numbers of blue beret troops to Macedonia in a symbolic but so far successful gesture of preventive diplomacy – UN peacekeepers were employed on the ostensibly humanitarian mission of ensuring that relief reached the victims of inter-ethnic violence in the besieged cities and those who had been 'ethnically cleansed'. But the provision of relief in the middle of a civil war is always contentious. Where the relief agencies see only innocent victims, the conflicting parties regard intervention as an attempt to alter the status quo. They may welcome it, or resist it, depending on their fortunes in the war, but will not in practice accept its disinterested neutrality. For those who put a city under siege, those inside are the enemy, not victims. Indeed, there can be no more telling illustration of the futility of confining intervention in a civil war to humanitarian objectives than the siege: the purpose of this ancient technique of warfare is, after all, precisely to starve the enemy into submission. The only way that Bosnia could have been preserved as a multi-ethnic state within its pre-existing (i.e. Yugoslav) boundaries would have been for an army of occupation to have moved in at the outset on a scale sufficient to demand the unconditional surrender of all local militias and to carry out their effective disarmament. This act of trusteeship was never a remote possibility.

To be fair, by the spring of 1993, the contradiction in UN policies had been recognised by the Security Council, which now concentrated on trying to find a face-saving formula which would first create a loose ethnic confederation and then allow it to split up peacefully. But for even this scheme to have a chance of success, it was vital that there should be no further ethnic cleansing: hence the policy of declaring Muslim safe areas in towns like Srebenica and Gorazde. This policy did not require an army of occupation, but to be credible it would have still needed a massive increase in the number of ground troops serving with the UN. The problem was no longer one of the mandate, but of the resources to carry it through. UN convoys had the authority to take 'all necessary measures' to ensure the delivery of relief aid. If they failed to force their way through against Serb opposition, it was because they knew they could not call up the reinforcements necessary to face down the stiffer resistance that they would be likely to meet on the next occasion. Shortly before he resigned as UN commander in Bosnia-Herzegovina in January 1994, Lieutenant-General Francis Briquemont complained publicly of the 'fantastic gap between the resolutions of the Security Council, the will to execute these resolutions, and the means available to commanders in the field'.[20]

The situation in Somalia was in some respects similar to that in Bosnia, and in others strikingly different. It was similar in that the UN was drawn into the crisis as the result of domestic pressure on governments in western countries to do something to relieve a humanitarian tragedy. It was also similar in that any solution to the humanitarian problem would require the UN to address the political and security crisis which was its main source. A strong case could be made for imposing a UN protectorate on the country as the only way of creating the conditions under which political reconstruction would be possible. But, as in Bosnia, so radical a solution was never seriously entertained. On the other hand, the basic problem in the Somali operation, at least prior to the American, French, Belgian and Italian withdrawals from UNOSOM II in the spring of 1994, was not inadequate resources but their inappropriateness and the manner in which they were deployed.[21]

---

[20] 'UN Bosnian Commander Wants More Troops, Fewer Resolutions', *New York Times*, 31 December 1993, p. A3.
[21] The confusion surrounding the engagement in October 1993 in which eighteen Americans were killed and seventy-five wounded was revealed by the two senior US military

When, at President Bush's request, General Colin Powell drew up the plans for Operation Restore Hope, he based them on the strategic doctrine that had been employed with such spectacular success in Operation Desert Storm. This doctrine required the task force to pursue precise and strictly limited objectives, which were much less obviously available in Somalia that they had been in the Gulf.[22] It also required a massive show of force, sufficient to overawe any possible opposition and minimise the risk of casualties. On this score his calculation initially proved correct. Once it became clear that the Americans had decided on intervention, all the warring factions professed to welcome their arrival and agreed to cooperate in their limited humanitarian mission in southern Somalia. The problem with the American approach was that the strategic doctrine did not easily translate into tactical principles for containing the conflict on a day-to-day basis.

Unlike the British and French, the Americans, who continued to dominate the UN forces even after they had formally handed over the operation to the Secretary-General, instructed their patrols to 'employ maximum controlled violence' when they encountered opposition rather than 'minimum necessary force'. Had this policy been accompanied by an even-handed and sustained effort to marginalise all the rival warlords, and to take control of their heavy weapons, it might have been justified. But after the killing of over twenty Pakistanis in June 1993, allegedly by Somali National Alliance militia, any pretence at impartiality was abandoned. Both the failure, and the lack of proportionality, of the American-led UN hunt for General Aideed brought the whole operation into disrepute and led to the premature withdrawal of all the major western contingents.

In his report to the Security Council in January 1994, the Secretary-General outlined possible options for the UN's future operations in Somalia. His own preference was for a 'continuation of UNOSOM II's current mandate with the addition of an extra brigade. It will call for disarmament, coercive if necessary, as well as capability for defence

commanders when they testified before the Senate Armed Services Committee on 12 May 1994. Major-General Thomas Montgomery, the former deputy UN commander, confirmed that the administration had refused to meet his requests for tanks and other armoured vehicles, and Major-General William Garrison, who commanded the task force of Delta Force commandos and army rangers which suffered the casualties, disclosed that he had been refused AC130 gunships. However, the generals disagreed on what difference the additional armour would have made. Montgomery believed that it would have reduced the number of casualties, but Garrison was sceptical: 'If we had put one more ounce of lead on South Mogadishu on the night of 3 and 4 October, I believe it would have sunk' (*Washington Post*, 13 May 1994).

[22] See chapter 4, pp. 110–12 below.

against UNOSOM II personnel.'[23] However, since his approaches to member states for contributions had failed to elicit a single positive response, he recommended a more modest option calling for 'voluntary disarmament and the deployment of about 16,000 troops to protect ports, convoys and refugees'. He also warned that its success would be crucially dependent on the improbable cooperation of the Somalis themselves. The acknowledgement of failure in advance was barely concealed.

### An interim diagnosis

It is beyond the scope of this volume to offer a prescription for what needs to be done to translate the Secretary-General's vision, with which we began, into reality. However, experience of the 'new interventionism' between 1991 and the end of 1994 may allow a preliminary, and interim, diagnosis. If by 'new world order' is meant structural change in the nature of international relations to allow effective coercive intervention on the side of the victims in civil conflicts, then the first and most obvious conclusion is that no such change has occurred.

The sad fact is that the end of the Cold War has not fundamentally altered the problem of power in international relations any more than did the end of World War I or World War II. On the other hand, as on these occasions, the outcome of the conflict shaped subsequent efforts to construct a new order based on legal principles and international norms. From this point of view, the history of the twentieth century can be seen as a series of attempts to come to terms with the implications of popular sovereignty and the concept of democracy for international relations. The collapse of the European empires, and the rise of the United States to world power after 1918, ensured that from now on international society would ostensibly be based on the principle of national self-determination and the attempt to proscribe the use of force as an instrument of foreign policy. The 'democratisation' of international society was carried a step further after 1945 with the withdrawal of European imperial powers from Asia, Africa, the Caribbean and Oceania, but the Cold War – and the contested conception of democratic government which underlay it – ensured that it would be a democracy of states only, and that no attempt would be made to enforce even minimum standards of domestic

---

[23] *Further Report of the Secretary-General Submitted in Pursuance of Paragraph 4 of Resolution 886 (1993)*, S/1994/12, 6 January 1994.

political behaviour. Only with the end of the Cold War was it possible to ask whether democratisation – in the fuller sense of an international society of peoples – was a feasible international objective at all.

In his *Agenda for Peace*, the Secretary-General argued that 'democracy within nations requires respect for human rights and fundamental freedoms, as set forth in the Charter' and that 'democracy, at all levels, is essential to attain peace for a new era of prosperity and justice'.[24] However, efforts to support these principles in cases of civil conflict have been bedevilled by two related problems. The first is how to devise realistic mandates in situations where the belligerents have not despaired of winning the conflict for themselves, and by force. During the Cold War, there were relatively few Security Council Resolutions, and those that passed the Council were in consequence carefully crafted to command respect.[25] Except in Korea, which was so exceptional as not really to count, and briefly in the Congo, UN peacekeeping forces were also never cast in a combative role. As a result, the authority of UN commanders in the field was not challenged, either by the parties to the conflict or by governments providing contingents for peacekeeping forces. By contrast, since the end of the Cold War, the number of Security Council Resolutions has steadily increased – over 50 in former Yugoslavia alone – but their authority has been progressively devalued.

To some extent, this is no doubt a result of organisational inexperience in a new and unfamiliar context, and therefore presumably susceptible to administrative reform. Indeed, much has already been done as a result of the lessons learned during the three operations reviewed in this volume. In particular, the Department of Peacekeeping Operations (DPKO), which is responsible for executive direction of all peacekeeping operations, has been upgraded. To quote from a recent report on these reforms, steps taken to strengthen the DPKO include:

a considerable expansion of staffing levels; the creation of a Planning Division under a new Office of Planning and Support; and the establishment of the Situation Centre. The Situation Centre, originally set up to support activities in Somalia, has since been upgraded and now operates round the clock in accordance with proper staff procedures. It acts as a communication channel between

---

[24] *Agenda for Peace*, paras. 81 and 82.
[25] Between 1947 and 1988 there was a total of 348 Security Council Resolutions concerning peacekeeping, an average of 8.5 resolutions per year. Between 1989 and the end of 1994, 296 Security Council Resolutions were passed, an average of 49.3 resolutions per year (from information provided by the Foreign and Commonwealth Office, London).

the headquarters in New York and missions in the field, while also providing a mechanism whereby information is disseminated within the Secretariat and to troop-contributing countries. In order to improve the UN headquarters' capability to monitor and support missions, measures have also been taken to increase the flow of information to the UN from member states (for this purpose the US has donated an information/intelligence processing system in the DPKO). Although the UN's capacities for collection and dissemination of information require further development, the creation of the Situation Centre (with an embryonic research and analysis capability) does represent a major step forward (not least psychologically) for the UN. A more flexible attitude within the UN to the issues of 'intelligence' is also discernible.[26]

Other organisational problems have proved more intractable. For example, the safe-area policy in eastern Bosnia was passed through the Council without any attempt to define, for the forces on the ground, what these areas actually comprised. Various methods of tightening up the drafting of future Security Council Resolutions suggest themselves. Two (not mutually exclusive) methods would be to ensure that the Secretary-General has the assistance of a senior military officer who could advise on the technical problems of implementation before any specific proposal was put to the Council, and that all draft resolutions should be vetted by a Scrutiny Committee made up of representatives from governments providing contingents to the peacekeeping force. This procedure might go some way to overcoming the tendency of national contingent commanders to refer back their orders to capitals before implementing them. Dual command was not a problem so long as the UN was not engaged in combat; but in June 1993 the delays caused by the Italians referring back to Rome before they went to the assistance of the surrounded Pakistanis meant that the latter suffered casualties that could almost certainly have been avoided, and set in train the sequence of events which undermined the whole Somali operation. Similarly fateful confusions, resulting from the absence of a single authoritative chain of command, have occurred with depressing regularity in former Yugoslavia.

No amount of improvement in the defining and technical drafting of mandates will be sufficient, however, unless UN commanders in the field are given the resources to carry them out. This is the second major problem which has frustrated UN efforts to turn principles into practice.

[26] Mats Berdal, *The United Nations at Fifty: Its Role in Global Security*, Ditchley Conference Report, 2–4 December 1994, no. D94/15. Berdal also points out that, as a result of the incorporation of the Field Operations Division into the DPKO, the new peacekeeping mission for Angola (UNAVEM III) is the first operation to have been planned by a military civilian staff in New York before the Security Council took a final decision on deployment.

Perhaps the most disquieting trend during the first half of the 1990s has been the willingness of the major, and therefore presumably most responsible, powers to will the end, but not the means. The problem of resources is not always merely a question of men and money, as the example of Somalia illustrates, but certainly it was shortages of both that made the full implementation of the mandates in Cambodia and former Yugoslavia impossible. As with the problem of the mandates themselves, some improvement could be brought about if the UN's finances were put on a proper footing.[27] But it is difficult to avoid the conclusion that the financial problems of the UN mask a deeper uncertainty within the governments of the major powers about the kind of international order they wish to support. As Brian Urquhart has commented, 'In 1992 the UN and all its peacekeeping operations throughout the world cost $2.4 billion – less than the cost of two days of Desert Storm or two Stealth bombers.'[28]

In large measure this uncertainty flows from the ambiguities inherent in democracy itself. By way of conclusion let us consider four of these. The first concerns the tension between the requirements of diplomatic prudence and democratic internationalism. Should foreign policy be driven by an interpretation of the national interest, including a proper regard for the likely consequences of major decisions such as the recognition of a new state, or should such decisions be taken primarily with regard to the democratic right of national self-determination and in response to popular pressures?

The creation of new states was sufficiently rare during the Cold War for democratic governments seldom to have been faced with the necessity of confronting this dilemma. But when Yugoslavia broke apart, the major powers did not know which way to jump. In the end, the sympathy of the German government – at the time when it held the European presidency – for Slovenia and Croatia almost certainly resulted in a premature recognition which had alarming humanitarian and political consequences for the entire region. Admittedly they were under strong pressure – there was a sizeable and vocal Croatian minority in Germany and the government was vulnerable to the argument that having just restored the right of self-determination to the people of East Germany, they had no grounds on which to

---

[27] See *Financing an Effective United Nations*, Report of the Independent Advisory Group on UN Financing, co-chairmen, Shijuro Ogata and Paul Volcker (New York: Ford Foundation, 1993).
[28] 'Who Can Police the World?', *New York Review of Books*, 12 May 1994. Urquhart continues, 'The average ratio of UN peacekeeping assessments to national defense expenditures is of the order of one dollar to one thousand dollars.'

deny this right to the peoples of former Yugoslavia. But it is precisely because democratically elected governments will be prey to a variety of regional and local pressures that there is a case for taking recognition away from national governments and subjecting it to a United Nations' procedure.[29] Such a major derogation from state sovereignty, as traditionally understood, would inevitably attract opposition from some members of the General Assembly, and perhaps for that reason has so far not been seriously entertained.

The second ambiguity concerns the role of public opinion in the international policies of the major powers. Public opinion – particularly when it is largely formed and articulated by the electronic media – is notoriously fickle. It is a curious fact that in the three cases where the UN has brought force to bear to protect the innocent victims of civil conflict – i.e. the creation of safe havens for the Iraqi Kurds and Shiites, and in Somalia and former Yugoslavia – it is western publics that have forced their generally reluctant governments to support international intervention. But it is also by reference to public opinion – above all by raising the spectre of returning 'body-bags' – that western politicians have sought to limit their involvement. The willingness of western populations to accept casualties for an international cause, in conflicts in which they themselves have no direct interest, has not been properly tested. It may also vary from country to country. However, the rapidity with which the Americans announced their final withdrawal from Somalia after the incident in October 1993, when eighteen American servicemen were killed, and their steadfast refusal to commit ground troops to Bosnia-Herzegovina until an overall ceasefire has been concluded, certainly supports the hypothesis that democratic politics constrains rather than encourages any major extension of the UN's peace and security role.

Thirdly, democratic uncertainty at home creates opportunities for the manipulation of the UN by undemocratic forces in the countries where it operates. This has been a feature of each of the interventions examined in this book. In each case the gap between the apparent strength of the mandate and the weakness of the will and/or capacity to carry it out, has been quickly perceived by unscrupulous local politicians seeking to use the UN presence to their own advantage. Thus in Cambodia, UNTAC failed to get control of many key functions of the Vietnamese-imposed administration that had been assigned to it, was forced to rely on much of the apparatus of the incumbent government and, as a consequence, was unable to prevent the physical harassment of opposition

[29] See chapter 3, pp. 90–2.

parties. In former Yugoslavia, the numerous ceasefires which were broken almost as soon as they were negotiated frequently provided a cover under which, usually, but not only, the Serbs, could regroup and move their heavy weapons to a new site. In Somalia, none of the local warlords showed any serious commitment to political reconciliation and reconstruction; and Aideed in particular turned the UN's attempt to identify him as the principal public enemy to his own advantage so effectively that he forced the UN into a humiliating reversal of its policy. In no case was the UN in a position to enforce what is widely regarded as an essential prerequisite of successful peacemaking (as distinct from peacekeeping), namely the disarming and demobilisation of rival factions.

Finally, there is a contradiction between the desire to build an international order based on democratic principles and the requirement of humanitarian intervention and political reconstruction, in societies where the collapse of the state has led to the criminalisation of society. This contradiction manifests itself in two ways.

Firstly, for historical reasons in Asia and Africa, and for reasons of immediate and short-run self-interest on the part of the western democracies, there is no support for the creation of UN protectorates or the revival of UN trusteeship. If there were, this would give the Organisation an explicit interest in nation-building, and would involve its leading members in expensive and long-run commitments. Secondly, if the UN cannot reasonably be expected to act like an empire, it must find itself handicapped whenever it becomes deeply embroiled in attempts to preside over the transformation or reconstruction of a political system. During the colonial period, the British, French and Italians employed administrators who developed a sophisticated knowledge of local languages and political cultures. The UN did not enjoy any of these advantages.[30] In both Cambodia and Somalia, its impact was seriously weakened by having to rely on personnel with only a superficial understanding of the cultures in which they were operating. Given the reluctance of the major powers to enter into open-ended commitments, it seems unlikely that the UN will be in a position to develop this kind of expertise in the future. And since the world is culturally extremely diverse, this lack of administrative capability will set limits to the new

[30] This is not to say that there is no room, even under existing circumstances, for an improvement in UN selection and training practices for administrative personnel who are employed in peacekeeping operations. In the Somali case, in particular, many of those employed appeared to have been inadequately briefed. See *Report of the Commission of Inquiry Established Pursuant to Security Council Resolution 885 (1993) to Investigate Attacks on UNOSOM II Personnel Which Led to Casualties Among Them*, 24 February 1994 (New York: United Nations, 1994), para. 255.

interventionism. There are thus formidable practical, as well as philosophical, obstacles to any early development of a more solidarist conception of international society.

## Postscript

After this book had been sent to press, American diplomatic efforts finally led to the convening of a peace conference on Bosnia-Herzegovina, at a US Air Force base in Dayton, Ohio. This conference led to a comprehensive peace agreement that was formally signed in Paris on 14 December 1995. Under the agreement, the UN will hand over peacekeeping responsibility to NATO, a move which was necessary to permit US ground troops to participate. A preliminary assessment of this 'final' stage in the crisis is to be found in Appendix D (pp. 226–33), together with the text of the agreement.

# 2    Cambodia

*Mats Berdal and Michael Leifer*

The United Nations operation in Cambodia during 1992–3 was, at the time, the most ambitious and expensive undertaking in the peacekeeping experience of the Organisation. At a cost of around US $1.7 billion, 22,000 military and civilian personnel were deployed to implement the Comprehensive Political Settlement of the Cambodia Conflict which had been concluded at an international conference in Paris on 23 October 1991.[1] That settlement made provision for a United Nations Transitional Authority in Cambodia (UNTAC) charged with holding the ring politically so that elections under its aegis could determine the future governance of a country long afflicted by violent upheaval and human suffering.

UNTAC was provided with exceptional resources but its mandate was restricted to peacekeeping. Peace enforcement, which had been demonstrated early in 1991 in Operation Desert Storm, was not any part of UNTAC's remit which was confined, in essence, to a quasi-administrative role. The critical problem confronted by UNTAC virtually from the outset of its deployment was how to discharge responsibility for filling a political vacuum in the face of obstructive violence by contending Cambodian parties.

The notorious Khmer Rouge refused totally to cooperate in implementing the Paris Agreement which it had signed, while the incumbent administration in Phnom Penh also used violence to force the outcome of the elections in which it would participate. In the event, UNTAC assumed a calculated risk in embarking on elections, which were conducted without serious disruption. No single party secured an overall majority, which paved the way for a coalition government which excluded the Khmer Rouge. They had repudiated the electoral process but failed to disrupt it with an effective military challenge. To that extent, the United Nations operation was an undoubted success. More

---

[1] *Agreement on a Comprehensive Political Settlement of the Cambodia Conflict*, 23 October 1991 (London, HMSO: 1991.Cm.1786). For text of agreement, see pp. 134–65, in appendix A.

problematic has been the viability of the political order in place at the completion of UNTAC's mission.

This chapter addresses the experience of United Nations' intervention in Cambodia after more than two decades of conflict. The involvement of the Organisation goes back over those decades but its physical intervention only took place as the Cold War was at an end; global rivalry had ceased by then to be a point of reference for the Cambodian issue. The regional dimension of conflict had diminished also, leaving the United Nations to address a domestic disorder among contending parties which had been incapable of an accommodation over power-sharing. To conventional peacekeeping was added the responsibility of democratic elections as a vehicle for conflict resolution, as well as a paradoxical reliance on the charismatic figure of Norodom Sihanouk.[2]

### First encounters

The United Nations operation in Cambodia has not had any bearing on the international status of the country, which was a French protectorate for nearly a century. Independence was conceded in November 1953 with international endorsement confirmed in July 1954 by the Geneva Conference on Indochina, which had not been convened under United Nations' auspices. Cambodia has been an established fact of international political life ever since it was admitted to the world body in 1955. The legitimacy of its governments has been subject to challenge at various times; it is this matter which engaged the attention and resources of the United Nations over two decades before the Paris Agreement of October 1991.[3]

---

[2] For some of the recent literature on the role of the UN in Cambodia, see Janet Heininger, *Peacekeeping in Transistion: The United Nations in Cambodia* (New York: Twentieth Century Press, 1994); Steven Ratner, 'The United Nations in Cambodia: A Model for Resolution of Internal Conflicts?', in Lori F. Damrosch (ed.), *Enforcing Restraint: Collective Intervention in Internal Conflicts* (New York: Council on Foreign Relations Press, 1993), pp. 241–73; Michael Doyle and N. Suntharalingam, 'The UN in Cambodia: Lesson for Complex Peacekeeping', *International Peacekeeping*, vol. 1, no. 2 (1994), pp. 117–47; William Shawcross, *Cambodia's New Deal* (Washington, D.C.: Carnegie Endowment for International Peace, 1994). For some of the operational lessons learned, see also Hugh Smith (ed.), *International Peacekeeping: Building on the Cambodian Experience* (Canberra: Australian Defence Studies Centre, 1994), and Trevor Findlay, *Cambodia: The Legacy and Lessons of UNTAC*, SIPRI Research Report, No. 9 (Oxford: Oxford University Press, 1995).

[3] For a discussion of the issue of international representation in the first decade of conflict, see Michael Leifer, 'The International Representation of Kampuchea', *Southeast Asian Affairs 1982* (Singapore: Heinmann Asia for Institute of Southeast Asian Studies, 1982), pp. 47–59.

Map 2.1 Cambodia, 1992–1994

The United Nations first became involved in the internal affairs of Cambodia following the coup that deposed Prince Norodom Sihanouk as head of state on 18 March 1970, when he was out of the country. The incumbent administration, led by the prime minister, General Lon Nol, which had mounted the coup, succeeded to the Cambodian seat in the United Nations. That seat was retained when the name of the state was changed in October 1970, from the Kingdom of Cambodia to the Khmer Republic. With Vietnamese Communist support, an armed challenge to the Phnom Penh administration was mounted by a Cambodian revolutionary movement, ostensibly on behalf of a government in exile in Beijing, headed by Prince Sihanouk. Abortive challenges to the credentials of the Phnom Penh delegation on behalf of that government were posed in the General Assembly in December 1973 and November 1974. In the event, the issue of the international representation of Cambodia was decided by *force majeure*.

On 17 April 1975, the armed forces of the revolutionary movement labelled by Prince Sihanouk as the Khmer Rouge took over the Cambodian capital. This internal transfer of power inaugurated a murderous era, but did not arouse controversy over legitimacy in Phnom Penh and representation in New York. One reason for the ready international acceptance of the new regime was its close identification with Prince Sihanouk, who had come to personify Cambodia to the outside world. Indeed, his domestic and international standing was to be an important factor in the calculations of permanent members of the United Nations Security Council when they assumed responsibility for restoring political order within the tormented country during the following decade. Although Prince Sihanouk was obliged to relinquish the office of head of state in April 1976, when the country was given a new constitution and renamed Democratic Kampuchea, the issue of the legitimacy and international representation of its government was not contested. It only revived within the United Nations with Vietnam's invasion of Cambodia in December 1978, the forcible removal of the government of Democratic Kampuchea and its replacement in January 1979 by a government of the People's Republic of Kampuchea.

### Close engagement

From that juncture, the United Nations became continuously involved in conflict in Cambodia. In principle, Vietnam's invasion had violated the cardinal rule of the society of states as enshrined in Article 2 (4) of the United Nations Charter. The Security Council was constrained by Soviet veto but the General Assembly passed recurrent adverse resolutions against Vietnam, calling for its military withdrawal; it also upheld the right of the ousted government of Democratic Kampuchea to occupy the Cambodian seat despite revelations of its gruesome rule.

Although cloaked in principle, the Cambodian conflict was, in essence, about the balance of power in Indochina, with global as well as regional significance. At issue with the invasion of Cambodia was whether or not Vietnam was to become the dominant state in the peninsula. That matter primarily involved a test of wills between Vietnam and China.[4] Vietnam's ruling Communist Party had long claimed a special geopolitical relationship with Laos and Cambodia arising from the experience of liberation struggle against France and America. China's objection to this assertion of entitlement had been expressed openly in the wake of Vietnam's unification in 1975. Sino-Vietnamese alienation in the context of Sino-Soviet antagonism and a countervailing Soviet–Vietnamese association was brought to a head by the xenophobic impulses of the government in Phnom Penh led by Pol Pot. The economic failings of Cambodia's political salvationism led to a paranoid search for enemies judged to be the Vietnamese and their internal agents. An open alignment between Cambodia and China in late 1977 concurrent with murderous attacks against civilian settlements across the border in southern Vietnam brought retribution in the form of invasion in December 1978.

That invasion was made possible through a Treaty of Friendship and Cooperation between the Soviet Union and Vietnam in November 1978. This protective alliance was concluded as Soviet–American detente had broken down and Sino-Vietnamese relations were deteriorating further. The attendant invasion of Cambodia was interpreted in both Washington and Beijing as clear evidence of Soviet expansionist intent through political proxy. China responded with a punitive military intervention into northern Vietnam in February 1979. The Soviet invasion of Afghanistan at the end of 1979 served to confirm Sino-American apprehensions. Vietnam's invasion of Cambodia also provoked a sharp diplomatic response from the Association of South-East Asian Nations (ASEAN) in support of their Thai regional partner faced with an unprecedented deployment of Vietnamese military power along its eastern border.

---

[4] For accounts of the origins and nature of the Cambodian conflict, see David W. P. Elliot (ed.), *The Third Indochina Conflict* (Boulder, Colo.: Westview Press, 1981); Grant Evans and Kevin Rowley, *Red Brotherhood at War* (London: Verso Books, 1984); Nayan Chanda, *Brother Enemy: The War After the War* (San Diego, Calif.: Harcourt Brace Jovanovich, 1986); and Michael Leifer, 'The Indochina Problem', in T. B. Millar and James Walter (eds.), *Asian-Pacific Security After the Cold War* (Canberra: Allen and Unwin, 1993), pp. 56–68.

A diverse anti-Vietnamese coalition materialised which set about seeking to impose breaking strain on the country's society and government in order to influence the outcome of conflict in Cambodia. The United Nations served as the arena for the diplomatic dimension of this strategy, with the leading role being assumed by ASEAN, whose regional credentials were employed to mobilise a recurrent voting challenge to Vietnam. Its spokesmen also pressed with success the right of the ousted government of Democratic Kampuchea to retain the Cambodian seat.

## The nature of the conflict

Central to the argument which raged over Cambodia within the United Nations was a fundamental disagreement over the nature of the conflict. Vietnam and its Soviet bloc supporters claimed that the government of Democratic Kampuchea had been overthrown by a so-called National United Front for National Salvation comprising dissident Cambodians determined to remove a genocidal regime. As civil war had been the agent of political change, the new government was entitled to occupy the Cambodian seat at the United Nations; it exercised effective power and control within the country, thus fulfilling conventional criteria for international recognition. Vietnam's adversaries rejected the representation of the conflict as a civil war, maintaining that the change of government in Phnom Penh had been effected by a blatant and illegal act of external military intervention which required liquidation. At issue, therefore, was not only the withdrawal of Vietnamese forces from Cambodia but also the removal of the government that had ridden to power on their backs.

The ability to shape the international understanding of the nature of the Cambodian conflict was seen by contending sides as directly relevant to the terms of its ultimate resolution. Contention over this matter had a direct bearing on the outcome of the next stage of United Nations' involvement which took the form of an international conference convened in New York in July 1981 under the auspices of the Secretary-General, Kurt Waldheim. That conference had been sought by an ASEAN-sponsored resolution of the General Assembly passed in the previous October. In the event, the conference did not provide an opportunity for conflict resolution. Vietnam and its supporters boycotted the conference, both because Vietnam considered the conference likely to condemn it as an aggressor and because the government in Phnom Penh had been excluded; the representatives of the ousted regime were accredited because of its retention of the Cambodian seat.

The conference generated more heat than light, while a proposal by ASEAN designed to accommodate the security interests of Vietnam was obstructed both by China and the United States.

That proposal merits mention because of its reappearance in part a decade later, when a formal settlement of the Cambodian conflict was concluded. It was suggested that in the event of Vietnam's military withdrawal from Cambodia, all warring Khmer factions should be disarmed and an interim administration set up before free elections were held under United Nations' auspices. China's representative argued strongly against such an interim administration, maintaining that Democratic Kampuchea was a legitimate member of the United Nations which did not have the right to establish a trusteeship over the country. The involvement of the United Nations at that juncture was clearly not intended to promote a negotiated settlement of the Cambodian conflict. The Organisation was being employed as an instrument of diplomatic pressure on the part of Vietnam's adversaries, who commanded an overwhelming majority in the General Assembly.

With the failure of the United Nations conference of 1981 to produce a full meeting of minds among the anti-Vietnamese coalition, its members turned their attentions to reinforcing pressure on Vietnam. A prime concern was to ensure that the Cambodian seat in the United Nations was retained, despite the murderous identity of Khmer Rouge representation. Political embarrassment was partially overcome in June 1982 by forging a tripartite coalition between the Khmer Rouge and two non-communist factions within a so-called Coalition Government of Democratic Kampuchea, presided over by Prince Norodom Sihanouk, which assumed the Cambodian seat in the United Nations. Joining the Khmer Rouge were the United National Front for an Independent, Peaceful and Cooperative Cambodia (Funcinpec in its French acronym), led by Prince Sihanouk, and the Khmer People's National Liberation Front, led by former prime minister Son Sann. This coalition contained the three main contending streams in Cambodian politics since the end of the Pacific War (1941–5): the royalist, the republican and the social revolutionary. They were united up to a point in their anti-Vietnamese endeavour, but were more of an incipient civil war than a government in waiting.

The United Nations retained a feeble initiative in the Cambodian conflict through its Austrian chairman of the 1981 conference, who made a number of fruitless attempts at mediation. In the main, it reverted to its arena role whereby each year a diplomatic ritual was played out with support mobilised for and against a resolution calling for Vietnamese troop withdrawals. The struggle for Cambodia then became a test of military resolve within the country, with a disparate insurgency operating with the benefit of territorial sanctuary in Thailand as well as attracting military assistance from China and military training from some ASEAN states and Britain. Vietnam demonstrated a countervailing ability to underpin the government it had implanted in Phnom Penh despite growing economic distress arising from its diplomatic isolation and attendant sanctions.

### A changing international context

The key to Vietnam's Indochina strategy was continuing material support from the Soviet Union. That support began to waver after the assumption of power in March 1985 by Mikhail Gorbachev, whose government set out to end its involvement in regional conflicts in order to improve its global relationships. Accordingly, the balance of advantage in the conflict began to change, prompting a radical response by Hanoi. In December 1986, the Sixth National Congress of Vietnam's Communist Party committed itself to a fundamental economic reform based on market principles, matching Soviet *perestroika*. This policy of *Doi Moi*, or renovation, was designed to safeguard regime security, but the required access to the international economy was obstructed by the Cambodian conflict. Vietnam addressed this obstacle by seizing the diplomatic initiative.

Vietnam was encouraged by Prince Sihanouk breaking ranks with his coalition partners during 1987 and entering into negotiations with Prime Minister Hun Sen of the Phnom Penh government. Indonesian and subsequently ASEAN support was then secured for an exclusive south-east Asian approach to a political settlement, involving all Cambodian factions as well as regional states. Vietnam attempted to trade off the withdrawal of its forces from Cambodia in return for regional endorsement of the government implanted in Phnom Penh. Talks between Sihanouk and Hun Sen, and then multilateral negotiations which ensued in Indonesia from July 1988 onward proved to be inconclusive. The tripartite Coalition Government of Democratic Kampuchea was internally divided, but was of one mind in insisting on the dismantling of the Phnom Penh government and its succession by an interim quadripartite coalition, which would conduct elections under international supervision. This proposal was rejected by the Phnom Penh government. Despite joining in negotiations with the Khmer Rouge, Prime Minister Hun Sen refused to accept their participation as an equal party to a political settlement and any provision for international peacekeeping. The failure of the regional approach to conflict resolution provided an opening for the permanent members of the United Nations Security Council to take up the diplomatic initiative, despite their mixed interests.

### From Paris to Paris

In April 1989, faced with mounting economic difficulty and external pressure, Vietnam offered an unconditional withdrawal of its forces from Cambodia by the following September. This concession provided the opportunity for convening an international conference in Paris at the end of July, under the auspices of the Secretary-General of the United Nations, Perez de Cuellar, chaired jointly by the foreign ministers of France and Indonesia. The anti-Vietnamese coalition reiterated their insistence on a comprehensive political settlement involving not only Vietnamese military withdrawal but also provision for an interim coalition to replace the Phnom Penh administration before national elections. The problem of interim power-sharing among Cambodian factions proved to be as intractable as ever, reinforced by the added objection from the Phnom Penh government, supported by Vietnam, to a United Nations role unless the Cambodian seat in the Organisation were declared vacant. The conference suspended its deliberations at the end of August.

The United Nations' initiative did not lapse, however, aided by a continuing linked improvement in Sino-Soviet and Sino-Vietnamese relations which served to change the structure of the conflict by diminishing its international dimension. At the end of the year, the Australian government began to explore and flesh out a proposal by American Congressman Stephen Solarz for a direct United Nations role intended to overcome the impasse over power-sharing. The Australian government envisaged the establishment of an interim United Nations administration in Cambodia, which would conduct elections to determine the political future of the country. The Australian plan was discussed and taken up in January 1990 at a meeting in Paris of senior officials from the five permanent members of the Security Council; the meeting endorsed 'an enhanced role' for the United Nations, but without indicating explicit provision for administration by the Organisation.

This initiative carried the germ of the ultimate peace settlement by identifying a symbolic device which might be employed to overcome the long-standing stumbling block to a political settlement. A Supreme National Council, on which all Cambodian factions would be represented, would embody national sovereignty and assume the Cambodian seat in the United Nations. Power-sharing would be circumvented between the onset and completion of a political settlement by that Council, delegating executive responsibilities to a United Nations administration which would run key ministries and also organise elections for a constituent assembly as well as supervising a ceasefire, the disarmament and demobilisation of contending forces and the withdrawal of foreign troops. The permanent members of the Security Council reached a framework agreement at the end of August 1990 in which original provision for a United Nations administration was diluted in the face of objections from the Phnom Penh government in particular. That agreement was then endorsed by the Security Council in September and by the General Assembly in October.

The Cambodian factions accepted this agreement as the basis for settling their conflict at a meeting in Jakarta in September 1990, including the general terms of reference of the twelve-member Supreme National Council to include the Khmer Rouge. The early implementation of the Security Council agreement was frustrated, however, because the Phnom Penh government with Vietnamese support persisted in standing out against its virtual dissolution through United Nations' control as well as seeking a specific provision barring the return to power of the Khmer Rouge. It took another year of political wrangling among the Cambodian factions before the Paris conference could reconvene to conclude a political settlement.

The momentum of accommodation was accelerated by Sino-Vietnamese rapprochement whereby a weakened Vietnam signalled a willingness to accept that its invasion of Cambodia had been a grievous mistake. The Supreme National Council overcame its deadlock at a meeting held in Beijing in July 1991, agreeing to a ceasefire and the despatch of a single delegation to the United Nations. Prince Sihanouk assumed the office of chairman, stepping down as leader of Funcinpec in favour of his son Prince Ranariddh. Terms of reference for the peace-keeping mandate were progressively worked out, but they stopped well short of interim administration and therefore did not challenge the nominal constitutional position of the Phnom Penh government, whose status had been at the heart of the conflict. By this juncture, the People's Republic of Kampuchea had changed its title to that of the more innocuous State of Cambodia. Correspondingly, shortly before the Paris Agreement was concluded, the ruling People's Revolutionary Party of Kampuchea changed its name to the Cambodian People's Party (CPP). These cosmetic changes were an attempt to make a virtue of political necessity in order to uphold the status quo established through Vietnam's military intervention.

To that extent, the term 'comprehensive' as applied to the ultimate settlement, was less than exact. The term had been employed by the anti-Vietnamese coalition as a code to indicate that a settlement required not only a withdrawal of Vietnamese forces, but also a change in the political status quo through the participation of all Cambodian factions, including the murderous Khmer Rouge. China's willingness to support a political settlement depended on such participation, viewed by the other permanent members of the Security Council as a necessary evil to avoid a continuing civil war. The attendant dismantling of the Phnom Penh administration did not take place, however. The United Nations plan was implemented with that administration still in place, despite its having been established as a direct consequence of Vietnam's invasion, which had drawn the Organisation into the conflict from the outset. China tolerated this concession because Vietnam, bereft of Soviet support, was no longer seen as a potential regional hegemon; the Khmer Rouge leadership almost certainly miscalculated that the Phnom Penh administration would fall apart with United Nations' intervention. In the event, the intervening presence of the United Nations Transitional Authority served to bolster the position of the incumbent administration to the fury of the Khmer Rouge.

### The nature of the Paris Agreement

The Paris Agreement on Cambodia concluded on 23 October 1991 envisaged a transitional period during which a constituent assembly would be elected through free and fair elections organised and certified by the United Nations. That assembly would be charged with drafting and approving a liberal democratic constitution; the constituent assembly would transform itself into a legislative assembly and create a new government, which would mark the end of the transitional period and the United Nations' mission. The intractable problem of power-sharing was to be bypassed through the Supreme National Council (SNC) delegating to the United Nations all powers necessary to ensure the implementation of the agreement. To that end, the Security Council was invited to establish a United Nations Transitional Authority in Cambodia (UNTAC), with civilian and military components under the direct responsibility of the Secretary-General. Apart from law-and-order peacekeeping duties relating to military arrangements and verification of withdrawal of foreign forces, UNTAC was given direct responsibility for ensuring 'a neutral political environment' conducive to free and fair elections. Under the terms of its mandate, all administrative agencies, bodies and offices acting in the field of foreign affairs, national defence, finance, public security and information were to be placed 'under the direct control of UNTAC', which would be exercised as necessary to ensure strict neutrality. This provision was intended to serve as an alternative to dismantling the Phnom Penh administration, which the United Nations did not have the resources to replace. Its degree of implementation proved to be highly controversial from early in UNTAC's tenure. The underlying problem was that the Cambodian factions to the agreement were bitter adversaries who had accepted the Paris Agreement with private reservations, because to abide strictly by their terms could lead to undoubted political disadvantage.

## UNTAC's mandate and the problem of implementation

On 28 February 1992, the Security Council established UNTAC, whose powers and responsibilities on paper exceeded those of all previous United Nations peacekeeping operations. By its Resolution 745 (1992), the Council committed the Organisation to the single most ambitious field operation in its history, aimed at producing a 'just and durable settlement to the Cambodia conflict' on the basis of free and fair elections in a neutral political environment within 'a period not to exceed eighteen months'.[5]

The UN operation was a success in its post-electoral outcome. A new constitution and government were created, while political violence had been reduced to a minimal level. Nonetheless, UNTAC had not been able to fulfil many of the terms of its mandate. For example, it had been unable to demilitarise and demobilise the armed factions, to protect human rights and to create a genuine 'neutral political environment' before conducting elections. It may be argued therefore that the Cambodian patient lived, but that the United Nations operation failed in a number of its responsibilities. Moreover, the political prognosis for the patient remains most uncertain. A structural problem of power-sharing has been only mitigated, and not resolved, through the intervening charismatic role of an ageing and infirm Norodom Sihanouk. The Khmer Rouge, who have been outlawed by the coalition government, continue to pose a military and political challenge.

UNTAC's shortcomings may be examined and explained on two levels. First, the non-cooperation of parties to the October 1991 Paris Agreement – principally the Khmer Rouge and the State of Cambodia – made key provisions of the peace plan virtually impossible to implement.

---

[5] Resolution 745, 28 February 1992.

Although the power-sharing problem in the transitional period was only set aside by enshrining the 'sovereignty, independence and unity of Cambodia' in the SNC, UNTAC's timetable was still predicated on the assumption that all four factions would be committed to the peace process. The UNTAC operation was thus based firmly on traditional principles of peacekeeping without provision being made for enforcing any aspect of the plan submitted by Secretary-General, Boutros Boutros-Ghali, for approval by the Security Council on 19 February 1992. As the Secretary-General himself put it shortly before the elections, UNTAC could only solve problems 'through dialogue, persuasion, negotiation and diplomacy'.[6]

Further complicating the UN's task of bringing stability to Cambodia was the erratic attitude and behaviour of Norodom Sihanouk throughout the transitional period. Although he was in poor health and domiciled much of the time in Beijing, UNTAC could not risk alienating the hugely popular leader who had long been revered by peasants as a 'God-king' and who had enjoyed a pivotal position both domestically and internationally as chairman of the SNC. Secondly, in terms of resources, planning and execution, the UN operation suffered from major limitations which were not conducive to a lasting settlement. With the notable exceptions of its electoral and repatriation components, as well as that part of the civil administration responsible for information, the UN operation in Cambodia demonstrated that the Organisation was ill equipped to initiate and sustain large-scale multi-component missions. UNTAC's operational efficiency was adversely affected by weakness in areas of logistics organisation and of command, control and communications. The quality of some of the troops and civilian personnel serving with the authority was also open to question.

The interaction of these two adverse factors, non-cooperation by the parties concerned and structural weaknesses in the UN peacekeeping machinery, resulted in a situation which, by the time the operation was completed in September 1993, differed markedly from that envisaged by the 18 signatories to the Paris Agreement in October 1991.

The plan for implementing the Paris mandate, approved by Resolution 745 (1992), set out the structure and functions of UNTAC.[7] It contained detailed provisions outlining the functions of seven distinctive components: electoral, civil administration, human rights, civilian police, repatriation, rehabilitation and military. The electoral component was charged with formulating, in consultation with the SNC, a

---

[6] Press Conference of the Secretary-General and Prince Norodom Sihanouk at the Royal Palace in Phnom Penh, 7 April 1993.
[7] Report of the Secretary-General on Cambodia, S/23613, 19 February 1992.

legal framework for the impending elections, consisting of an electoral law, regulations and codes of conduct. Additionally, it was to conduct civic education programmes, voter registration and the polling itself. The basis for the elections was to be proportional representation by province.

In order to facilitate the transition to a popularly elected government, the Paris Agreement emphasised that 'a neutral political environment conducive to free and fair general elections' had to be created. To this end, UNTAC's civil administration would exercise 'direct control as necessary to ensure strict neutrality' over all 'agencies, bodies and offices acting in the field of foreign affairs, national defence, finance, public security and information'. Moreover, 'direct supervision or control' would also be exercised over those administrative structures that 'could directly influence the outcome of elections'.[8]

To promote a climate conducive to free and fair elections, UNTAC's human rights component was also given a role through education programmes, monitoring and investigation in fostering 'an environment in which respect for human rights and fundamental freedoms ensued'. Allied responsibility for ensuring that law and order was 'maintained effectively and impartially' in all 21 provinces was allocated to UNTAC's civilian police. Its strength was 3,600 officers from more than 30 police forces world-wide. The repatriation component was given the task of ensuring that some 360,000 refugees from camps along the Thai–Cambodian border were resettled within a nine-month period, while the rebuilding of basic infrastructure, public utilities and essential services was entrusted to the rehabilitation component.

By far the largest of UNTAC's components was the military one. The original tasks entrusted to it were both far-reaching and unprecedented in UN peacekeeping history. Its responsibilities covered four major areas: (1) verification of the withdrawal of foreign troops and their arms and equipment; (2) supervision of the ceasefire and the regroupment, cantonment and disarming of armed factions; (3) weapons control, including measures to locate and destroy caches throughout the country; and (4) a mine-clearing and education programme. According to UNTAC's timetable, 70 per cent of the existing armies of all four factions were to be cantoned and disarmed by September 1992. In addition, the military component was given important support tasks for other mission components relating, in particular, to security at reception

---

[8] *Agreement on a Comprehensive Political Settlement of the Cambodia Conflict*, Annex 1, Section B, paras. 1–2 (for text, see p. 142 in appendix A).

centres for Cambodian refugees and the rebuilding of the country's basic infrastructure.

To achieve these objectives, UNTAC was allocated 12 enlarged infantry battalions (each supposedly with integral first-line and second-line support), responsible for establishing and manning regroupment and cantonment areas. At the same time, 485 military observers – posted at fixed locations or working as mobile 'verification teams' – were given responsibility for physically verifying adherence to the provisions relating to the regroupment, cantonment and demobilisation processes.[9] To assist these operations, an air-support group with 10 fixed-wing aircraft and 26 helicopters was attached to UNTAC. Because of the collapse of much of the country's existing infrastructure, an engineering unit of more than 2,000 soldiers was given responsibility for providing support to infantry battalions with water-purification systems, site preparation and track and road maintenance. Additional logistics support was provided by a logistics battalion charged also with supporting the civilian component 'as required'. Assistance to the civilian elements was to be provided by UNTAC's signals units whose primary task was to establish and maintain the force communications net.

It is clear in retrospect that the implementation plan, unprecedented in scope and complexity, contained some major weaknesses. In the first place, as will be discussed more fully later, it was not based on a coherent logistical estimate of the situation on the ground. Furthermore, it did not take sufficient account of the political and practical difficulties inherent in trying to assume a quasi-administrative role with existing government structures still in place. Most importantly, the extremely compressed timetable for elections came to act as a straitjacket on the activities of all the other components regardless of the difficulties encountered. Although one of the principal reasons for sticking so rigidly to the electoral schedule was financial, a systematic process of pre-deployment planning would have made it clear that UNTAC's mandate as set out in the Paris Agreement could not possibly be implemented responsibly within the space of 18 months, even had the parties to the Agreement been cooperative. After initial surveys by Australian and UN technical survey teams, it was decided that elections could only be held during the dry season in the first half of the year. This meant that any postponement would have generated particularly acute financial diffi-

---

[9] To verify the withdrawal and non-return of foreign forces UNTAC originally planned to post forces at 24 fixed locations or 'ingress/egress points': seven along the border with Thailand, nine along the border with Vietnam and two along the border with Laos. See S/23613, para. 58.

culties, a fact which undoubtedly added to the sense of urgency that characterised UNTAC's concept of implementation. As one report accurately noted, the timetable presented by the Secretary-General in February 1992 would have required 'almost perfect efficiency to succeed'.[10] This was clearly too much to ask of the UN.

There is a further consideration to be addressed. Under the Paris Agreement, the SNC would offer 'advice to UNTAC' provided there was consensus among its members. Failing such consensus, however, Prince Norodom Sihanouk, president of the SNC and the 'legitimate representative of Cambodian sovereignty', who was declared head of state in November 1992 upon his return from exile, would be 'entitled to make decisions on what advice to offer UNTAC'. Although the SNC was in many ways a legal fiction, the standing of Sihanouk among ordinary Cambodians made it necessary for the UN to ensure his continuing support for the operation. His volatile moods, absences from Phnom Penh and frequently contradictory statements complicated his relationship with the special representative of the Secretary-General and head of UNTAC, Yasushi Akashi.[11] For example, although the Paris accords made no mention of a presidential poll, Sihanouk at one stage 'persuaded' the UN to accept the idea. He did so by withdrawing his cooperation from the UN and by refusing to sign agreements in his capacity as president of the SNC for loans from the World Bank. He subsequently abandoned the idea for presidential elections after the adoption of a new monarchical constitution by the constituent assembly.[12]

### The Khmer Rouge and the abandonment of the military provisions

Given the exceptionally ambitious nature of UNTAC's mission and the compressed schedule for the elections, it was hardly surprising that the implementation plan emphasised that the military component had to be 'assured that all the Cambodian parties will scrupulously fulfil the commitments that have been made in signing the agreements and will

[10] *The Lost Agenda: Human Rights and UN Field Operations* (New York: Human Rights Watch, June 1993), p. 44.

[11] At a joint press conference with Boutros Boutros-Ghali, Sihanouk himself noted how journalists referred to him as the 'changing prince or the mercurial prince': Press Conference of the Secretary-General and Prince Norodom Sihanouk at the Royal Palace in Phnom Penh, 7 April 1993.

[12] *Report of the Secretary-General on the Implementation of Security Council Resolution 792 (1992)*, S/25289, 13 February 1993, para. 49. Similarly, to the dismay of UNTAC and diplomats in the capital, during a critical and violent stage in the run-up to the elections, Prince Sihanouk left for North Korea to attend the birthday celebrations of Kim Il-Sung.

extend full cooperation to UNTAC at all times'.[13] In fact, throughout the entire period of the UN operation in Cambodia, fighting continued within the country. Moreover, UN forces were themselves subject to deliberate attack and sustained 56 fatalities. The kidnapping of UN personnel and the theft of their equipment was another frequent occurrence throughout the transitional period. The ceasefire, supposedly in effect from the signing of the Paris Agreement, only resulted in a reduction in the level of fighting which followed a cyclical pattern of dry-season government offensives succeeded by wet-season attacks by the Khmer Rouge.[14] Before the election, Khmer Rouge military operations against the Cambodian People's Armed Forces (CPAF) were often at battalion level and were accompanied by systematic acts of terror directed in particular against ethnic Vietnamese settlers.

Even before UNTAC began its deployment, the Khmer Rouge had launched a series of 'unusually well-coordinated offensives' in the countryside in an attempt to enlarge their base areas in the north of the country and secure strategic roads (National Highways 6 and 12) before the arrival of UN troops.[15] In provinces such as Battambang in the north-west, the Khmer Rouge successfully expanded its area of operations into State of Cambodia (SOC)-controlled territory beyond the agreed ceasefire line. Government forces in turn responded by counter-offensives and showed an increased determination not to relinquish administrative and government control. Throughout March and April 1992, large-scale fighting in Kompong Thom Province between the Khmer Rouge and government forces delayed the deployment of Indonesian peacekeeping units.[16]

In spite of an inauspicious start, when UNTAC became operational on 15 March 1992 it was still hoped that all four factions would abide by the military provisions of the implementation plan. Khmer Rouge offensives against the CPAF were dismissed by UN officials as 'tactical manoeuvring' before the disarmament process. This optimism resulted from the Khmer Rouge's willingness to permit UNHCR-directed repatriation of refugees from three camps under its control and also for

---

[13] S/23613, para. 81.
[14] See 'Renewed Fighting in Cambodia Places UN Truce in Peril', *International Herald Tribune*, 17 June 1992; 'Khmer Rouge Widens Its Attacks . . . Ceasefire at Risk Nationwide', *International Herald Tribune*, 16 July 1992, and 'Phnom Penh Offensive Threatens Peace Plan', *Independent*, 2 February 1993.
[15] 'Khmer Rouge Reported to Grab for Territory', *International Herald Tribune*, 14–15 March 1992; 'UN Representative Sounds Cambodia Warning', *Financial Times*, 16 March 1992.
[16] An estimated 18,000 people were driven from their villages in the province of Kompong Thom between January and May and many of these have been unable to return because of the mines which have since been planted in the area.

some limited inspection by UN observers of its base areas. The repatriation process, which began on 30 March, was an inter-agency effort headed and organised by the UNHCR in the field. By April 1993, more than 96 per cent of the 360,000 targeted refugees had been repatriated. This achievement, while praiseworthy, serves to highlight the fact that continuous cooperation from all contending parties is the basic condition for successful peacekeeping. When it came to implementing the military provisions' of the Paris Agreement, such cooperation was not forthcoming.

On 9 May 1992, UNTAC formally announced that Phase I of the ceasefire would be followed on 13 June by Phase II, under which regroupment and cantonment of all four factions' military forces would take place. Reporting in July 1992 on the progress of the UNTAC operation, Boutros Boutros-Ghali observed that it was 'becoming increasingly clear' that the Party of Democratic Kampuchea (Khmer Rouge) would not honour the assurances it had originally given. Indeed, by this time the Khmer Rouge had already refused UNTAC entry to the areas under its control and had failed to provide figures on the number of troops and material there, as required by the Paris Agreement. Although various measures were taken to bring the Khmer Rouge into the process – including an informal proposal for discussion drawn up at a Ministerial Conference on the Rehabilitation and Reconstruction of Cambodia on 22 June in Tokyo, designed to meet some of the specific concerns set out by the Khmer Rouge – Khieu Sampan, its nominal leader and principal representative on the SNC, refused to rejoin the peace process. It is worth noting that the option of enforcement – briefly advocated by the French deputy force commander, Michel Loridon, who urged that UNTAC 'should call the Khmer Rouge's bluff' – was quickly rejected by the UN because troop-contributing countries (notably Australia, Japan and Indonesia) made it clear that they were not prepared to consider the use of force, except in self-defence.[17]

The immediate result was that UNTAC was denied entry to some 15 per cent of the country, specifically in Pailin close to the Thai border and in parts of north-western Siem Reap, northern Preah Vihear and central Kompong Thom. More seriously, the Khmer Rouge's attitude derailed the process of demilitarisation, gradually forcing the UN to abandon completely its demobilisation programme in the summer and

[17] Private discussion with UNHCR and DPKO officials. Lieutenant-General Sanderson was also keenly aware of the importance of not being drawn into enforcement-type operations within what was essentially a peacekeeping mission. See John M. Sanderson, 'UNTAC: Successes and Failures', in Smith, *International Peacekeeping*, pp. 29–30.

autumn of 1992.[18] By mid-November, only some 55,000 troops of the three cooperating parties had been cantoned. The collapse of the military provisions of the Agreement meant that less than 5 per cent of the estimated 200,000 troops had been cantoned by the target date. Those who did register in the regroupment areas were thought by UN officials to be untrained teenagers with old, often useless weapons, while superior forces and caches of weapons remained in the field. Nonetheless, in late 1992, the Security Council decided, despite the incomplete application of the Paris accords, to authorise preparations for elections in all areas to which UNTAC would have access as of 31 January 1993.

The reasons given by the Khmer Rouge for not participating were twofold. First, it argued persistently that Vietnamese forces had not been fully withdrawn from the country. UNTAC, anxious to keep the 'door open for full and constructive participation by the PDK in the peace process', took the charge extremely seriously and intensified efforts to 'uncover' Vietnamese forces in hiding but found little basis for the charge.[19] By 'Vietnamese forces', the Khmer Rouge meant all ethnic Vietnamese inside Cambodia, including second-generation immigrants and those attracted temporarily by the boom created by the massive foreign presence, especially in Phnom Penh. The second reason advanced by the Khmer Rouge carried more force: namely, that 'real' power had not been transferred from the Phnom Penh government and that the UN's exercise of so-called 'direct control' had not prevented the SOC from using the state apparatus, and especially the secret police, for party political ends.

### The failure of UN 'direct control' and SOC intimidation

It had been agreed in Paris that for a 'neutral political environment' to emerge before elections, some form of UN control had to be exercised over the SOC administration. The formula chosen was that of 'direct control' in the areas of foreign affairs, national defence, finance, public security and information. Conscious of the fluid nature of bureaucratic and administrative boundaries, UNTAC hoped that a 'functional analysis would yield an identification of existing administrative structures concerned'.[20] By definition, this task required intimate knowledge of and sensitivity to the host culture. Yet both were in short supply and

[18] 'UN to Halt Cambodian Disarmament', *International Herald Tribune*, 22 October 1992.
[19] Interviews with UNTAC officials.
[20] S/23613, para. 94.

UNTAC's attempts to control the administration with any effect were wholly unsuccessful.

This failure of control obtained in part because SOC ministries and officials deliberately obstructed UNTAC. It was made impossible, for example, for it to 'work as a partner with all existing administrative structures charged with public security' as stipulated in the implementation plan. The failure of direct control, however, was also the result of inadequate preparation on the part of UNTAC's civil administration component, whose lack of qualified staff and knowledge of the nature of the SOC bureaucracy and the Khmer language hampered its activities from the outset. Many civilian administration positions simply remained empty. Moreover, even when appropriate personnel were available, a study by Asia Watch found that UNTAC administrators did not always carry out their duties when actually stationed in the ministries to which they had been assigned.[21]

The most serious failure of the civil administration component was its inability to monitor, let alone control, the activities of 'agencies, bodies and offices dealing with public security at the highest levels'.[22] Indeed, throughout the transitional period, the SOC secret police operated much as it had done before. The UN assigned two administrators to the Ministry of National Security who 'relied on periodic briefings by the Ministry itself to learn of its activities'. Moreover, the UN never specified standards of accountability, something which made control difficult to effect. As a result, the government was able to use the state apparatus against political opponents. A particularly bloody campaign of assassinations was directed against Funcinpec functionaries when the political popularity of the party of Prince Norodom Sihanouk's son, Prince Norodom Ranariddh, increased dramatically in late 1992.

To counter this breakdown in law and order, the UN could have employed its 3,600-strong police force whose mandate included the continuous monitoring of the internal security forces and local police forces at all levels. With a few isolated exceptions, however, UNTAC's CIVPOL was the least successful of its components.[23] An important reason for this failing was the lack of pre-deployment planning and agreement on standard operational procedures and the lack of a working language among its officers: a multinational force drawn from more than 30 different police forces world-wide.

The most serious weakness of the civilian police operations, however, stemmed from the inability to prosecute. Following a significant

---

[21] *Lost Agenda*, p. 51.
[22] S/23613, para. 101.
[23] Private interviews.

increase in violence throughout the country in November and December 1992, UNTAC Directive 93/1 of 6 January 1993 established a Special Prosecutor's Office with 'powers to arrest, detain and prosecute persons accused of politically motivated criminal acts and human rights violations'.[24] For the first time in UN peacekeeping history, UN civil police forces were given powers of arrest. This provision marked a potentially significant departure from the principle of non-enforcement. The efficacy of the Prosecutor's Office turned out to be very limited, however. In the first place, the directive was strongly opposed by other UNTAC components, most prominently by the civil administration, which argued that it went beyond UNTAC's mandate. Similarly, UNTAC's military component was unwilling to use force when making arrests. A more serious obstacle was the failure to find any independent local court that could hear cases brought by the Prosecutor's Office. Added to this, the absence of any witness protection programme, proper defence council or criminal laws under which to prosecute suspects all served to undermine the value of this innovation in UN practice. While UNTAC was able to place a SOC policeman and a Khmer Rouge soldier in custody early in February 1993, their cases had not come to court by the end of 1994.

As indicated earlier, the failure to obtain cooperation from the parties to the Cambodian conflict was not the only factor impairing the effectiveness of the UN operation in Cambodia. Although preparations for a major UN commitment began before the Paris Agreement were signed, they did not prevent acute problems from developing in areas of logistics support, command, control and communications. Furthermore, financial problems, the lack of systematic procedures for collecting and processing intelligence (or 'information' to use UN terminology) and the highly uneven quality of the troops and civilian staff serving with UNTAC further weakened its effectiveness.

## Planning, logistics preparations and initial deployment

The ambitious nature of UNTAC's mandate placed a premium on obtaining accurate data on which pre-deployment planning could be based. This task was severely complicated by Cambodia's long period of isolation from the outside world and, in particular, by the absence of reliable government records and statistics (most of which had been destroyed by the Khmer Rouge between 1975 and 1978). It was partly

[24] S/25289. See also 'UN to Combat Political Murders in Cambodia', *Los Angeles Times*, 8 January 1993.

for this reason that the Security Council, even before the final agreements were signed in Paris, had authorised the deployment of several technical survey missions to reconnoitre the area of deployment.[25] The gathering of planning data, however, was fragmented and not effectively organised, with the result that UN forces arriving in Cambodia did not have sufficient knowledge about conditions on the ground.

During 1990, the Secretary-General sent three separate technical survey teams to Cambodia to examine 'emerging operational issues' relating to the rebuilding of the infrastructure, civil administration and the repatriation of refugees from Thailand. Another military survey mission was sent in September 1991 to explore the conditions for a stable ceasefire prior to the arrival of the United Nations Advance Mission in Cambodia (UNAMIC). Another three survey missions – on military arrangements, civil administration, and police and human rights – visited the country between October and December 1991. UNAMIC established its headquarters in Phnom Penh on 9 November 1991 in order to 'maintain the momentum' of the peace process and prevent any 'untoward development' in Cambodia. It was also established with a view to providing more data for mission planning in New York.[26] Once UNAMIC personnel arrived back in New York, the paucity of staff within the DPKO and the preoccupation of planners with the Croatian deployment delayed the process of detailed mission-planning.[27] The activities of various survey missions sent to Cambodia before UNTAC's deployment were clearly not coordinated. This prevented the development of an integrated plan. The lack of civil–military integration, in particular, remained a serious problem throughout the entire operation, and was only partly overcome by the creation of Joint Operations Centres throughout the country.[28] Indeed, assessing the operation as a whole, the Force Commander, Lieutenant-General John Sanderson,

---

[25] The first fact-finding mission, which also looked into the requirements of UN field operations in the country, was sent by the Secretary-General in August 1989.

[26] UNAMIC consisted of a civilian and military liaison staff as well as a military mine-awareness unit and support personnel.

[27] Private interviews. See also J. Chopra, J. Mackinlay and L. Minear, *Report on the Cambodian Peace Process* (Oslo: Norwegian Institute of International Affairs, February 1993), p. 19. For an account of the weaknesses of UN logistics support and planning generally, see Mats Berdal, *Whither UN Peacekeeping?*, Adelphi Paper 281 (London: Brassey's, for the International Institute for Strategic Studies, October 1993), pp. 32–5. See chapter 3 for a discussion of the Croatian deployment and other aspects of the UN mission in former Yugoslavia.

[28] For a more detailed account of the weaknesses in the area of planning, see *UN Peacekeeping: Lessons Learned in Managing Recent Missions* (Washington, D. C.: General Accounting Office, December 1993), pp. 30–5.

identified the complete lack of 'any strategic planning within UNTAC' as a major source of the 'many practical problems experienced'.[29]

The most serious planning problem, however, and one which directly influenced the deployment of UNTAC's various components, was the absence of any centralised logistic planning unit within the UN Secretariat where the provision of logistics support was coordinated by the Field Operations Division (in the Department of Administration and Management) which was only obliged to 'consult' with the DPKO.[30] Although the implementation plan noted that the assessment of resources required for the operation had taken account of 'the varied nature of the topography and vegetation, climatic conditions, the nature of warfare which has been waged . . . the disposition of the forces of the parties and, above all, the degradation or non-existence of infrastructure', this did not amount to a proper logistical estimate. The size of the force, especially its air and engineering component, was simply too small to cope with the range of tasks assigned to it in a country without an effective transport network during the rainy season and with limited refuelling depots and sanitation facilities. Once the specialised logistics elements had been deployed, problems of supply continued because of the existence of different supply doctrines and incompatible equipment among the three countries providing logistics support.

Some of the aforementioned problems might have been overcome by the early deployment of qualified engineers. In fact, the lack of an effective engineering capability was a major problem throughout the operation and illustrates many of the weaknesses in UN planning procedures. For example, no engineering reconnaissance aimed at identifying tasks and local resources took place before UNTAC commenced its deployment. Moreover, apart from the early deployment of the Thai battalion, UNTAC's other engineering units from China and Poland only began to deploy after the regular infantry units had arrived. At the same time, neither the Chinese nor the Polish contingent was adequately equipped for operations in Cambodia, while the French engineering company was too small (only some 150 men) and the well-equipped engineers provided by Japan were restricted in their deployment to an area south of Phnom Penh. In addition to this, the UN headquarters in New York had not developed appropriate guidelines for the engineering elements. Such guidelines should have been issued to contributing countries before their units deployed.

[29] Sanderson, 'UNTAC: Successes and Failures', p. 22.
[30] 'Cambodian Peace Plan "Threatened" by UN Delay', *Daily Telegraph*, 14 January 1992 and private information from UNTAC officials.

A further and critical impediment to movement inside the country was the huge number of land-mines and sub-munitions in Cambodia. UN's initial de-mining programme, as well as subsequent measures taken to remedy the problem, provide perhaps the clearest example of the inadequacy of pre-deployment planning.[31] The UN's failure to address this problem early on critically undermined the humanitarian relief efforts of the UNHCR, UNDP and ICRC. As one UNHCR representative put it in late 1991: 'the only de-mining going on now is when people tread on them'.[32] In the course of 1992, land mines were planted in Cambodia at a faster rate than they were being removed, and by the time of the elections UNTAC's small Mine Clearance Training Unit (MCTU) had only disposed of some 15,000 mines and 'other pieces of unexploded ordnance'.[33] After the end of UNTAC's operation, it has been estimated that some 8–10 million mines remained.[34]

The UN's failure to anticipate ground conditions and the obvious disadvantages that stemmed from the lack of any systematic reconnaissance capability raises the issue of whether the UN should develop more effective means of gathering intelligence. Anxious to preserve the image of strict neutrality, the UN has traditionally refrained from activities which may be interpreted as involving the collection of military intelligence about the parties to a conflict. In politically fluid and militarily complex situations such as in Cambodia, more advanced technologies and procedures for collecting and assessing intelligence, and the development of a *local* intelligence apparatus, would undoubtedly have enhanced UNTAC's effectiveness. Specifically, once UNTAC began to deploy, it suffered from the lack of a tactical intelligence capability incorporating advanced surveillance and tracking techniques required for the monitoring of movement across borders in dense, malaria-ridden jungles, as well as for the location of arms caches throughout the country. Without such a capability, it was impossible to determine with any degree of accuracy the strength, organisation and operational efficiency of the Khmer Rouge.[35] It also made it difficult for UNTAC to

[31] 'UN Blamed for Delay in Clearing Mines', *Guardian*, 22 November 1991.

[32] For an account of the early de-mining efforts in Cambodia, see 'Political Control, Human Rights and the UN Missions in Cambodia', *Asia Watch* (New York: Asia Watch, September 1992), pp. 61–5.

[33] Craig Etcheson, 'The "Peace" in Cambodia', *Current History*, vol. 91, no. 569 (December 1992), p. 413; and *Fourth Progress Report of the Secretary-General on the United Nations Transitional Authority in Cambodia*, S/25719, 3 May 1993, paras. 52 and 53.

[34] *Cambodia Times* (Phnom Penh), 31 October–7 November 1993, p. 3.

[35] The question of the Khmer Rouge's strength has been a continuing source of controversy and speculation. UNTAC's own military observers rejected the estimates of western institutes as exaggerated, claiming that the Khmer Rouge strength was no more

ascertain whether Vietnamese forces, paramilitary or clandestine units, remained hidden within Cambodia as the Khmer Rouge claimed. Equally important, however, such a capability would also have enabled the UN to monitor the performance of its own operation, making sure that the deployment was proceeding smoothly and that the logistics flow was efficiently directed.

This quality of monitoring did not occur. Instead, the lack of accurate planning data, the extremely limited logistical capabilities available to the UN Secretariat and, in particular, the absence of a centralised logistical planning unit within the Secretariat in New York, led to an extremely drawn-out deployment process.[36] Although UNTAC's mandate had been agreed in Paris in October 1991, the UNTAC headquarters in Phnom Penh only became operational on 15 March 1992 when Yasushi Akashi took up his position as head of UNTAC. More serious still were the delays in the deployment of UNTAC's other components. Although priority was given to its military component, it was not until August that all 12 infantry battalions had been deployed. Moreover, military units were also deployed in an inverse order of effectiveness, with infantry troops arriving before logistics and engineering components. By August 1992, only about half of the civilian administrators had arrived and the civilian police component was still some 36 per cent below its planned strength. Initial difficulties in securing sufficient funds for UNTAC, whose operation eventually came to absorb more than two-thirds of the total UN peacekeeping budget, further delayed the deployment of troops. This problem was partly a consequence of the automatic delays built into the UN's complex budgetary allocation procedure. It also reflected, however, reluctance on the part of member states to provide necessary financial support, a problem that was resolved to a limited extent by the pledges made at the International Conference on the Reconstruction of Cambodia held in Tokyo in June 1992.[37]

## Command, control and direction from New York

The performance of any UN field operation has always been intimately linked to the effectiveness of its command and control arrangements, both within the theatre of operations and between the headquarters in

than 14,000–15,000 troops organised in divisional strengths of about 400. See 'Khmer Rouge Bogey Gets Cut Down to Size', *Business Times*, 16 April 1993.
[36] For some of the other sources of delay, see Yasushi Akashi, 'The Challenges Faced by UNTAC', *Japan Review of International Affairs*, vol. 7, no. 3 (Summer 1993), p. 188.
[37] The 31 countries attending pledged a total of US $880 million.

New York and the field. UN arrangements, however, are subject to a combination of technical and political constraints which invariably reduce the degree to which unified direction can be provided.[38] The size and complexity of UNTAC's mission meant that these constraints had a more detrimental effect on UN operations in Cambodia than on traditional peacekeeping operations. On the technical side, the UNTAC operations revealed just how difficult it is to establish reliable communications within a combined force where contingents arrive with their own equipment stocks, standards and specifications. Communications within Cambodia – that is, the links between the mission headquarters in Phnom Penh and individual battalions in the provinces – were hamstrung not only by the incompatibilities in communications equipment but also by the lack of standardised communications procedures and joint-level planning *before* deployment, which might have eased the problem. The destruction of the local infrastructure meant that the amount of signals traffic which could be carried on the civilian radio network, on which the UN usually relies, was extremely limited.

A further complication arising from the increasingly wide range of countries from which contingents were drawn – more than 40 countries provided military and police personnel to UNTAC – was that of language. In Cambodia, several battalions arrived with no knowledge of either French or English, and this in itself gave rise to major communications difficulties. UNTAC also suffered from a general lack of bilingual operators (i.e. proficient in Khmer) which UN's complex recruitment policies were unable to remedy.[39]

As noted above, command and control arrangements depend not only on technical factors. In Cambodia, the absence of clear and unambiguous chains of command *internal* to UNTAC, as well as proper coordination between the Secretariat in New York and the field, resulted in a loss of operational efficiency. Within UNTAC, a major challenge confronting Akashi and, especially, the force commander, Lieutenant-General Sanderson, from the outset, was how to ensure the loyalty of individual battalion commanders while making them accept the chain of command within the mission. By referring matters to national authorities, or even taking orders from embassies in Phnom Penh, it was often impossible for Akashi to coordinate effectively activities in the field. The Indonesian battalion, for example, was notorious for its tendency to take directions from the Indonesian ambassador in Phnom Penh

[38] For a discussion of UN command and control problems more generally, see Berdal, *Whither UN Peacekeeping?*, pp. 39–43.
[39] 'Leichtsinnig, schwerfällig, teuer – Die UN-Operation in Kambodscha: Kein Modell für Afghanistan', *Frankfürter Allgemeine Zeitung*, 3 July 1993.

rather than from the force commander.[40] While the disposition of national authorities to intervene in the day-to-day running of their own contingents is certainly not new, the hostile and dangerous operational environment in Cambodia, as well as the large number of new and inexperienced troop-contributing countries, made that practice more than usually unacceptable.[41]

The relationship between the Secretariat in New York and UNTAC exposed a fundamental problem (which has plagued other contemporary UN field operations) over the lack of clearly defined reporting channels back to the UN headquarters. This failing stemmed in part from the decentralised nature of UN management practices and the lack of horizontal coordination among the four principal departments most directly involved in peacekeeping operations: the DPKO, the Department of Political Affairs, the Department of Humanitarian Affairs and the Department of Administration and Management (DAM). In particular, as in other peacekeeping operations, the separation of the DPKO and the Field Operations Division (FOD) caused delays and confusion in Cambodia. Even had the reporting channels been properly specified, the general lack of political and military officers in New York, as well as the outdated procurement procedures of the organisation, made it extremely difficult to provide effective guidance and support for an operation on UNTAC's scale. For example, the purchase of medical supplies centrally through the FOD in New York resulted in delays until late September 1992. In the meantime, critical supplies had to be purchased locally in Bangkok. Cumbersome and centralised procurement regulations and decision-making procedures also delayed the introduction of a satisfactory air-control system to support UNTAC air operations for some nine months.

It is worth noting in this context that the efficiency of the UNHCR-led repatriation of refugees owed much to the fact that, by delegating financial and administrative responsibility from New York to the UNHCR in the field, a degree of flexibility in planning and execution was achieved which did not exist for any other of UNTAC's components. As noted above, these were forced to rely on insufficient and poorly coordinated administrative support from the DAM and the DPKO in New York. The experience of UNTAC clearly suggests, therefore, that a greater degree of financial, administrative and operational authority should be delegated to the field in future operations.

---

[40] On one occasion, when the Khmer Rouge held a group of Indonesian soldiers hostage, the ambassador negotiated directly with the captors and after their release requested a helicopter from UNTAC to fly them to safety.

[41] Private interviews.

## Training and quality of UNTAC personnel

The dramatic increase in UN peacekeeping operations in the first half of 1992 meant that the UN could no longer rely only on traditional troop-contributing countries for its operation in Cambodia. Similarly, the composite nature of the UNTAC mission required a high number of civilian personnel and experts recruited directly by the UN or seconded by member states on short-term contracts. In the words of one senior official, the Secretariat could 'not afford to be choosy' when it began to put together a force for Cambodia. The attendant danger was that insufficient attention would be given to the need for familiarising troops with peacekeeping procedures and the specific challenges of operating in Cambodia. Indeed, this turned out to be a major problem as several units failed to maintain even minimum standards of discipline while showing little or no sensitivity to religion or local customs in their area of deployment. In many cases, lack of training and poor disciplinary standards were compounded by the UN payment and allowances system which created very substantial income differentials between civilian and military officials in the field. An additional problem stemmed from the fact that once the cantonment process had collapsed in summer 1992, several infantry battalions were left with little to do. In the eyes of ordinary Cambodians, many UN soldiers appeared to be spending most of their time in bars and brothels or to be driving recklessly in UN vehicles.[42]

Certain contingents did considerable damage to the overall objectives of the operations by undermining the credibility of the UN in the eyes of the local population. The first Bulgarian battalion, and to a lesser extent contingents from Tunisia and Indonesia, are unofficially regarded as having done as much to damage as to advance the cause of UNTAC.[43] The Japanese police contingent was felt by some to be excessively concerned about the domestic political impact of sustaining casualties, especially during the early stage of its deployment. Ideally, UN policy with regard to the hiring of civilian staff should be governed by the relevant Charter provision which holds that 'paramount consideration in the employment of the staff . . . shall be the necessity of securing the highest standards of efficiency, competence, and integrity'.[44] In

---

[42] 'UN Cambodian Force Is Malfunctioning', *International Herald Tribune*, 5 October 1992; 'Sex and Inflation End the UN Honeymoon in Cambodia', *The Times*, 26 November 1992. The behaviour of the Bulgarian battalions, the first of which had to be sent back, has been particularly commented upon (interview with UNTAC officials).

[43] 'Leichtsinnig, schwerfallig, teuer'.

[44] Article 101, UN Charter.

practice, however, the stress on merit has become subordinate to that of geographical distribution and, more depressingly, to that of bureaucratic patronage and personal favouritism. This practice, combined with the difficulty of finding sufficient staff to fill specialist functions, explains why the quality of UNTAC staff was so uneven, with the highly competent and dedicated working alongside inexperienced and, worse, unmotivated personnel. This factor is important to an understanding of the mixed performance of UNTAC's different components. There is little doubt, for example, that a major reason for the impressive record of UNTAC's electoral component, which succeeded in registering more than 90 per cent (4.7 million) of the total number of eligible voters, lay in the quality and determination of those working for it (including 460 highly dedicated volunteers). Conversely, the overall performance of the civilian component has been attributed, at least in part, to the lack of proper organisation and motivation and to the poor quality of its staff.

There is a further important dimension to the UN's role in Cambodia which was not properly foreseen: the UNTAC presence was in itself economically and socially destabilising because it fuelled an artificial boom and generated massive inflation in the poverty-stricken country.[45] The dangers of hyperinflation and the 'distorting impact of UNTAC expenditure' on the Cambodian economy more generally, should have been anticipated since the civilian per diem 'mission subsistence allowance' (MSA) was as high as US $145 while the average per capita income in the country in 1991 was estimated at only US $150 a year.[46] It has been estimated that the 'total UNTAC budget was of the same order of magnitude as the total Cambodian GDP for the three years 1991–1993' and that this promoted a 'speculative private sector response' more than it encouraged the strengthening of the 'productive and administrative capacity of the economy'.[47] The economic boom in construction also led to an influx of ethnic Vietnamese who were disliked by many Cambodians and therefore inflamed ethnic tensions. The boom and the UNTAC presence also attracted a large number of prostitutes from Thailand, Vietnam and Laos, especially to Phnom Penh. Indeed, several reports indicate that cases of HIV infection, largely unknown in the country before the arrival of UN forces, rose dramatically during the transitional period and that the UN bureaucracy was

---

[45] 'With the UN in Town, Phnom Penh Booms – Is This a Good Thing?', *International Herald Tribune*, 23 June 1992.

[46] For a good account of the economic and social consequences of the UNTAC operation, see E. V. K. FitzGerald, 'The Economic Dimension of the Peace Process in Cambodia', in Peter Utting (ed.), *Between Hope and Insecurity: The Social Consequences of the Cambodian Peace Process* (Geneva: UNRISD Report, 1994).

[47] Ibid., pp. 78–85.

exceptionally slow in taking preventive action.[48] Such developments generated widespread resentment among the local population, resentment which naturally was exploited by the Khmer Rouge.[49] In February 1993, Prince Sihanouk, in a blunt and forceful attack on the UN performance, said that while the Cambodian people initially had been very willing to support the UN, they now 'detested' and 'hated UNTAC'.[50]

### Elections and political aftermath

Some 4.7 million Cambodians were registered for the elections despite the difficulties inherent in that process, but the collapse of the military provisions and the inability of UNTAC's civilian police to maintain law and order meant that a 'neutral political environment' as envisaged did not emerge in the country. Indeed, in the run-up to the elections the security situation deteriorated dramatically throughout the country. Between March and May 1993, incidents of political violence, including attacks on UNTAC representatives, resulted in 200 deaths, 338 injuries and 114 abductions.[51] Many of these fatalities were Vietnamese settlers murdered by Khmer Rouge guerrillas, with the most serious attack taking place on 11 March, when a massacre of 33 people in a fishing village sparked off a mass exodus of Vietnamese. At the same time, both Funcinpec and the Buddhist Liberal Democratic Party (an off-shoot of the Khmer People's National Liberation Front) electoral workers were subject to intensified government violence and obstruction of their campaigning. When, in mid-April, Khieu Sampan left the capital and formally withdrew the Khmer Rouge from the peace process, doubts arose as to whether the elections could be held at all, with foreign diplomats predicting the imminent resumption of full-scale civil war. UNTAC took a calculated risk to proceed, however.

In spite of the upsurge in violence, the elections were held between 23 and 27 May in a relatively peaceful atmosphere. This unanticipated outcome was partly a product of Khmer Rouge inaction, possibly with the greater prospect of a Funcinpec than a CPP victory which had been anticipated with apprehension. It also owed much to the UN presence,

---

[48] See 'Die Kambodschaner sterben still', *Frankfürter Allgemeine Zeitung*, 1 June 1993, and 'Child Sex Boom Blamed on UN', *Guardian*, 4 November 1993. See also Judy L. Ledgerwood, 'UN Peacekeeping Mission: The Lessons of Cambodia', *Asia-Pacific Issues* (East–West Center), no. 11 (March 1994), p. 7.

[49] 'Cambodians Fall out with UN Peacekeepers', *Independent*, 26 January 1993.

[50] 'I Want to Retake Power', *Far Eastern Economic Review*, 4 February 1993, p. 21.

[51] See 'Statement by the Director of UNTAC Human Rights Component on Political Violence', 23 May 1993. See also 'Pre-Poll Violence Overwhelms UN in Cambodia', *Independent*, 6 April 1993.

in particular the role of the electoral component whose volunteers risked life and limb in the countryside. Moreover, the intoxicating idea of political choice in free elections had been communicated with great effect by Radio UNTAC, a remarkable innovation in peacekeeping practice. It broadcast 16 hours a day and reached an extensive audience which responded on polling day.[52] Bravely defying threats of violence, an unanticipated 89.56 per cent of the registered voters cast their ballots and on 15 June 1993 the Security Council formally endorsed the election results declaring the balloting to have been free and fair. The votes cast and the attendant distribution of seats in the assembly gave Funcinpec a near majority:

| Party | Seats in assembly | Proportion of votes |
|-------|-------------------|---------------------|
| United National Front for an Independent, Peaceful and Cooperative Cambodia (Funcinpec) | 58 | 45.47% |
| Cambodian People's Party (CPP) | 51 | 38.23% |
| Buddhist Liberal Democratic Party (BLDP) | 10 | 3.81% |
| Molinaka and Nakataorsou Khmere for Freedom | 1 | 1.37%[53] |

In late May, the apparent outcome provoked protests from the CPP, which questioned the administration of the elections and called for fresh polls. Before the elections could be officially endorsed by the Security Council, Prince Sihanouk struck a deal with communist veteran hardliner, Chea Sim, declaring himself head of state in charge of an interim coalition government comprising the CPP and Funcinpec. Although justified from a fear of a military coup, Sihanouk had acted unilaterally without consulting Akashi, UN officials in New York or his own son, Prince Ranariddh, whose party had just won a plurality in the elections. In face of opposition from both Funcinpec and UNTAC officials, who privately deplored his action as a constitutional if bloodless coup, Sihanouk abandoned the idea some 12 hours later. The abortive initiative indicated the limitations of UNTAC's role. Sihanouk's retreat did not put an end to UNTAC's immediate difficulties. For a brief period, the CPP leadership appeared to endorse the formation of 'autonomous zones' in seven eastern provinces following a secessionist attempt led by Prince Norodom Chakrapong, the estranged half-brother of Prince Ranariddh and SOC's deputy prime minister, and General Sin Song, its minister of national security. That gambit was part of a concerted

---

[52] Akashi, 'Challenges Faced by UNTAC', p. 195.
[53] Cambodia Election Results, UN DPI/1389 – June 1993.

attempt by the CPP to ensure its participation in government, despite losing the elections.

With the collapse of the secessionist move by mid-June, the CPP grudgingly accepted the outcome of the elections and willingly participated in the establishment of a provisional national government of Cambodia with Funcinpec. Prince Ranariddh and Hun Sen jointly assumed the office of co-prime minister which was approved by the new constituent assembly on 1 July. To its credit, the UN had prevailed politically up to a point in refusing to reconsider the election results in spite of threats from the CPP. The post-election interim solution then became a working political compromise encouraged also through Prince Sihanouk's intervention. On 21 September, the constituent assembly approved a new liberal democratic constitution which reinstated the monarchy. Norodom Sihanouk was enthroned as constitutional monarch in Phnom Penh on 24 September 1993, nearly four decades after he had abdicated the throne. This ironic development institutionalised his facility for political intervention which in the last resort worked in the interest of stability, albeit not exactly as UNTAC had intended. The constitutional assembly then transformed itself into a national assembly on 28 September. But it was only at the end of October that a new government was announced with Prince Ranariddh and Hun Sen respectively as first and second prime minister, with the other posts being allocated also on a power-sharing basis. Delay in its announcement occurred primarily because of tensions within the CPP. That party obtained control of the Ministries of Home Affairs, Justice and Defence, while Chea Sim became chairman of the national assembly with a place on the Throne Council, which decides royal succession.

The post-election governing structure comprised a vulnerable political stalemate with the CPP still dominant in the administration, armed forces and police. The Khmer Rouge has been conscious of the tensions and imbalance within the fragile coalition and has sought to exploit them, including the ambitions of King Sihanouk who returned from medical treatment in Beijing in January 1995. It had refused all cooperation with UNTAC but from July 1993 attempted to negotiate a return to public life by offering to provide forces for a new unified army if given 'advisory posts' in the cabinet, which King Sihanouk encouraged in the interest of national reconciliation. Negotiations on the terms for such reconciliation came to nought by mid-1994, after which the government outlawed the Khmer Rouge, which reacted by setting up a competing provisional government. The military resilience of the Khmer Rouge was demonstrated in their successful counter-attacks to government offensives during the 1994 dry season, although a surge of defections took place at the beginning of the following dry season. Thus, within a year of the elections, Cambodia had reverted to civil conflict despite the evident achievements of United Nations peacekeeping.

When Yasushi Akashi left Cambodia on 26 September 1993 on the completion of his mission as head of UNTAC, he claimed that the United Nations had succeeded in its objective of 'laying a firm foundation for Cambodian democracy'. Allowing for the inevitable rhetoric which such a valedictory occasion demanded, Akashi had good reason to be pleased with UNTAC's overall performance compared to that of United Nations peacekeeping in former Yugoslavia and Somalia. That performance, however, revealed a host of shortcomings which should be part of the learning experience of the Organisation.

## Conclusion

The demise of the Cold War and the apparent achievements of the UN in Afghanistan, Angola, Namibia and Iraq between 1988 and 1991 generated a strong sense of optimism about the future role of the organisation. This optimism reached a symbolic high point at the first-ever Security Council summit held in New York in January 1992. It also shaped the approach taken by the principal sponsors of the plan to settle the Cambodian conflict. Underlying the Paris Agreement was the belief that by decoupling Cambodia's civil war from the wider pattern of regional and global confrontation the basis would be provided for a political settlement. The assumption was also made that in order to bring an end to the civil war, the Khmer Rouge had to become a legitimate party to the Agreement. The external sponsors involved the United Nations in a peacekeeping role in Cambodia despite the nature of the internal conflict and the political culture of the country with which they were dealing. They proceeded on the premise that through a comprehensive agreement and democratic rationalism, a lasting settlement could be achieved.

Ironically, a settlement of a kind was attained through UN intervention although the terms of UNTAC's mandate were not upheld. But the responsibility accorded to UNTAC was not underpinned either in authority or capability so as to ensure that all the Cambodian parties kept both to the spirit and letter of the Paris Agreement. Peace enforcement was not, of course, within its purview because the United Nations had not assumed a trusteeship role with UNTAC as a provisional government. To that extent, the mandate in terms of quasi-administrative responsibility was not matched by that in terms of power. Accordingly, Cambodia should not be regarded as a model for UN intervention. One important lesson of UNTAC's experience, however, is that given the conventions and limitations of peacekeeping, democratic multiparty elections within a short and finite time period are not necessarily a replicable means with which to secure so-called comprehensive political settlements.

This chapter also points to two further lessons from the UN's involvement in Cambodia. First, the UN still lacks the capacity to plan, deploy and administer large-scale multi-component operations. Secondly, the political will still does not exist among the major powers for the UN to take a more activist, intrusive and long-term role in dealing with internal conflicts, particularly if they are likely to demand enforcement operations. To that extent, the world of the United Nations at the end of the twentieth century would not be unfamiliar to the pioneers of the League of Nations who struggled against corresponding shortcomings shortly after its advent.

# 3    Former Yugoslavia

*Spyros Economides and Paul Taylor*

The experience of the United Nations in former Yugoslavia up to the end of 1994 was a depressing one, especially as it followed the success of the Gulf War, and the prospect of a 'new world order' in 1991. Regional organisations like the European Union (EU) and NATO were also infected by the miasma of failure. In this chapter the wreckage is examined: what caused the disappointment of the high hopes of a successful intervention? Was the failure as total as some feared? What lessons can be extracted about relations between the regional and the global organisations in protecting the peace?

In the body of the chapter the main currents in the UN's drift to disaster are charted, not in terms of the incidents on the ground, but in the decisions of those who controlled the agenda. In a concluding section some lessons for the future are deduced.

## The break-up of the Yugoslav Federation

Following Tito's death, the rigidities of the Cold War international system held Yugoslavia together for a while, but the demise of communism and the ensuing cataclysmic changes in eastern Europe released the centrifugal pressures which had previously been contained. By the beginning of the 1990s there was rising tension between the republics of Serbia and Croatia, the two dominant segments of the old state.

Yet it was Slovenia which took the lead in the race for independence, by holding a plebiscite in December 1990, which produced an overwhelming majority in favour of severing links with the Yugoslav Federation. Despite attempts by all parties to renegotiate the constitution of

The authors wish to express their gratitude to all the officials in Geneva and New York who gave generously of their time and judgement during the preparation of this essay, but who naturally wish to remain anonymous. Interviews were carried out in September 1992 in New York. Any errors are, however, entirely the responsibility of the authors. They would also like to thank the large number of friends and colleagues who provided information and invaluable comments.

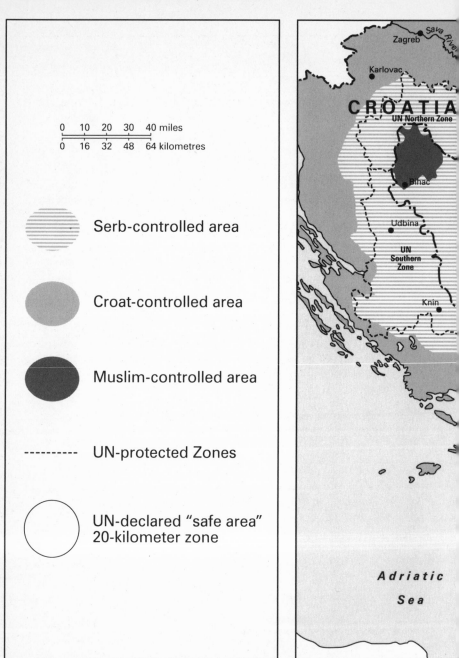

0   10   20   30   40 miles
0   16   32   48   64 kilometres

Serb-controlled area

Croat-controlled area

Muslim-controlled area

---------- UN-protected Zones

UN-declared "safe area"
20-kilometer zone

Map 3.1 Bosnia-Herzegovina, December 1994

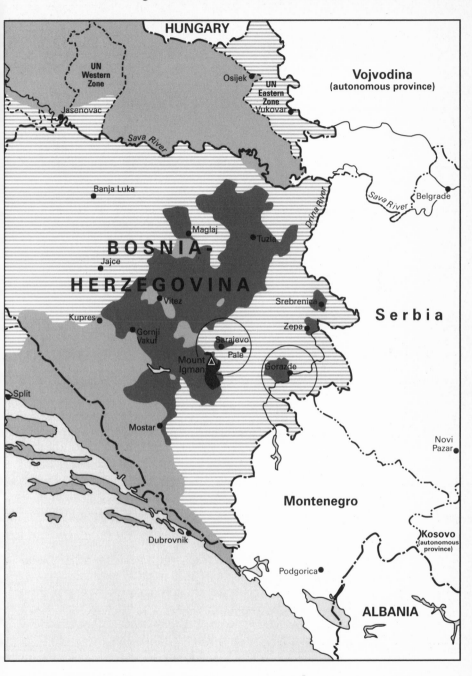

Yugoslavia along looser confederal lines, the political, economic and ethnic fissures between the various republics deepened. On 25 June 1991, Slovenia and Croatia carried out their intentions and declared independence. Rejecting what they considered to be the economically stifling, politically archaic and nationalistically divisive policies of Belgrade – now dominated by Slobodan Milosevic – Slovenia and Croatia seceded, prompting the outbreak of warfare.

The war waged by the Yugoslav National Army against Slovenia lasted a mere 10 days, after which the former surprisingly withdrew. But in Croatia the ruptures in Yugoslav society, and the territorial and ethnic divisions bequeathed by Tito to his country, emerged with greater force. The war there was a vicious affair, presaging the descent into inter-ethnic violence which was to be witnessed later in Bosnia-Herzegovina. The fighting arose because the 12 per cent Serbian minority was determined not to relinquish its links with Serbia. But the fighting was not confined to the areas of the Krajina and Eastern Slavonia which harboured these minorities. It extended into other parts of Croatia, thus widening and deepening the more profound political and nationalist divisions between Serbia and Croatia. The fighting was between Croatian armed forces and the Yugoslav National Army, but it looked as if the latter was an instrument of Serbian policy. It was this conflict which brought initial international involvement in the Yugoslav crisis.

As a consequence, the outbreak of violence in Bosnia-Herzegovina was sadly predictable. The rights and interests of the three ethnic groups – Muslims, Serbs and Croats – had been guaranteed under Tito's constitutional arrangements, which maintained their equality within a multinational Yugoslav state. As this edifice was now crumbling, the unstable ethnic mix within its frontiers could no longer be held together. The referendum in Bosnia-Herzegovina on 1 March 1992 was boycotted by the Serbian population, but it provided an overwhelming majority in favour of independence. There were ominous signs of what was to follow: Serbs rejected the result of the referendum, indicated their preparedness to escalate the level of protest to defend their interests, and raised barricades around Sarajevo. They had decisively rejected an independent Bosnian republic in the knowledge that they would constantly be outvoted by the other two ethnic groups, and that electoral contests would always result in voting along ethnic rather than political lines. The chances of violence were enhanced by an international mechanism: recognition of Bosnia-Herzegovina by the member states of the EC, precipitated by Germany, which heightened the Serbs' sense of confinement in a framework they were not prepared to tolerate.

This was the situation in which the international community was to become involved: first through the Conference on Security and Cooperation in Europe (CSCE), then the EC/EU and finally through the UN. From the outset the international community faced the difficulty of mediating on the basis of two contradictory principles: the sanctity of the frontiers of states, once recognised, and the right to self-determination and protection of the rights of ethnic minorities. The regional situation in the Balkans made the dilemma worse. A crisis was developing in Kosovo; and the former Yugoslav Republic of Macedonia (FYROM) was also a likely flash point, not least because of the Greek government's refusal to accept its name.

Therefore, by early 1992, the situation in former Yugoslavia was one of increasing chaos and conflicting principles. From the perspective of December 1994 it was clear that the international community was then also afflicted by uncertainty and a matching irresolution. The 'new world order' of George Bush had quickly faded and the lack of a distinct international order led to a vacuum which various international organisations and states struggled to fill. There were two unfortunate aspects of the intervention: the crisis in Yugoslavia was brutally complex, and the UN and the regional organisations utterly inexperienced and unprepared for dealing with problems of peace and order in the post-Cold War world.

### Obstacles to successful intervention in the crisis in former Yugoslavia

When UN-sponsored action in the Gulf in response to the invasion of Kuwait by Saddam Hussein is compared with the intervention in Yugoslavia, three kinds of special difficulties in the latter are highlighted. The first concerns the problems of identifying clearly the territorial dimensions of the problem. The peculiar mix of populations and the uncertainty created by rival claims to territory made it difficult to identify and accept territorial and administrative demarcations; this was the legacy not only of traditional ethnic and territorial problems in the Balkans but also of the Yugoslav federation constructed by Tito which involved a whole series of compromises aimed at making sure that no single constituent republic dominated the state.[1]

---

[1] See, for example, James Gow, *Yugoslav Endgames: Civil Strife and Inter-State Conflict*, London Defence Studies No. 5 (London: Brassey's, for the Centre for Defence Studies, June 1991), and John Zametica, *The Yugoslav Conflict*, Adelphi Paper 270 (London: Brassey's, for the International Institute for Strategic Studies, May 1992).

It was difficult for any agency contemplating intervention to see a clear point of entry; no frontier could be established behind which the intervening force could safely be assembled, and from where it could move against a clearly located antagonist on the other side. The options of the international community were further complicated by the ethnic diversity within the new entities, even after they had been formally recognised as states. While their borders had previously been generally accepted as internal administrative frontiers without much political significance, when they were transformed into international frontiers they represented a threat to the ethnic minorities living within them, who hence questioned their legality and historical authenticity. Furthermore, any military action which was contemplated ran the risk of incurring unacceptably high levels of collateral damage because of the nature of the conflict which was spread out in small pockets, involving mainly small-arms combat among neighbouring ethnic communities.

A second problem, which emerged very quickly, was that of deciding upon the purpose and style of such an intervention, a problem later developed in the context of the ever-changing mandate of UNPRO-FOR. In the history of the UN two forms of intervention had emerged: namely, *enforcement* under Chapter VII of the Charter, involving the use of force to pursue an agreed end, such as the exclusion of an invader – as in the Gulf War – and *peacekeeping*, being the interposition of UN forces between the warring parties with the purpose of encouraging them to negotiate a settlement. The latter had no clear basis in the Charter, but was usually thought to derive from Chapter VI which concerned the pacific settlement of disputes. Both procedures could be accompanied by *peacemaking*, the active involvement of the UN in the search for a peaceful settlement, through mediation and the use of good offices.

From the earliest phases of the Yugoslav crisis the intervening agency faced a problem in this context. Should the purpose be humanitarian, intended to alleviate the sufferings of the civilians affected by the dispute, or should it be the assertion of the principle of the sanctity of frontiers? Or should it be a combination of the two? Each of these purposes implied a particular style of intervention, but pursuing the humanitarian goal interfered with the assertion of the principle of the sanctity of frontiers. The former implied negotiation, mediation and peacekeeping, while the latter required enforcement and implied that there should be no compromise or impartiality. It is shown below that the humanitarian concerns made it more difficult to sustain the principle of the sanctity of frontiers (made especially difficult in the light of the question of their validity).

A third set of difficulties may be found in the diplomatic background of the conflict. Throughout the crisis successive US governments were ambivalent about how to respond, and tended to oscillate between support of enforcement and an anxiety not to be drawn into yet another war. In the early phase the Pentagon was the more cautious, and the State Department more activist.[2] But the prevalent consensus was that this was something for the Europeans to do: the Americans had made their contribution to the maintenance of international peace and security in the Gulf War.[3] At the outset of the problems in the Balkans in 1991 this was also the view of the Europeans, especially the French and the Germans, who were inclined to see the crisis as an opportunity to demonstrate and test the emerging machinery for foreign policy cooperation in the EC/EU, be it the existing European Political Cooperation (EPC) or the envisaged Common Foreign and Security Policy (CFSP), and the CSCE,[4] and to create a stronger joint conflict resolution and military capacity.

The Russians were, of course, greatly concerned about the crisis and fearful about its implications for the Russian Federation, and for the frontiers of a number of the recently independent states in the Commonwealth of Independent States (CIS), if the principle of the sanctity of frontiers was compromised in Yugoslavia. But circumstances within Russia, and the bankruptcy of the Russian economy, meant that the Russians were unable to adopt an activist line. This became more apparent in spring 1993, especially as the referendum about President Yeltsin's future approached.[5] Indeed, the Russians became more hostile to military action against the Serbs as the crisis developed.[6]

In consequence the permanent members of the United Nations (the United States, Russia, France, China and the United Kingdom, known as the P5), which had taken a firm lead in the Gulf crisis, were from the beginning not inclined to support firm UN action in the Balkans: their view was that the Europeans should take the lead. This position, which proved to be a serious abdication of responsibility, was reinforced in the early stages by the view of the UN Secretary-General, that this was an occasion when Chapter VIII of the Charter, on cooperation

---

[2] Interview with an official, US mission to the UN, New York, September 1992.

[3] See Paul Taylor and A. J. R. Groom, *The United Nations and the Gulf War: Back to the Future*, Discussion Paper No. 38 (London: Royal Institute of International Affairs, February 1992).

[4] See Geoffrey Edwards and Chris Hill, 'European Political Co-operation, 1989–1991', in A. Barav and D. A. Wyatt (eds.), *Yearbook of European Law 1991* (Oxford: Clarendon Press, 1992), pp. 489–519.

[5] See *The Times*, 23 April 1993.

[6] The reasons behind this gradual shift are highlighted in an ensuing section, pp. 71–2.

between the regional and global organisations, could be tested. In a number of his reports the Secretary-General had proposed an extended role for regional organisations in the maintenance of international peace and security, and the obvious regional organisations in Europe were the EU and the CSCE.[7]

### The purpose of United Nations' intervention: the evolving mandate

One of the greatest difficulties encountered by the UN in its involvement in former Yugoslavia was that the mandate agreed by the Security Council altered as the crisis developed. It was, therefore, impossible to evaluate the success of the UN by enquiring about the *statement of mission* and then measuring the achievement in this light. The mission statement, in the form of the mandate contained in Security Council resolutions, was constantly changing and being modified during the various stages of the crisis. This point is expanded through this chapter, but at this stage it can be briefly developed.

The initial mandate of the UN in former Yugoslavia included Resolution 713, which established a uniform arms embargo on 25 September 1991; it was intended to assist in the preservation of the frontiers of the state of Yugoslavia, unless changes could be agreed by peaceful means and with the consent of all parties. At this stage this was to be done in cooperation with the member states of the European Community. This action was taken under Chapter VII of the Charter, and it was explicitly stated that the situation in Yugoslavia represented a threat to international peace and security. It also noted that the action followed from the request of the government of Yugoslavia, acting through its representative in New York.

These conditions were attached to a number of resolutions, including that establishing the United Nations Protection Force (UNPROFOR) in Croatia, approved on 21 February 1992 (Resolution 743). The force was created in response to the recommendation of the Secretary-General, who in his report of 15 February 1992 judged that, in the context of the ceasefire then in effect, such a force could succeed in consolidating the ceasefire and facilitating the negotiation of an overall settlement (para. 28, S/23592).

---

[7] In particular see his report, *Agenda for Peace: Preventive Diplomacy, Peacemaking and Peacekeeping. Report of the Secretary-General Pursuant to the Statement Adopted by the Summit Meeting of the Security Council on 31 January 1992* (New York: United Nations, 1992).

As mentioned, there was in this resolution specific reference to the request of the government of Yugoslavia, an indication of the view that the operation was to facilitate the adjustment of the frontiers of an existing state with the agreement of that state. The force was to be established in areas to be determined by UN agents, with a number of administrative responsibilities, and a duty to stop action that could disturb public order. It was to ensure that local police forces reflected the national composition of the populations in the protected areas. The mandate looked, in other words, like that of a traditional peacekeeping force: to be interpositional and impartial, and to provide the framework for negotiations. It nevertheless raised hopes which went beyond traditional peacekeeping in that according to paragraph 5, the force was to 'create the conditions of peace and security required for the negotiation of an overall settlement of the Yugoslav crisis'. In due course this was to be a source of great disappointment to the Croatians, who interpreted the UNPROFOR mandate as being proactively anti-Serbian, but saw UNPROFOR carrying out a more traditional peacekeeping role despite the reference to Chapter VII.

By May 1992, the form of words in the ensuing mandates had changed. For example, Resolution 752 referred to the *former* Socialist Federal Republic of Yugoslavia, and demanded the withdrawal of the Yugoslav National Army from republics other than Serbia and Montenegro and the cessation of operations by Croatian forces in Bosnia-Herzegovina. The UN now dropped the pretence that it was dealing with problems of adjusting the existing frontiers of an established Yugoslav state. In the month following, in Resolution 757, the mandate of UNPROFOR was altered to include a much more active security role with regard to the protection of Sarajevo airport after the withdrawal of the Bosnian Serb forces. It was to be reopened and fortified with a UN special regime (S/24075, para. 5), with the assistance of an extra 1,100 UN troops. The mandate now included the supervision and control of facilities, organisation and security inside the airport; supervision and control of all local civilian personnel; and the dispatch of humanitarian assistance.

In Resolution 770, of 13 August 1992, the mandate of UNPROFOR was further expanded. The force was now asked to deliver humanitarian assistance and was empowered to use 'all measures necessary' to do this: this operation in Bosnia-Herzegovina was to become known as UNPROFOR II. What did this mandate entail in detail? In the words of the Secretary-General it was to 'support UNHCR's efforts to deliver humanitarian relief *throughout Bosnia and Herzegovina*, and in particular to provide protection, at UNHCR's request, where and when UNHCR considered such protection necessary'. 'It would remain UNHCR's responsibility, as at present, to determine the priorities and schedules for the delivery of such relief, to organise the relief convoys, to negotiate safe passage along the intended routes, with UNPROFOR's assistance as required, and to coordinate requests from non-governmental organisations and other agencies wishing to join UNPROFOR-protected convoys. UNHCR, after consulting UNPROFOR, would decide which convoys needed protection, and protection would be provided only at UNHCR's request. Other humanitarian agencies seeking UNPROFOR protection for their deliveries of relief supplies would have to address their requests to UNHCR' (paras. 3–4, Report of Secretary-General, S/24540, 10 September 1992). This was the division of labour between UNHCR and UNPROFOR, at least through the end of 1994.

As will be seen below, by late 1993 and 1994 a further question arose with regard to the mandate of UNPROFOR. Was the force authorised to order outside military assistance in pursuit of a further mandate from the Security Council, such as the enforcement of the air exclusion zones created by Operation Deny Flight in late March 1993, or the elimination of weapons which were attacking territory declared by the Security Council to be a 'safe area', as Srebrenica was in mid-April of the same year? UNPROFOR leaders were formally required to address requests for such assistance to the Secretary-General's Special Representative in the region who, as the senior local UN official, would decide whether to authorise them in the context of the Security Council mandate. He would consult with the military leaders of the force before doing so.[8]

## The escalation of the crisis and the greater involvement of the UN

On 16 October 1992, a leading article in *The Times* contained the following proposals: that there should be air strikes against the Serbian warlords and Serbian planes involved in the war in Bosnia-Herzegovina; that there should be active defence of convoys if an attempt were made to prevent them from reaching their destinations in pursuit of their mandate; that the peacekeeping activities in the area should be positively coordinated under the French commander of UNPROFOR II through NATO; and that there should be clear support for the then more moder-

---

[8] The mandate of UNPROFOR was further expanded through Security Council Resolution 795, 11 December 1992, which authorised the initial deployment of 700 troops on a more traditional peacekeeping operation in FYROM, separating Serbia proper from the new republic.

ate prime minister of the remnant of federal Yugoslavia, Milan Panic, against the leader of Serbia, Milosevic, who was seen as being responsible for the attempt to create a Greater Serbia at the expense of Croatia, but especially of Bosnia-Herzegovina.

These proposals are indications of trends in the crisis which may be summarised as an escalation from minimum peacekeeping to a more activist peacekeeping, tending toward enforcement, culminating in strikes against Serbian heavy weapons;[9] the more positive identification of an enemy in the form of the Serbian activists under Milosevic and, in Bosnia-Herzegovina, Radovan Karadzic; a striking increase in the scale of the presence of the intervening forces in Bosnia – by mid-November 1992 they amounted to 6,500 men – as earlier in Croatia, and the closer involvement of NATO. This was a process of *creeping escalation*, with a component of more activist peacekeeping, accompanied by an increasingly clear realisation that the regional agencies were incapable of retaining control.

The enhancement of the role of the UN, at the expense of the EC/EU, may be traced through four phases.

1. In the first phase, up until late November 1991, the UN was involved only in that it condemned the violence, and reinforced positions adopted by the EC, as with the approval by the Security Council of an embargo on supplies of arms to all parties in the rapidly disintegrating Federal Republic of Yugoslavia.[10] The EC was more proactive up until November 1991, and was the lead organisation, in the sense that its role combined peacemaking with peacekeeping.[11] This took the form of attempting to mediate a peaceful solution to the break-up of Yugoslavia, the negotiation of ceasefires – which were constantly broken by all parties – and the provision of EC monitors. (The EC had been delegated by the CSCE to take over primary responsibility following the failure of the consensus-seeking CSCE mechanism to make any progress with regard to the fighting in Slovenia and then Croatia.) From the early phase of the conflict the regional organisation sought to attribute primary responsibility for the crisis, first in Croatia, then in Bosnia-Herzegovina, to the Serbs. It directed various pressures against the Serbs, and came to be seen

---

[9] See *The Times*, 24 April 1993.
[10] According to Resolution 713 (1991), 25 September 1991. For text of the resolution, see pp. 173–5 in Appendix B.
[11] This was reflected in the preamble to Resolution 713, which commended 'the efforts undertaken by the European Community and its member States . . . to restore peace and dialogue in Yugoslavia . . .'

quite quickly by the latter as an enemy, possibly an instrument of Germany, traditionally hostile to Serbia.[12] This was quite starkly reflected in the role attributed to Germany in the EC's recognition of the secessionist republics of Slovenia and Croatia.

2. At the start of a second phase, in November 1991, Cyrus Vance was asked to intervene as the Secretary-General's personal representative, and the UN played a key peacemaking role in the ending of the first Serbo-Croatian War. This followed the failure of the EC's efforts to end the crisis in Croatia, in part because it was now seen, not as an unbiased mediator, but as an opponent of Serbia. The EC also made mistakes in concluding and administering ceasefires: it did not have the mechanisms or experience of the UN in such matters. Hence the UN became more actively involved with the creation of UNPRO-FOR and its initial deployment in Croatia.

Nevertheless, in this second phase, the UN role was mainly concerned with *peacekeeping*; it reinforced an effort that was still being directed and conducted primarily by the regional organisation. But the warring sides saw the global organisation as being more impartial in holding the ring. They were also more conciliatory toward the UN position, as espoused by Vance, to ensure that they were not alienating the United States, which was assumed to be backing Cyrus Vance. At the same time, the *peacemaking* function of the EC remained intact; even though the EC had failed in its initial peace-brokering mission, it still retained the authority delegated to it by the CSCE.

3. In a third phase the UN found itself being pushed into a more proactive role, and was invited to take the lead by Lord Carrington and others, especially after a meeting in London on 17 July 1992.[13] The Secretary-General indicated that he accepted the need for a greater UN role in his report of 6 June 1992, though in this phase, as will be shown, there was quarrelling between the regional and global organisations.[14] Greater UN involvement coincided with the more general acceptance of the view that Serbia–Montenegro was the violating state, and the first big step taken was the approval of mandatory sanctions against Serbia–Montenegro at the end of May

---

[12] See James Gow and James D. D. Smith, *Peace-Making, Peace-Keeping: European Security and the Yugoslav Wars*, London Defence Studies No. 11 (London: Brassey's, for the Centre for Defence Studies, May 1992), p. 36.

[13] This meeting lead to the London Agreement of 23 July, described as 'a plan to hand over the baton to the UN with dignity': *Independent*, 3 July 1992.

[14] *Report of the Secretary-General Pursuant to Security Council Resolution 757 (1992)*, S/24075, 6 June 1992.

1992,[15] followed, on 13 August, by the granting of a mandate to activist states to use 'all measures necessary' against the Serbs if they tried to prevent the provision of humanitarian assistance.[16]

4. In late August 1992 a fourth phase was visible. On his appointment to succeed Peter Carrington as head of the EC's Commission on Yugoslavia on 27 August 1992, David Owen said that any distinction between the role of the two organisations was now defunct. The UN's role as *peacekeeper* was to be merged with the EC's role as *peacemaker*. The two organisations were to set up a joint operation in Geneva to conduct negotiations and research possible forms of settlement on the terms agreed at the London Conference in late August 1992.[17]

After the conference the two organisations worked together in this tandem arrangement, and links with the United Nations were tightened by the direct participation of the permanent members of the Security Council and the Secretary-General's representative Vance, and by the role of the British and French governments in New York. The latter became responsible for orchestrating diplomacy among members of the Security Council, particularly the P5, to obtain support for resolutions indicated by the London Conference, and any subsequent proposals.

## From peacekeeping to near-enforcement

Several states, including the United Kingdom, declared that their commitment of troops to the crisis would be limited, and that their actions would be confined to the protection of the convoys carrying scarce supplies to those trapped in the conflict areas; they were to protect the UN's humanitarian work in Bosnia. But for a while the possibility of moving beyond the support of convoys to more coercive military action was not positively excluded.

At a cabinet meeting on 18 August 1992 to authorise the use of British troops in Bosnia following the 13 August resolution, and the use of British war planes to create an exclusion zone for Iraqi aircraft in southern Iraq, four stages of commitment in Bosnia were identified.[18] The weakest was preferred as the other three could lead to an escalation of involvement. Nevertheless, it was thought that the British could yet

[15] Resolution 757, 30 May 1992, China and Zimbabwe abstaining. For text of the resolution, see pp. 179–84 in Appendix B.
[16] Resolution 770, 13 August 1992, adopted with three abstentions, China, India and Zimbabwe. For text of the resolution, see pp. 185–6 in Appendix B.
[17] *The Times*, 28 August 1992.
[18] See Colin Brown, 'British Troops Will Protect Aid Convoys', *Independent*, 19 August 1992.

change their minds, and other states, such as the United States and France, occasionally advocated a more muscular approach. But only military assistance for humanitarian missions was explicitly allowed, and only minor further military actions were proposed in the UN, such as the agreement to set up no-fly zones in Bosnia. A decision was also taken to enforce a naval blockade against Serbia–Montenegro, and to monitor the sanctions.

As the line dividing active peacekeeping and peace enforcement was approached, there were often hints that it might be overstepped, especially from the United States, then hesitation and retreat. A major problem was that there was no agreement on the political objective of enforcement: the optimism which had followed the recognition of Croatia was quickly overtaken by evidence of Croatian intentions to share the carve-up of Bosnian territory with Serbia. Although the primary guilt of Serbia was widely acknowledged, the sense that there should be a plague on all their houses was widespread.

The form of words used in the resolution of 13 August 1992, which permitted the use of greater force to protect the humanitarian convoys, was reminiscent of Resolution 678 of November 1990, which had sanctioned the use of force against Saddam Hussein, but, for those who framed it, it had almost the opposite implications. The 1992 resolution included the phrase 'all measures necessary' to protect the convoys, whereas the 1990 resolution mentioned 'all necessary means'. The 1990 resolution was intended to convey the threat of the use of force to eject Saddam from Kuwait, whilst appearing sufficiently ambiguous as to allow those who opposed force to support it. In contrast the 1992 resolution threatened more force than the states were prepared to use, but it was hoped that the Serbs would interpret it in the light of the earlier resolution. But unlike Resolution 678, the threat was not backed with any convincing evidence that it was real.[19]

Until the London Conference of 26–28 August 1992, it was possible to maintain the position that the use of force to impose a settlement in Yugoslavia had not been excluded. But one consequence of that conference was to reinforce the Serbs' doubt that force would be used. The agreement specified the use of sanctions up to and including the complete isolation of the Yugoslav rump state, if that state failed to comply with the agreed terms, but statements by the British and others, and the failure to refer to enforcement, implied that there would be no military coercion. This message was reinforced by the precision with which the

[19] It was reported on *The World at One*, BBC Radio 4, 27 August 1992, that the people of Belgrade had feared that attacks on their city would follow shortly after the approval of the resolution.

non-coercive sanctions were spelled out: they amounted to total isolation for Serbia–Montenegro, but as the sub-text implied, not more
than that.[20]

By late 1992 it had become apparent that the scale of threat posed
by the intervening UN forces had been significantly increased since the
creation of UNPROFOR in February. The big step was resolution Resolution 770 of 13 August 1992, but an earlier resolution, Resolution
761, of 29 June 1992, had pointed the way when it held that the Security
Council 'does not exclude other measures to secure aid'. On 11 September the Security Council confirmed that the new UN force in
Bosnia-Herzegovina of up to 8,500 men, UNPROFOR II, could remove
those obstructing the convoys by force if necessary. This had been foreseen in the Secretary-General's Report of 10 September.[21]

By the end of the year several other indications of the escalation of
preparedness to use force were evident. For instance, in early October,
UN forces were authorised to use force to resist an attempt to return
home by Croatians who had been driven out of UNPROFOR I territory.
A senior UN official in charge, Cedric Thornberry, blamed the Croatian
government for encouraging this, but stressed that even more trouble
would arise if the refugees were allowed back.[22] By mid-November 1992
the British force of 2,400 men had arrived in Bosnia equipped with
heavy armoured personnel carriers, Warriors, and lighter vehicles,
Scimitars. This level of armament was a clear – if to some a symbolic –
indication of a determination to be more proactive in protecting troops
and removing opposition to the convoys, despite the statement by the
British defence minister, Malcolm Rifkind, on 23 November that British
forces would keep a low profile. By December serious incidents involving Serbs and British forces had taken place and although these had
not involved casualties, there was a real danger of this happening. This
situation considerably sharpened the dilemma: it could lead either to a
sudden increase in commitment, and enforcement, as part of a process
of retaliation, or to withdrawal.

In Britain, in late 1992, the former response seemed possible. There
had been *creeping escalation* toward a strong version of peacekeeping: if
a serious incident took place it was hard in mid-December to predict
the outcome. But public opinion and the style of government response

---

[20] *The Times*, 29 August 1992.
[21] *New York Times*, 11 September 1992. The Secretary-General interpreted the rules of
engagement as follows: 'self defense is deemed to include situations in which armed
persons attempt by force to prevent United Nations troops from carrying out their
mandate'. See S/24540.
[22] *The Times*, 2 October 1992.

in France and Britain suggested they could be provoked into enforcement. Initially this could have involved air strikes against Serbian positions, as recommended in the *Times* leader mentioned above.

### Plans for peace: the retreat from principle

By January 1993 a plan for peace had been produced by the Vance–Owen team, which for the first time could be seen as representing a clearer statement of a political goal. The plan involved keeping the existing frontiers of Bosnia-Herzegovina and a central government with modest powers but also divided the territory into ten cantons which would have a high degree of autonomy. The difficulty was that it allowed the Serbs to retain some of the territory they had captured militarily, and indeed allowed some of the ethnic cleansing carried out by the other groups to be kept in place also. Despite being the biggest territorial victors, the Serbs were the main opponents of ratification, because they would have to relinquish part of the conquered land, especially the vital land corridor linking the Krajina to Serbia proper through parts of northern Bosnia.[23] The plan preserved a basic tenet of international relations – the sanctity of international frontiers – but it accepted some measure of ethnic cleansing. The new Clinton administration in the United States therefore hesitated to endorse it and the general failure to agree on implementation of the plan squandered one of the few real chances of peace.

The approach of the dividing line between active peacekeeping and enforcement had frightened many in the governments of the leading western states involved. But even this 'para-escalation' made the control of the global organisation more necessary to the hesitant states. Using violence required that the UN be in charge; restraining its use also had to be pursued through the global organisation. The earlier somewhat unreal oscillations of the EC/EU countries between coercive and non-coercive measures had gradually given way to a similar oscillation in the UN, where it was thought the key decisions ought to be taken. The transfer of the Vance–Owen talks from Geneva to New York in spring 1993 facilitated closer teamwork between representatives of the United States, the P5 and the EC/EU states, but also emphasised the importance of the UN as the lead organisation.

While the two main mediators continued in their fruitless efforts to persuade all the three Bosnian groups to agree to the Vance–Owen peace plan, the UN passed a string of resolutions in early 1993, which

[23] See *Observer*, 3 January 1993.

did not positively move to enforcement, but edged in its direction and kept the pressure on the Bosnian Serbs. Security Council Resolution 807 extended the mandate of UNPROFOR until the end of March 1993 initially, and then until the end of June 1993. More importantly, this same resolution affirmed that UNPROFOR was acting under Chapter VII of the UN Charter – i.e. that it was there to maintain security, and that the Secretary-General should take all necessary measures for the protection of the force and the provision of heavier weaponry for defensive purposes. Pressure was also maintained by two further resolutions; Resolution 808 which set up an ad hoc war tribunal and requested information about war crimes, and Resolution 816, which finally enforced the no-fly zone over Bosnia. It asked NATO war planes to intercept Bosnian Serb planes in the zones. It had taken over six months for the agreement to acquire these teeth. President Clinton also declared himself prepared in spring 1993 to authorise strikes by US aircraft against Serb positions, for instance, around Sarajevo, a move that the United States argued was sanctioned by Resolution 770. It was resisted with some anxiety by those with troops on the ground.

### Problems in maintaining the UN's impartiality

Once UNPROFOR was involved, the UN was faced with the difficulty that any proactive role ran the risk of attracting retaliation against the existing UN forces, both in Croatia and Bosnia, thus making it increasingly difficult for the organisation to maintain a reputation for impartiality. The UN Secretary-General was at pains to stress this point in his report of 26 May 1992 to the Security Council,[24] which implied a preference for mediation rather than enforcement, though in later reports on 30 May and 6 June, whilst still stressing the risks, he reluctantly accepted the need for a more active role for UNPROFOR,[25] on condition that the parties to the dispute (in Sarajevo) accepted and abided by the terms of a ceasefire, and more personnel and resources were allocated.

But the Secretary-General became very irritated (in late July 1992), by what he saw as the EC's unilaterally committing the UN to actions which could increase the chances that UNPROFOR would be seen as partisan. He also noted that Croatia was extremely unhappy about what seemed to be an international validation of the enclaves captured by Serbian forces in Croatia as a result of the positioning of the UNPRO-

---

[24] Security Council, *Report of the Secretary-General pursuant to Security Council Resolution 752 (1992)*, S/24000, 26 May 1992.
[25] Ibid.

FOR forces around those specific enclaves. A rather cynical joke after the initial deployment of UNPROFOR in Croatia was that this force should be called 'UNPROSERB' or 'SERBPROFOR', to illustrate its true role as seen through Croatian eyes. In late November 1992, the Croatian government threatened not to agree to the renewal of the UNPROFOR mandate in February 1993, a tactic which the Croats have persistently pursued ever since. The Secretary-General also expressed great concern at the UN's close involvement with the Balkan crisis at the expense of its involvement in crises elsewhere in the world, particularly in Somalia.[26]

One reason for Croatian complaints was that the UN, through Cyrus Vance, had allowed responsibility for the civilian administration of the UNPROFOR region in Croatia to be placed in Serb hands. The plan called for a reversion of power into the hands of an authority representative of the local populations. Under this specific plan populations would have been returned to their homes and lands, allowing for representative local government. But as the displaced populations were not returned, because of Serbian intransigence, the Serbs retained control of these areas. There was also clear evidence of serious infringements of human rights by Serbian groups in the area under the authority of the so-called Serbian Republic of Krajina. As the crisis evolved the UN, like the EC before it, began to attract accusations of partisanship.

At the London Conference in late August 1992, the Bosnian Serbs were allowed a victory, in that discussions about the frontiers of Bosnia with Serbia, and other terms of a possible settlement, were to begin in a week's time (4 September 1992) in Geneva, and there was no guarantee that seized lands would be returned. There was indeed a promise to 'respect the integrity of present frontiers, unless changed by mutual agreement', and the US acting secretary of state, Lawrence Eagleburger, said that the United States would not accept anything other than a return to the status quo ante. But, in the context of the conference, there had been a sell-out: the agreement allowed the Serbs to continue to put pressure on Bosnia in the name of finding general agreement, and to fudge and postpone settlement. A ceasefire was yet to be agreed, and although a scheme for placing heavy weapons under UN supervision at 11 centres was accepted by the Serbian leadership in Bosnia, there was no guarantee that all the weapons could be located and disposed of in this way.

By late 1992 the Bosnian Serbs had begun to show a two-fold reaction in their judgement of the UN. The dominant strain, encouraged by

[26] See *International Herald Tribune*, 4 August 1992.

Slobodan Milosevic in Belgrade, was that they could now play the long game, more confident that they would not be subject to coercive military sanctions, and reassured by the evidence that those who could act were hesitating and that any pressure toward enforcement in the UN was being contained. The UN became vulnerable to the charge that it was continuously chasing after the frontiers of mediation: too often it seemed to be implying mediation on the basis of the most recent gains by the Serbs, a problem which arose in part from its humanitarian role. Agreeing to negotiations about frontiers was a concession to the transgressors, which had been excluded in the Gulf crisis.

On the other hand the Serbs continued to express doubts about UN intentions and impartiality. There were accusations that the single UN convoy into Gorazde had conveyed arms to the Muslim defenders; this had led to a retreat by the Serbs. The Serbs also complained that some broader, clandestine deal had been struck at the London Conference at their expense and 'this had a shocking effect on Serbian morale'.[27] This also led to a transformation of the image of the UN forces.

The lead states had declined to enforce principles or peace, but despite this the Serbs were beginning to see the UN forces as opponents. Attacks on them seemed to be increasing and on 4 September an Italian military transport aircraft carrying blankets into Sarajevo crashed after having been hit by an anti-aircraft missile. Even though there was strong evidence to suggest that the aircraft had been downed by either Croatian or Muslim forces, the Bosnian Serbs were to bear the brunt of accusations. Their feeling of persecution by the international community as embodied by the UN mission in Bosnia was heightened.

All this reinforced the latent fears within the governments of the lead states about greater involvement. Unlike in Iraq, as the crisis proceeded they became more, rather than less, tortured by the agonies of choosing between mediation and enforcement. By late April 1993 this dilemma had become unbearable, as the world witnessed the fierce attacks of the Bosnian Serbs on the Muslim town of Srebrenica, and gross violations of human rights.[28] As of December 1994, the agony remained with the Serb aggression against the 'safe area' of Bihac.

But both concern with the humanitarian dimensions of the crisis, and acceptance of the Secretary-General's enhanced role, were the result of an ambivalence at the heart of the intentions of the lead states in the UN and the EC/EU: on the one hand they wanted to defend fundamental principles without reserve or hesitation, but on the other, they were

[27] *The Times*, 3 September 1992.
[28] See *The Times*, 21 April 1993.

inexorably driven to seek compromise to save costs and lives for themselves. Through spring 1993 the UN was the forum for debate about whether principle should be defended through enforcement, or whether it should play a more limited role. Much of this debate was fuelled by the vacillations in US policy, sometimes suggesting a preparedness to fight to the last Fijian – or European – sometimes implying an active commitment to enforce themselves, and sometimes drawing back from all options. But the United States stopped short of actually providing troops on the ground.

For a number of reasons the precise mix of mechanisms and policy in former Yugoslavia proved to be unstable. Involvement to promote humanitarian assistance spilled over into a more active role, which in turn made it more difficult to protect the organisation's reputation for impartiality, despite the determined efforts of commanders such as General Sir Michael Rose. It also made mediation harder.

### Regional and global agencies: forms and fictions

In his report of June 1992 Boutros Boutros-Ghali interpreted the somewhat vague provisions of Chapter VIII of the Charter on relations between regional organisations and the United Nations:[29] the UN should lead. The Secretary-General complained in mid-July 1992 that the EC–UN relationship was the opposite of this. The EC was in some ways directing the UN, but failing to provide the resources for the policies it approved.

This complaint was partly financial. At the London Conference on 26–28 August 1992, the Secretary-General, now a joint chairman of the conference, complained that the EC members, which were among the richest states in the world, had been slow to provide enough resources for the tasks that had been agreed. This was a disastrous failing: in summer 1992 the UN was owed US $530 million by member states – mainly the United States.[30] But the EC states showed no sign of being prepared to provide the resources for any more effective role in former Yugoslavia, despite claims that it was primarily their concern.[31] The financial plight of the UN remained serious in 1994. Around US $992.8 million was owed on the peacekeeping fund on 31 December 1993, and US $478 million was owed in unpaid assessments to the regular

---

[29] *Agenda for Peace.*
[30] Paul Taylor, 'The United Nations System Under Stress: Financial Pressures and Their Consequences', in Paul Taylor, *International Organization in the Modern World* (London: Pinter, 1993), pp. 159–79.
[31] See Hella Pick in *Guardian*, 29 October 1993.

budget, about 50 per cent of which was owed by the United States.[32] The EU remained unmoved by the need to match concerns with resources.

But it would be misleading to see the EU, or NATO, and the UN as discrete organisations. Two of the permanent members of the Security Council, France and Britain, were also members of the EU, which took a leading role in the regional organisation's work concerning former Yugoslavia. Three members of the Security Council belonged to NATO. But throughout the development of the EPC and CFSP mechanisms the two EC/EU states had insisted that they had the right to act in their individual capacity with regard to issues that were before the Security Council, and on these questions they declined to be bound by any form of instructions from the EC/EU states.

Agreements between the members of the EC/EU, including the Single European Act of 1985, and the Maastricht Treaty of 1991, confirmed this privileged position for the British and the French. EC/EU member states on the Security Council therefore protected the formal separation of the two organisations in New York and, oddly, declined to appear to act there on behalf of the EC/EU. Within the UN framework they agreed only to inform the other EC/EU members about developments in their weekly meetings in New York. What could have been a useful connection between the regional and the global organisations – overlapping membership of the EC/EU and the Security Council – became a limitation on inter-organisational communication.

In fact the overlapping memberships and discontinuities meant that distinctions between the regional and universal organisations were unreal, and states in Europe and the UN in practice had no organisational affiliation: in neither case was there any mandate. On the Contact Group it was unclear how far, or in what sense, the five permanent members of the Security Council represented the United Nations. They had not been authorised to attend in the name of the UN by the Security Council, and did not seem to be acting in the framework of a specific UN mandate, and in any case two of them were also members of the EC/EU. They were there in their individual capacity.

In like vein the meaning of the term *the UN* was also flexible. The UN could mean the Secretariat and the Secretary-General, or the collectivity of states working through that organisation. When he spoke of the interests of the UN in former Yugoslavia, Boutros-Ghali seemed to

---

[32] See Anthony Mango, 'Finance and Administration', in *A Global Agenda: Issues Before the 49th General Assembly of the United Nations* (New York: United Nations, 1994), pp. 304–5.

mean those of the permanent institutions, and his representatives.[33] This interpretation became a convenient device for those states which were becoming anxious to avoid firmer action, as it made it easier to attach blame to the institution rather than to themselves. In this way humanitarian assistance, being a function of the UN more narrowly defined, became part of a formula by which the cautious elements in member governments sought to abdicate responsibility. In contrast, in the Gulf War the Secretary-General was excluded and the image of the United Nations presented by the governments was of the group of states in alliance with the government of Kuwait.

There were also a number of problems in the relationship between NATO and the UN. NATO had been mandated by Security Council resolutions to enforce the air exclusion zones, and to attack weapons in use against the UN-declared safe areas on the authorisation of the senior UN officer in former Yugoslavia, Yasushi Akashi. Two issues arose. First, it was clear that NATO was the most obvious available mechanism for carrying out these tasks and after it was discovered that the alliance could act out of area, there was no impediment to its doing so under a Security Council mandate. The UN had to authorise such actions, based however on Article 51 in Chapter VII, and not Chapter VIII, of the Charter: the alliance was merely a framework within which a group of states happened to be joined.

Second was the implications of this way of working for the future. There were obvious dangers in accepting the two linked principles of using an organisation like NATO to act, even under licence, outside its own area, and of contracting out the job of maintaining international peace and security to a state or an organisation. Where did the field of NATO action stop? Could it act *anywhere* in the world? In the Middle East, the Far East, or just where the interests of members were directly affected? How was this to be decided? Was it merely a hired gun, or given overlapping membership, simply Security Council power without the Russian or Chinese veto? Was there not the risk that 'contracting out' would reinforce the older *spheres of interest* idea, with local powers asserting their primary responsibility to the exclusion of the global authority? It seemed that the way forward had to be supporting the enhancement of the authority of the UN, and that the option of 'contracting out' discredited the global organisation and licensed local bullies. In the final section of this chapter these points are discussed further.

[33] *The Times*, 3 September 1992.

## Alarms and excursions: the main actors in the first half of 1993

In late 1992 the United States seemed to be prepared to mount a massive response to the Serbs, but they were not supported in this by the Europeans, and the proposal evaporated as the Bush election campaign got under way. In fact, it was argued in some circles that the Bush administration's hints at massive intervention were nothing but a ploy in the presidential election campaign, an area in which Bush was emphasising his experience.

The incoming Clinton administration had explicitly placed domestic political and economic options at the top of the agenda and was loathe to announce a major foreign policy decision with regard to the conflict in Bosnia as the government's first important action. Pressure was on Clinton to revive the American economy, to 'put America back to work' and to move away from a primary concern with external affairs. Yet the United States could not simply discard its international role, and there existed some hope within Clinton policy-making ranks that victory for Milan Panic against Milosevic in the Serbian presidential election in late 1992 could be the turning point in former Yugoslavia. Moral support was provided for Panic, not least in implying that sanctions against Serbia could be loosened if he won. With the defeat of Panic the Clinton administration was paralysed with indecision: the Vance–Owen peace plan dividing Bosnia into cantons was unacceptable, as it sanctioned ethnic cleansing, the new leadership in Belgrade had a poor track record and in any case foreign affairs was of secondary importance.

By this time the United States had become involved in the Somalian imbroglio – at the behest of the UN. Clinton's attention on US peace-keeping and humanitarian relief missions abroad was dominated by this particular dispute, and for a while the crisis in Bosnia took the back seat. Yet at the heart of American policy still lay the dilemma of not wanting to extend US commitments in terms of ground troops to Bosnia until a political settlement was reached on the ground; but the flawed premises of the Vance–Owen plan could not be accepted.

Therefore, the United States again pushed for tighter sanctions, but added an air-drop of vital supplies to beleaguered populations. An American envoy was sent to the peace talks in the person of Reginald Bartholomew; and, as mentioned, the Vance–Owen talks were moved to New York, where the participants would be closer to the UN and the US administration. Bartholomew's first action was to travel to Moscow, an indication of American concerns over what they saw as an emerging obstacle to strengthening sanctions against Serbia and enforcing the no-fly zone over Bosnia. This was the increasing alignment of the Russians with the Serbs in Bosnia.

Indeed, as the crisis evolved, the Russians became more prepared to resist increasing the pressures against the Serbs. The Yeltsin government, and the Russian people, were profoundly divided in their loyalties. There was sympathy for the Serbs, but at the same time a great anxiety about allowing a sovereign state to be destroyed without general consent. There was also a hankering after a more independent role among some of Yeltsin's opponents, involving hostility to the west, and certainly opposition to any expansion of NATO to the east as was shown at the December 1994 CSCE meeting, when Yeltsin himself objected to adding eastern European states to NATO. Any demonstration of NATO fire power close to Russian frontiers, as with attacks on Serbian heavy weapons, caused unease. In the Security Council, one factor which discouraged further expansion of the mandate in mid-1993 was the fear that the Russians might prove obdurate. There was a tendency to argue that the general terms of older mandates, like the 'necessary measures' of Resolution 770, could be the legal basis of specific new actions.

Despite deep reservations about the nature of the Vance–Owen plan, by April 1993 the United States was left with no other alternative and showed a willingness to accept it as the best possible bargain that could be struck, if it were to be accepted by all parties. The no-fly zone was pushed through the Security Council on 31 March, and Warren Christopher pressed for the lifting of the arms embargo on Bosnia to allow the Muslims to defend themselves and thus provide, in his words, 'a level playing field'.[34] There was even a hint that the United States would consider using force to ensure compliance, especially through air strikes against Serbian heavy weaponry. Yet the basic premise remained that until a political settlement was found, which the United States then could assist in policing through the employment of a massive NATO-based peacekeeping force, there were no immediate plans for direct US military enforcement measures.[35]

And in Europe, there were, of course, a number of reasons for doubting the others' support if the going got tough. Right at the centre of the problem was the refusal of Germany to provide troops for enforcement purposes in former Yugoslavia, because of the restrictions on activities outside the NATO area then thought to be in the German consti-

[34] *Independent*, 6 April 1993.
[35] See *The Times*, 11 February 1993.

tution.[36] The EC/EU therefore lacked several of the conditions of successful collective action.

David Owen also now argued for limited air strikes – a nod toward enforcement. Through the two years of the crisis the Bosnian Serbs had been increasingly, and with mounting vigour, identified as the main transgressors. The UN Security Council had accepted the proposal that information about war crimes should be collected, a policy targeted explicitly at the Bosnian Serbs.[37] The earlier uncertainties about who was guilty had been clarified, at least in the minds of western governments, despite some muddying of the waters as a result of a renewal of fighting between Croats and Muslims in central Bosnia in late April 1993.

### Intimations of settlement: from summer 1993 until summer 1994

From summer 1993 into the winter, the warring parties were all embroiled in small-scale fighting to capture or recapture tracts of territory. Despite the repeated extension of the UNPROFOR mandate in Croatia, there were constant rumblings that the Croatian armed forces were preparing for a major military operation to recapture those areas of Croatia in which the Serbian minority lived under the peacekeeping aegis of the UN force. Tripartite fighting in Bosnia, and tension between Serbia and Croatia over the fate of the Serbian enclaves in Croatia, had horrid implications both for the inhabitants of the region and the international community.

Nevertheless, the Serbs, both in Serbia proper and in Bosnia, were becoming more amenable to a solution, albeit for differing reasons. Serbia was increasingly feeling the uncomfortable effects of the comprehensive UN sanctions imposed in March 1992, while the Bosnian Serbs were concerned with consolidating their gains. Similarly, the Croats, both in Croatia and in Bosnia, were contending with problems of their own which leant toward some sort of solution in Bosnia. Croatia's policies on the Serbian enclaves in Croatia, and Croatian president Franjo Tudjman's repeated threats to terminate the UNPROFOR mandate, attracted critical attention; there was even a threat from the international community to impose economic sanctions on Croatia to stop it assisting Croat forces in Bosnia. As with the Bosnian Serbs, the Croats in Bosnia were now more or less content with the ground they had

---

[36] The German Constitutional Court, in summer 1994, ruled that such action was in fact compatible with the German Constitution.
[37] In Security Council Resolution 771 (1992).

captured and were now primarily interested in defending this territory in the face of increased Muslim military activity. Bosnian Muslims had the least to lose in continuing the fighting, but were still unable to build up a strong enough international coalition to overturn the blanket arms embargo on all former Yugoslav republics, which would provide the so-called 'level playing field', or to provoke a massive military intervention.

In summer 1993 a further plan for the division of Bosnia was proposed by the Owen–Stoltenberg team (Vance having been replaced by Stoltenberg as the Secretary-General's envoy to the peace talks). This plan was a further retreat from the principles on which the international community had originally insisted, a further indication of an increasing anxiety to be out at the minimum acceptable cost.

Peacemaking had initially aimed at keeping a unitary Bosnian republic, thus maintaining the rule that frontiers were not to be changed by force. When this failed, the cantonisation plan was proposed by Vance and Owen, aimed at keeping Bosnia unitary but in a complex puzzle of ethnic divisions, governed by a relatively weak central government. The original intention had been to avoid the division of Bosnia into ethnic provinces, as this would have been seen as a capitulation to armed force and a vindication of the policy of ethnic cleansing. In the new plan this was exactly what was proposed by the EC/EU–UN team. Bosnia was to be divided into three ethnic units, with a loose, and powerless, confederal government in Sarajevo.

A further concession was that after a probationary period of two years, the ethnically based republics would have the right to secede from the confederation with the consent of the other signatories. This would mean that the Republika Srpska (the Serb Republic of Bosnia) and Herzeg-Bosna (the Croatian counterpart) could join their respective parent states of Serbia and Croatia, something which the international community had previously rejected. By winter 1993, therefore, the conclusion could not be avoided that the main states had acted on the principle of regressive mediation, always offering to bargain on the basis of the most recent gains of the aggressor. They had avoided the alternative: enforcement on the basis of principle.

Again there was much discussion between the warring parties and the negotiators about the territorial demarcation of each entity – a problem that had plagued all previous tentative agreements – even when the three groups had in principle agreed to the constitutional side of the arrangement. If the three parties agreed to the plan, the international community was willing to enforce the peace through the deployment of NATO forces under the UN. The Muslim leadership of Izetbegovic rejected the plan, however, because of inadequate territorial concessions by the Serbs. Humanitarian missions continued, but the UN contingents were kept under continuing pressure as the peacemaking efforts of the UN and the EU failed.

In the winter of 1993–4, the fighting on the ground was primarily dominated by hostilities between the Croats and the Bosnian Muslims in central Bosnia, which illustrated the new-found vigour and military organisation of a growing and increasingly better-armed Muslim force. Similarly, on 28 February 1994, international military involvement in the Bosnian crisis took a new twist with the enforcement of the no-fly zone with the use of NATO military aircraft to attack and destroy four Serbian warplanes. This illustrated the increasingly antagonistic stance of the outside world to the Serbian position, but it also put into question the role of the UN operation in the region. This was a clear-cut instance of *creeping escalation* from peacekeeping to peace enforcement by the UN and it naturally reinforced Serb doubts about the acceptability of the global organisation as an impartial peacemaker and peacekeeper, whilst encouraging the Muslims to hope for forceful military intervention on their side. Negatively, it also contributed to the declining reputation of the UN for impartiality.

At the same time, the United States brokered – some would say directed – conciliation between Croatia, the Bosnian Croats and the Bosnian Muslim government, which led to a confederal arrangement between these parties. This reflected in part the rising pressure on the Clinton administration from domestic public opinion and Congress to pursue a strategy which would favour the victims of Serb aggression. The Bosnian Serbs were thus now faced with a united front in negotiations, which was given added strength by the recommendations made by Congress to Clinton to lift the arms embargo against the Bosnian government. By this time, however, the Serbs had taken most of the territory they wanted in Bosnia, and had no interest in pursuing further large-scale offensive deployments. The conclusion had to be that the anti-Serb coalition was encouraged to fight on precisely when the Serbs themselves would have been prepared to negotiate a peace – though on their terms.

### Finessing the principles: from summer 1994

Nevertheless, in July 1994, yet another peace plan was announced by the Contact Group comprising Britain, France, Germany, Russia and the United States – now returned to Geneva from New York. Agreed by the group in July 1994, this plan would have divided Bosnia into mini-ethnic states while keeping the facade of a unitary Bosnian state; it was backed by an explicit threat by the Contact Group that if the Bosnian Serbs did not accept the latest variant of the plan by 20 July 1994 the arms embargo against the Bosnian Muslims would be lifted and further sanctions would be imposed on Serbia itself.

The peace plan demanded that the Bosnian Serbs relinquish some 20 per cent of the territory in Bosnia under their control, and called for the division of Bosnia between the new Croat–Muslim Federation and the Bosnian Serbs on the basis of a 51 per cent to 49 per cent territorial split. The Serbs at this time controlled some 70 per cent of Bosnia. In principle, the plan would apparently keep in place a unitary Bosnian state along loose confederal lines with the two units allowed a great degree of freedom in managing both their domestic and international affairs. The Contact Group proposal accepted that although territorial acquisition through the use of force was unacceptable, some compromise with this principle had to be made.

Pressures against the Serbs were now accumulating. They were facing an international organisation which seemed to be threatening to move from peacekeeping to enforcement with the overt use of the military might of NATO under UN supervision; a united presence from the Croats and Muslims both in the military and diplomatic spheres, which also added extra emphasis to the internationally held view that the Serbs were the villains of the piece; an increase in military activity by the Muslims with the tacit consent of the international community and an increase in the supply of arms entering Bosnia through the Croatian coastline. And Milosevic, now president of Serbia–Montenegro, put pressure on the Bosnian Serbs to settle on the terms of the most recent plan, by closing the frontier between Serbia–Montenegro and Bosnian Serbia, thus putting a stranglehold on the latter's supplies. In return Milosevic, who was increasingly afraid that the Bosnian Serb leader had larger ambitions to replace him as leader of a Greater Serbia, bargained for the loosening of the international sanctions on Serbia–Montenegro which were producing increasing political and economic strains.

For their part the western Europeans were now quite willing to partition Bosnia, if it meant an end to the fighting. But the United States remained adamant that no partition that was the result of the use of armed force could be condoned. Nevertheless in the deal the United States went as far as to concede that the constituent units of a confederal Bosnia might secede at a future date. In return the United States extracted from the Europeans the concession that the arms embargo would be lifted if the Bosnian Serbs rejected the plan. The US acceptance of the possibility of partitioning of Bosnia was the biggest shift in

American policy since Bush first had to deal with this issue in early 1991.

The first Serb response was neither to accept nor to reject the plan: they demonstrated yet again their skills in diplomatic procrastination. On 20 July 1994, Radovan Karadzic rejected the possibility of a 51–49 per cent territorial split; demanded guarantees for the Serbian corridors joining Serbia proper with the Krajina; demanded access to the Adriatic Sea; and, most importantly, stressed that any acceptance of the plan must include provision for future review of the plan with the right of secession for the two constituent ethnic states. Karadzic also stressed that this was not an outright rejection of the plan but rather part and parcel of an ongoing negotiating process in which the Serbs were asking for certain points of clarification and certain guarantees.

By December 1994, it seemed that all the parties to the dispute and the international mediators had accepted that Bosnia would be divided, sooner or later, in one form or another, formally or informally. But, as with all the plans for the resolution of the conflict since 1992, the maps proved to be the insurmountable obstacle. The continuation of fighting seemed to be the order of the day.

### Conclusions: the position in December 1994

At the time of writing, in December 1994, it was possible to draw two different sets of conclusions from the crisis about former Yugoslavia. These concerned first the role and contribution of the UN presence in former Yugoslavia, and second the lessons which may be extracted from this experience about the appropriate relationship between the UN and regional organisations in future interventions.

#### The UN presence in former Yugoslavia

There are some conclusions which must remain a matter of judgement rather than proof. These include the view that humanitarian inter-vention is a moral obligation, and that as long as it cannot be proved that it costs more lives than it saves, it is incumbent on humanity to do what it can to protect life through all available mechanisms. The argu-ment that intervention in former Yugoslavia has not done this is imposs-ible to prove, and therefore cannot be supported. How can the net bal-ance be calculated of the numbers who have survived because of UN convoys?

The judgement that the UN helped to keep the crisis on the agenda, and that this was itself of benefit, was also impossible to prove. The attention of the international community offered a marginal disincentive to offences against humanity, and some actions that might otherwise have been taken probably were not taken. But this was not just about Bosnia-Herzegovina. UN involvement there was necessary if only to remind other potential malefactors that an international response was always possible, and that the law of the jungle was not the norm.

Lessons about the mistakes of UN intervention may also be deduced by reference to the range of *conceivable* ways of intervening in former Yugoslavia and their implications. First was large-scale intervention to enforce a solution, but this would have required resources which the states working with the UN were unwilling to provide. In any case such a level of intervention could have been counter-productive in the long term as it would simply have pushed grievances underground, as if one of the parties had 'won' by force of arms.

Second was a mode of intervention which committed sufficient resources to make it probable that goals agreed in the Security Council, short of enforcement, would be achieved. This was often not the case: for instance, Resolution 770 promised, as has been seen, more than it was intended to carry out. 'All measures necessary' were never taken to make sure that humanitarian assistance was delivered, and this was probably the first step in the decline of the credibility of the UN. Similarly the decision to introduce safe areas was taken by the Security Council in a kind of resource vacuum: the means necessary to maintain them if attacked were not provided. But such a level of commitment would not have been impossible, and it would have been well short of that necessary for enforcement.

Third was negative intervention: that is avoiding the commitment of UN forces, though encouraging settlement by diplomatic means, with intervention by the friends of the parties resisted, and peacekeeping forces provided after ceasefires. In this situation, however, there would have been the risk that the Serbs would have been lavishly armed by the Russians and the Bosnian Muslims by the Muslim states and the United States. Bosnia would have been destroyed in a proxy war.

Fourth was direct intervention by the large states, say the Russians on the Serb side, at the risk of counter-intervention on the side of the Bosnian Muslims by the West and the Islamic states. This was, of course, the worst-case scenario, and it was precisely because of the horrors it implied that it was an unlikely eventuality. The same rules applied as during the Cold War: each side would avoid too obvious and direct an involvement because of the risk of counter-intervention and escalation to general war.

What conclusions emerge from these possibilities? The best course of action, in that it combined what was practicable with what was the least undesirable, would have been the second option outlined above. This course also assumed the impartiality of the UN: it positively committed resources to the pursuit of impartial goals. But there needed to be a sufficient level of force to make it look as if goals agreed by the UN, short of enforcement, would be vigorously pursued. The mistake of the UN was to choose goals without being prepared to do this, and, as is usually the case with hollow threats, they were found out.

Intervention in former Yugoslavia probably had the effect of prolonging the crisis at a lower level of engagement, and discouraged a more rapid conclusion at a higher level. But this was the best that could have been achieved. It avoided the problem of finding massive external forces to impose a settlement which would then have needed policing in the long term at great cost. But it also combined a vigorous pursuit of humanitarian goals, and measures for isolating areas of peace, without compromising with the harsh truth of such conflicts – that the parties to them have to resolve them, even if this means war. The UN was right to intervene, right to fall short of enforcement but go beyond traditional peacekeeping, but wrong in that it failed to match realisable ambitions with affordable means.

The UN could be said to have *managed* the crisis for reasons which add up to the point that intervention was both ineffective in stopping the war *and* required by *both* the main parties to the dispute. The Serbs preferred that the UN stay rather than go, because they retained a preference for a legitimised settlement: hence the tendency for them to continue to push, when given any opportunity, and to make tactical concessions – accepting ceasefires, handing over heavy weapons, etc. – when it looked as if there could be a more powerful response. The UN's departure would also have freed the Islamic countries to arm the Muslims on a much larger scale, probably with the support of the United States. But the threat by the US Congress in late 1994 to allow arms to flow to the Muslims, in defiance of the UN arms embargo, was paradoxically helpful from the point of view of the UN: it encouraged the Serbs to placate the United Nations in the face of greater dangers. At the same time – and this also tended to prolong the war – the Serbs were constantly encouraged to do what they could to gain territory up to the point at which this was clearly at the risk of UN departure. But the Muslims also wanted the UN to stay because it could be an ally against Serb attack, and a skirt from under which the Serbs could *be* attacked, as in the case of the provocative excursions from the Bihac safe area in November–December 1994.

But the animosity between Milosevic and Karadzic, increasingly visible through 1994, was probably also a consequence as much of the structure of the conflict as of personalities. The restraints imposed by the UN presence, without actually preventing Serbian aggression, meant that the Serbs got increasing gains but never enough. Settlement in the framework of Bosnia-Herzegovina, on terms judged acceptable by the Serbs, was always unlikely in the context of UN intervention: the Serbs were always capable of getting enough to encourage them to seek for more, as mediation on the basis of the next gain was always an option. There was, however, bound to come a point when Bosnian Serb leaders would realise that their ambitions, growing as they were, could never be accommodated in Bosnia-Herzegovina: hence a bid for leadership of a Greater Serbia under Karadzic.

It follows in turn that it was always unlikely that a settlement could be reached without the positive support of the Belgrade government on the side of the UN. This was true under Panic as under Milosevic. The former should have been more rewarded for his support of the UN, but in late 1994 so should the latter, for instance, by lifting sanctions on Serbia–Montenegro: any settlement in Bosnia-Herzegovina would require the support of Belgrade. Without the whole-hearted support of Milosevic, sufficient pressure on Karadzic could not be exerted. But more importantly perhaps, Milosevic needed to be brought, and kept, on side, because of what could happen in other parts of the Balkans, especially in Kosovo and in Macedonia (FYROM). The latter crisis could be even more damaging than that in former Yugoslavia, and to contain it the support of Belgrade was essential.

It became apparent, during 1994, that any settlement on former Yugoslavia would be at the expense of the state of Bosnia-Herzegovina. This prospect had ambiguous implications for the UN. From one angle it will be seen as a disastrous betrayal of the key principle on which the UN was founded – respect for the frontiers of nation-states once recognised. But, from another, if this principle had to be suspended, as looked likely in December 1994, it will become clear that it is only the global organisation which has the authority to grant this dispensation, and to promulgate its basis.

If there are to be new ways of thinking about the bases of United Nations' intervention and humanitarian assistance these will have implications for the process whereby states are recognised.[38] The process of recognising the break-away republics in Yugoslavia was, however, controlled by the states of the EC/EU according to tests enunciated by the Badinter Commission attached to the EC Conference on Yugoslavia.[39] This produced a quandary: on the one hand the UN was the primary forum for the definition of the criteria of statehood, but, on the other hand, their relevance to the circumstances in former Yugoslavia was determined by the regional organisation. In consequence there was the risk of placing the application of general principles in thrall to local contingency; or even at the mercy of particular state interests within the regional organisation.

In Yugoslavia the recognition process was mishandled by the EC, a lesson which the EU will not easily forget, and was perhaps reflected in its initial reticence to recognise the former Yugoslav republic of Macedonia as an independent state, despite its having seemingly fulfilled all the conditions set out by the Badinter Commission. The major problem was that the EC recognised the regions of former Yugoslavia as successor states before any agreement about frontiers or assuring the rights of minorities, including the Serbs in Bosnia-Herzegovina.

The Badinter Commission had implied recognition before this had happened de jure, by dealing with the central governments in the break-away territories and accepting the central authorities' statements about the way in which the rights of minorities were to be protected. For instance, evidence of adequate protection for the minority rights of the Serbs was taken merely from assurances contained in a letter from the Bosnian government to say that it had been incorporated in the constitution. There was little direct contact with the minorities, because it might have offended the central regimes. Indeed the Badinter Commission was asked by Lord Carrington to make political judgements, as opposed to strictly legal ones, precisely because the EC states had been subjected to undue pressure in 1991 from the Germans, and asking Badinter to take this on was a useful evasion.

What conclusions follow from these observations? One is that any relaxing of the strict prohibition of intervention in international relations carries with it clear implications for the recognition process. If increasingly there is to be intervention, the global organisation should also have

[38] See Paul Taylor, 'The Role of the United Nations in the Provision of Humanitarian Assistance: New Problems and New Responses', in James T. H. Tang (ed.), *Human Rights and International Relations in the Asia Pacific* (London and New York: Pinter, 1995), p. 141.

[39] See various press releases issued by the Commission of the European Communities on behalf of the Commission for Yugoslavia under reference CEECAN 270066DGO8 and 09, February–March 1992.

the right to approve states in the first instance, and to de-recognise them if they fall short. If tests to be applied are widened, and applied more explicitly to the rights and welfare of peoples, the global organisation should also have the right to decide upon the justification of a claim to statehood. The reason, as shown by the example of former Yugoslavia, is that it will have to pick up the pieces if that state fails. This is the case for making the recognition of states a global responsibility to be exercised through the UN. Security Council approval would both reflect and enhance its authority. Conversely, it follows that if states cannot accept the transfer to the UN of this traditional prerogative role, then the strict rule of non-intervention cannot be relaxed.

A more modest conclusion, however, was that a point has been reached in Yugoslavia, when the global organisation will eventually have to be asked to correct the error of the regional organisation, the EC/EU, which had helped to precipitate it. Only the UN can place the seal of legitimacy upon the resulting new states.

### Regional–global organisation relationships

The crisis in former Yugoslavia also provides some lessons on the appropriate relationship between regional and global organisations. The regional organisation should normally act as the agent of the UN, always within a mandate approved in the Security Council, but subject to closer and more direct control as the scale of military intervention moves from that appropriate to traditional peacekeeping toward enforcement. Enforcement should always be managed by the global organisation. Similarly decisions of a constitutive nature, creating new rules or legitimising new actors, for instance through recognition, should be taken by the United Nations.

Much has been written about the reform of the global organisation and this is not the place to pursue the matter. But two points may usefully be added: first, if regional organisations are to be a fundamental part of a reformed global security architecture, the arrangements of the Security Council should reflect this; second, the crisis in former Yugoslavia demonstrates the overwhelming importance of relating policies to resources. The Security Council simply should not take decisions without adequate resources. Perhaps there should be a separate Technical Evaluation Authority to confirm that resources and policy match.

Regional organisations should only act on problems between members, and not out of their area in crises among non-members. But action by the member states of an out-of-area organisation may be sanctioned by the local regional organisation to act on its behalf in their region.

Hence in former Yugoslavia, or other parts of Eurasia, NATO could act if this were requested by the Organisation of Security and Cooperation in Europe (OSCE), which is the responsible inclusive regional organisation. These various forms of supervision are necessary in order to avoid either a return to the spheres-of-influence idea, which creates no-go areas for international authority, or the appearance of the hired gun with overtones of what would look like imperialism.

Such principles mean that in a number of areas of the world regional security organisations need to be created where they do not now exist. They should be legitimised by the global authority, and their decisions subject to UN authority, both under the Security Council and the jurisdiction of the International Court of Justice.

Developing the role of regional organisations on the lines of this interpretation of the principles of Chapter VIII can only be carried out in the context of the overall reform of the United Nations, especially the membership of the Security Council and its relations with the General Assembly. The model of the EU is a useful model of links between the regional organisations and the UN, though the French and British insistence on acting on their own account in the Security Council should be abandoned; other regional security organisations should also be represented in the Security Council. The United Nations and regional organisations should be linked by overlapping memberships, and related through legitimised hierarchies.

# 4    Somalia

*Ioan Lewis and James Mayall*

The involvement of the United Nations in Somalia was a product of the new international climate created by the end of the Cold War and by the dramatic success of Operation Desert Storm, and its aftermath in 1991. For the UN, the Somali operation, which at its height employed a force of 28,000 at an estimated cost of US $1.5 billion, broke new ground in two ways. Under Resolution 794 of 3 December 1992, the Security Council invoked Chapter VII of the Charter to authorise the establishment of an Unified Task Force (UNITAF), under United States command and control, 'in order to establish a secure environment for humanitarian relief operations in Somalia'. This was the first time that an unambiguously internal and humanitarian crisis had been designated as a threat to international peace and security, thus justifying peace-enforcement measures.

Secondly, with this and subsequent resolutions, the UN dropped the pretence that its involvement in Somalia arose out of an invitation from the government – although the Council continued to refer to 'urgent calls from Somalia . . . to ensure the delivery of humanitarian assistance' – since no government existed with the authority to issue such an invitation. For the first time, statelessness was acknowledged to be a threat to an international society composed of sovereign states.

The United Nations did not extend its prerogatives in these ways either willingly or as the result of a deliberate and carefully worked out international strategy. Indeed, although the Security Council resolution[1] which established UNOSOM II gave the Organisation a wider mandate than UNITAF, from which it took over in May 1993, its political content was sufficiently imprecise to offer many hostages to fortune. If support for UN intervention arose because of the disintegration of all government and the ensuing 'anarchy', the official view remained that 'the people of Somalia bear the ultimate responsibility for national rec-

---

[1] Resolution 814, 26 March 1993. For text of the resolution, see pp. 202–7 in Appendix C.

onciliation and reconstruction of their own country'.[2] There were periodic suggestions that the UN should establish a formal protectorate for Somalia, or resume the trusteeship responsibilities that it relinquished in 1960. However, no government was prepared to support this view publicly, partly, no doubt, for fear of taking on an open-ended and costly commitment, far removed from their own vital interests, and partly out of respect for Third World sensitivities on the issue of colonialism.

This chapter examines the experience of United Nations' intervention and its local, regional and global implications. As with the other case studies in this volume, more is involved than an assessment of UN peacekeeping in a country where the general commitment to peace barely exists. In Somalia the issue was whether political reconstruction could be engineered in the absence of a clear-cut political authority, and in a society in which there were a dozen or more major factions, none of which were above manipulating the UN for their own ends.

### Somalia as an international problem

Somalia became independent in 1960, when the British Somaliland Protectorate joined with the trusteeship territory administered by Italy to form a single republic. In the aftermath of World War II, the then British foreign secretary, Ernest Bevin, had advanced a plan that all the Somali territories should be prepared for independence within a single state. This proposal had its origins in Britain's control of the region during World War II, but it fell foul of disagreements amongst the four powers (France, the United Kingdom, the United States and the USSR) which had been charged by the newly formed United Nations Organisation with devising a solution to the problem of Italy's former colonies.[3]

The international status of the country was thus not a direct issue in the crisis that led to UN intervention. From a historical point of view, however, it must certainly be counted amongst the indirect causes. Somalia has been a problematic member of international society from the beginning. Although the principle of national self-determination was enshrined in the UN Charter as an inalienable human right, it was interpreted in practice as western European de-colonisation, ruling out any subsequent territorial revision as a result of irredentist or secessionist claims, except in the unlikely event that these could be peacefully nego-

---

[2] Ibid.
[3] See I. M. Lewis, *A Modern History of Somalia: Nation and State in the Horn of Africa* (Boulder, Colo.: Westview Press, 1988), chapter 7.

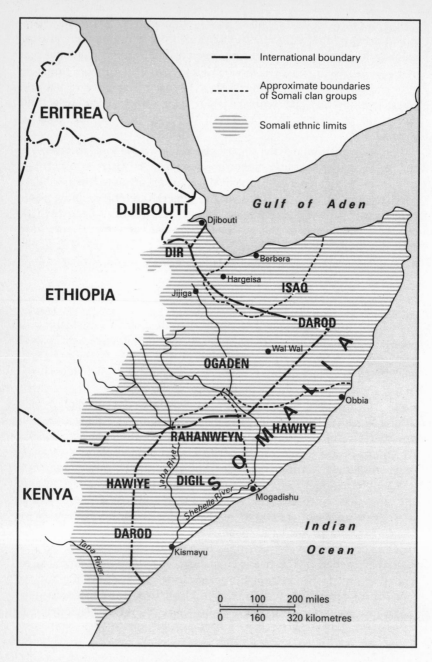

Map 4.1 Somalia, 1991–1994

tiated between the parties concerned.[4] The Somali nationalists had settled for what they could get, but they remained committed to uniting all Somalis under a single government. This objective was written into the constitution and was symbolised by the national flag, a five-pointed star in which each point represented one of the centres of Somali population. Three remained outside the republic: the Ogaden region of Ethiopia, the north-eastern province of Kenya, and Djibouti, at that time still ruled directly by France.

Successive Somali governments attempted to secure the 'return' of the lost territories by diplomacy; by supporting both low-level insurgency within the Ogaden and the *shifta*, bandits who operated across the Somali–Kenya border; by directing propaganda and conducting political warfare against the Kenyan and Ethiopian governments; and finally by seeking a military and political alliance with each of the superpowers in turn.

None of these strategies worked. At the founding meeting of the Organisation of African Unity in May 1963 Somalia failed to gain any support for its irredentist claims. Indeed, the short border war which broke out in the Ogaden in October 1963 not only failed to modify the status quo but led the OAU to adopt a resolution the following July binding all African governments to respect the frontiers they had inherited at independence.[5] A resumption of the fighting in 1967 was equally unsuccessful, and Kenya and Ethiopia signed a defence pact against their common enemy. Such was the antagonism between Somalia and its neighbours that this pact survived the Ethiopian revolution in 1974.

The military coup by which General Siyad Barre came to power in 1969 temporarily stabilised the regional conflict, although it also involved Somalia more deeply in Cold War rivalries than previously, and, by giving the regime access to plentiful and relatively sophisticated military supplies, contributed over the longer term to the destruction of the state. Barre announced Somalia's conversion to Marxism-Leninism and signed a long-term treaty of friendship and cooperation with the Soviet Union. No reliable evidence exists that the Soviet Union, which gained port facilities at Berbera and other military installations, ever encouraged the regime to press its irredentist claims, and indeed for the first few years of his rule, Siyad himself actively discouraged popular provocation of the Ethiopian and Kenyan governments. That he would have been unlikely to succeed for long

---

[4] See James Mayall, *Nationalism and International Society* (Cambridge: Cambridge University Press, 1990), pp. 50–7.
[5] For text, see Ian Brownlie (ed.), *Basic Documents in African Affairs* (Oxford: Clarendon Press, 1971), pp. 360–1.

will become clear when we consider the nature of Somali society in relation to the current crisis. Here it is sufficient to note that Somali nationalism differs from that in most African countries in that it is in essence a popular (albeit contradictory) rather than merely an elite phenomenon.

Siyad Barre's restraint did not long outlast the Ethiopian revolution. The fall of Emperor Haile Selassie was followed, after a chaotic interlude, by the establishment of another self-declared Marxist dictatorship under Mengistu Haile Marriam. During this interlude which also saw the gradual withdrawal of US patronage, Ethiopia seemed to be on the point of disintegrating into the state's multiple ethnic components. Given the hostility which the international community had previously demonstrated toward Somalia's irredentist ambitions, it was not surprising that Siyad apparently concluded that the Ethiopian revolution had created an opportunity that was unlikely to recur. For a time, the Soviet authorities tried to consolidate their influence in the Horn of Africa by attempting (in March 1977) to broker a confederation of socialist states to include Ethiopia, Somalia and Yemen. Had it been acceptable, this formula would have reduced the diplomatic costs of shifting their patronage from Mogadishu to Addis Ababa since they had previously supported not only the Somalis but the Eritrean separatists as well. However, when the scheme predictably failed to win regional support, the Soviet government was forced to choose between clients. Equally predictably, it chose Ethiopia.[6]

Meanwhile, Ethiopian–US relations had deteriorated to the point that in April 1977 Mengistu closed US installations in Ethiopia and Eritrea and expelled US personnel. Ethiopia increasingly sought military support from the Soviet Union and, in May, Mengistu visited Moscow and issued a declaration of mutual collaboration against 'imperialist' and 'reactionary' forces which he held responsible for aggravating tension in the Horn. Djibouti's independence from France on 26 June triggered the ensuing Somali–Ethiopian struggle for control of the ethnically Somali Ogaden and the looming seismic shift in superpower allegiances in the region. When the Western Somali Liberation Front (WSLF) rose in revolt in the Ogaden in July, Siyad (whose mother was Ogadeni) first supported it financially and politically and then invaded the territory with his regular forces.

The United States eventually accepted the Somali offer of the vacated Soviet strategic real estate, although not before they had made it clear

---

[6] For a full discussion, see Robert G. Patman, *The Soviet Union in the Horn of Africa* (Cambridge: Cambridge University Press, 1990), pp. 190–254.

that they would not support Somali expansionism. By this time the war was over. Unfortunately, the state of alarm in Washington at what was perceived as a new forward Soviet strategy in Africa was such that there had been influential advocates of the United States in favour of doing whatever was necessary to stop the advance. The national security advisor, Zbigniew Brzezinski, even talked ruefully of the SALT II treaty being buried in the sands of the Ogaden. It is impossible to say whether the Somalis really believed the Americans would come to their assistance. Certainly, the noisy foreign policy debate in Washington allowed them to listen to those they wanted to hear.[7]

In reality, the danger of direct American intervention on the Somali side was remote. The tacit ground rules that had emerged during the first Cold War continued during the second: only one superpower at a time could be directly committed to a regional conflict. In 1977, Moscow was the first to move. Early Somali successes were reversed when the Soviet Union mounted an air-lift of heavy armour and Cuban troops from Aden. The outcome was a crushing military defeat in March 1978. The United States refused to come to Siyad's assistance until Somali forces had been withdrawn from the Ogaden. Thereafter Somalia had American support – after 1979 it was even recruited along with Sudan and Kenya to the favoured group of states that provided facilities for the American Rapid Deployment Force – but it was also effectively forced to abandon the irredentist claims which had formed the corner-stone of the state's international policies since 1960. A new constitution, which substituted support for all oppressed peoples for the earlier commitment to liberate Somalis, was an attempt to secure the kind of international recognition and support that the southern African liberation movements enjoyed.[8] But the conceit was so obvious that it impressed no one, and indeed served to illustrate, not for the first or last time, the depth of Somali misunderstanding of the nature and working of international society.

Somalia is both riven with conflict and politically volatile at the best of times (see below, pp. 101–3) but without the potential safety valve of irredentist enthusiasm, all of these conflicts imploded within the state

---

[7] See James Mayall, 'The Battle for the Horn: Somali Irredentism and International Diplomacy', *The World Today*, vol. 34, no. 9 (September 1978), pp. 336–45.

[8] See James Mayall, 'Self-Determination and the OAU', and Sally Sealy, 'The Changing Idiom of Self-Determination in the Horn of Africa', in I. M. Lewis (ed.), *Nationalism and Self-Determination in the Horn of Africa* (London: Ithaca Press, 1983), pp. 77–92 and 93–109.

itself and eventually destroyed it. It was thus that unsuccessful Somali irredentism paved the way for the internal crisis of the 1990s.

### The nature of the conflict

The Somali defeat in 1978 had two interlocking consequences. First, it saddled the country with a seemingly permanent refugee population, as over 500,000 people followed the retreating army out of the Ogaden. Secondly, Siyad was soon faced by an insurrection of northern clans in the former British Protectorate and north-east. The first of these developments helped to create an economy of dependence on humanitarian aid; the second locked the country into the pattern of regional and global rivalries that persisted until the end of the Cold War.

Support for dissidents from neighbouring countries has long been an established feature of the political landscape in the Horn. For example, Eritrean and Tigrean separatists were regularly provided with Somali passports. Mengistu was merely following precedent in seeking to relieve the pressure on his own regime from the Eritrean and Tigrean insurgencies by supporting internal conflict in Somalia. However, the end of the Cold War weakened Siyad's ability to resist. Even as an ally, he had always been regarded with suspicion in Washington, and, under fire from their own human rights activists, the Americans now had no compelling reason to support him. In Ethiopia, Mengistu was also having to contemplate survival in a post-Cold War world. In 1988 the two leaders agreed to resume diplomatic relations and to stop helping each other's insurgent movements. The rot had gone too far to be arrested by such tactical diplomatic manoeuvring, although it may have helped Siyad cling on to power for another two years. Indeed, this Ethiopian–Somali agreement spurred on the Somali National Movement (SNM) to a final effort, which, at considerable cost in civilian lives, led eventually to the overthrow of Siyad's forces in the north-west. By August 1990 the three major Somali opposition movements – the SNM, the United Somali Congress (USC) and the Somali Patriotic Movement (SPM) – had joined forces with the aim of ousting Siyad Barre from power, an objective which they finally accomplished on 27 January 1991.

Their loose alliance proved incapable of holding together long enough to bring about the economic and political reconstruction of the country. On the contrary, its falling apart was responsible for an humanitarian disaster of even greater proportions than that over which Siyad had presided, and finally brought about United Nations' intervention. To understand the nature of the Somali conflict and how victory could be turned so quickly and decisively into national disintegration and chaos, it is necessary first to grasp the unique character of Somali political culture.

### Somali political culture

The Muslim Somalis (numbering about 5 million) are essentially nomadic herdsmen, roving with their prized camels, sheep and goats (and sometimes cattle) over the plains of the Horn of Africa. Only in the relatively fertile region of the Shebelle and Juba Rivers in southern Somalia, where the Italian colonisers established banana and sugar plantations, is agriculture practised traditionally on any extensive scale. Elsewhere in this semi-desert land, where petrol exploration has proceeded apparently unsuccessfully since World War II, Somalis are accustomed to fight for access to pasture and water. Before European colonisation, despite a strong sense of linguistic and cultural identity, they did not constitute a state, but were divided into an elaborate series of clans and sub-clans without strongly developed dynastic rule. Their uncentralised political organisation belonged to the type classified by political anthropologists as a 'segmentary lineage system' where political identity and loyalty are determined by genealogical closeness and remoteness.[9] A genealogy here was less a historical document than a political charter. The ideological principle was identical to that expressed in the Bedouin Arab maxim: 'Myself against my brother; my brother and I against my cousins; my cousins and I against the world'.

The nineteenth-century English explorer and Arabist, Richard Burton, described the Somalis accurately as a 'fierce and turbulent race of republicans' who lacked both chiefs and experience of centralised government. If he had been a modern travel writer, he might have added that, with their constantly changing political loyalties – at different levels in the segmentary system – the Somalis lived in what amounted to a state of chronic political schizophrenia, verging on anarchy. Instead, Burton dwelt on what he saw as a redeeming positive characteristic, the pervasive importance of oral poetry in Somali popular culture.[10] He failed, however, to stress sufficiently the crucial role of poetic polemic in war and peace.[11] Burton might also have emphasised the prominence

---

[9] See I. M. Lewis, *A Pastoral Democracy* (New York: Afrikana Press, 1982), and *Blood and Bone* (Trenton, N. J.: Red Sea Press, 1993), for detailed accounts.

[10] See B. W. Andrzejewski and I. M. Lewis, *Somali Poetry* (Oxford: Oxford University Press, 1964); B. W. Andrzejewski and S. Andrzejewski, *Somali Poetry* (Bloomington: Indiana University Press, 1993).

[11] S. S. Samatar, *Oral Poetry and Somali Nationalism* (Cambridge: Cambridge University Press, 1982).

in Somali politics of a form of political contract or treaty, as a means of binding diffuse kinship loyalties at a particular level within and between clans.

### Somalis and the outside world

As a fiercely independent people, with a powerful sense of ethnic exclusiveness and superiority, notwithstanding their myriad internal divisions, the Somalis have lived for centuries outside, or on the edge of, world history and the literate tradition. Characteristically, they have usually impinged on the world outside in contexts of confrontation and conflict. Thus, the earliest extended account of the Somalis in written history is in a sixteenth-century source recording the part they played on the Islamic side in the religious wars of the period between Christian Ethiopia and the surrounding Muslim principalities. It strikes a very modern note in reporting that Somali warriors were particularly famous for their skills in organising ambushes. It also mentions a prominent Somali battle leader belonging to the same clan which in 1969 provided the military dictator of Somalia, Mohammed Siyad Barre.

Muslim 'fundamentalism' is likewise hardly a novel, modern phenomenon in Somali politics. Immediately after the French, British, Italians and Ethiopians had carved up the Somali lands at the close of the nineteenth century,[12] a fiery Somali fundamentalist sheik, who was the most brilliant poet of his age, proclaimed a holy war against the Christian colonisers which dragged on for twenty years. This protracted anticolonial rebellion, retrospectively considered by Somalis as a protonationalist movement, survived four major British military expeditions and the first use of air strikes in colonial Africa, before it collapsed when Siyad Mohammed, known to the British as the 'mad Mullah', died of influenza in 1920 at a remote village in the Ethiopian Ogaden.

Although it ranged more widely afield, the Dervish War was centred in the north of the Somali region, in the British Somaliland Protectorate and eastern Ethiopia, inhabited by the ethnically Somali Ogaden, the clan of the Dervish leader himself. The Italian colony of Somalia, to the south, was less affected, although the extension of Italian authority was from time to time subject to attacks by Siyad Mohammed's forces. Nevertheless, Somali conscripts were recruited into Mussolini's armies for the long-awaited conquest of Ethiopia. The Italo-Ethiopian War of 1935–6, which became part of the run-up to World War II, was triggered by a minor confrontation between Ethiopian and Italian forces at

---

[12] See Lewis, *Modern History of Somalia*, pp. 63–91.

the oasis of Wal Wal in Ogaden territory in an area disputed by Italy and Ethiopia.

The Italian defeat by the Allies in 1941 brought their Somali colony together with those of Ethiopia and Britain under a single British military administration which promoted Somali nationalism, directly and indirectly, particularly through Ernest Bevin's plan proposing that all the Somali people should be administered as a single state and prepared for self-government. When, as we have seen, this pan-Somali plan had to be abandoned, the Somali territories resumed their former colonial statuses, except for the Italian colony of Somalia which became a UN trusteeship, administered by Italy under a ten-year mandate (1950–60). At independence, ex-Italian Somalia merged with the former British Somaliland Protectorate, which had been hastily prepared for self-government, to form the Somali Republic. The new state was thus based on the principle of self-determination applied to a single ethnic group, parts of which still languished under foreign rule. Unlike the majority of ethnically heterogeneous African states dedicated to 'nation-building', Somalia's predicament was its incomplete statehood, the spur to pan-Somali unification which neighbouring states found so threatening.

### The limits of Somali political cohesion

While pursuing these external goals, with little success, the nationalists who dominated the political scene in Somalia strove to maintain the pretension that divisive clan ties had withered away. There was, thus, no serious attempt to address and come to terms with the realities of clan allegiance which had been sharpened rather than diminished by their encapsulation in the exotic structure of a centralised state which provided a new and enlarged arena for clan competition and conflict. These contradictions had even become part of the new political language where politicians spoke of each other's basic allegiance in terms of 'ex-clan', a historical phenomenon which no longer affected them.

After a decade of parliamentary democracy, the seething tensions of antagonistic clans which undermined national cohesion provided the setting for the military coup of October 1969 led by the army commander, Mohammed Siyad Barre. He invoked a crude home-grown version of 'scientific socialism' to consolidate his power, officially outlawing all forms of clannish behaviour.[13] Although the people's inspiration was now supposed to be the curious trinity of 'Comrades Marx, Lenin and Siyad' (the dominant state emblem), Siyad's actual power base was a

---

[13] See Lewis, *Blood and Bone*, chapter 7.

more traditional trinity: his own clan, his mother's clan and the clan of his son-in-law, commander of the secret police. These three clans all belonged at a higher segmentary level to the Darod clan-family which had highjacked the Somali state, and now dominated all the other clans. There was no precedent in Somali history for such clan hegemony.

Siyad's maternal clan allegiance to the Ogaden made him particularly vulnerable to Ogadeni pressure which, as Ethiopia fell apart following the revolution which overthrew Haile Selassie, became increasingly insistent. While his commitment of Somalia's army to help the WSLF guerrillas in their 1977 uprising was initially very popular at home, the crushing defeat which had quickly followed in March 1978 prompted an upsurge of suppressed clan tensions. A critical factor here was the huge refugee influx which flooded Somalia in the wake of the Ethiopian reconquest of the Ogaden. The majority of these Ogadeni refugees (belonging to the Darod clan-family) were grouped in large refugee camps in the north-west regions of the republic, traditionally occupied by the Isaq clansmen who had proved the most recalcitrant subjects of Siyad's dictatorial rule. For centuries, the Isaq and Ogaden had jostled for access to pastureland and water along the Ethiopian border.

In the immediate wake of the Ogaden debacle, it was, however, an abortive coup in April 1978 by predominantly Mijerteyn (Darod) officers which signalled the beginnings of armed insurrection against Siyad's regime. In 1982, the Mijerteyn opposition regrouped with the formation of the Somali Salvation Democratic Front (SSDF),[14] closely followed by the Isaq-based Somali National Movement (SNM).[15] This brought armed insurrection to the north-east and north-west regions, which became increasingly subject to harsh military rule. Both movements organised their guerrilla operations inside Somalia from bases in Ethiopia, with the tacit agreement of Mengistu's government which, despite its dedication to socialism and close ties to the USSR, was after the Ogaden War more rather than less hostile to Somalia than the old regime of Haile Selassie.

Having guardedly replaced the USSR as Somalia's patron, the United States and its western allies (especially the Italians) added new equipment to what remained of Siyad's Soviet arsenals, with Saudi Arabia and other Gulf states meeting some of the bills. This was used to counter the

---

[14] D. Compagnon, 'The Somali Opposition Fronts', *Horn of Africa*, vol. 13, no. 1/2 (1990), pp. 29–54.

[15] D. Compagnon, 'Somaliland, un ordre politique en gestation?', *Politique Africaine*, no. 50, June 1993, pp. 9–20; G. Prunier, 'A Candid View of the Somali National Movement', *Horn of Africa*, vols. 13/14, nos. 3/4 (1992), pp. 107–20; Lewis, *Blood and Bone*, chapter 8.

insurrections in the north-east and north-west and growing disaffection in other parts of the country, where the dictator's survivalist divide-and-rule tactics relied heavily on the dangerous expedient of bribing and arming friendly clans to attack his enemies. The increasingly desperate fighting in the north eroded the strength of Siyad's forces which became more and more dominated by his own clansmen. In common with the rest of the state, these forces depended critically on supplies of relief food aid for the refugee population – whose size was thus a very controversial issue with UNHCR.[16] The official economy, based primarily on the export of livestock from the war-torn north was collapsing, and was no longer as important as the informal sector based on livestock trading and migrant labour (what Somalis called the 'muscle-drain') in the Gulf states. Banana exports from the riverain plantations in the south had earlier dwindled into insignificance through a mixture of incompetence and corruption. Still paid at essentially the same rates as in the 1960s before the years of hyperinflation, the civil service had virtually ceased to function by the end of the decade.

### The descent into chaos

The peace accord signed by the Ethiopian and Somali dictators in April 1988, which obliged each side to stop supporting the other's dissidents, was, ironically, the final precipitant to the full-scale civil war which had already destroyed the Somali state months before the actual overthrow of Siyad in January 1991. The pressure of human rights activists on western governments, appalled at the ferocious suppression of northern dissidence, led to the virtual cessation of aid by 1990 when the area under Siyad's control hardly extended outside Mogadishu. When the Darod dictator was finally dislodged from the already severely battle-scarred capital by USC forces of the Hawiye clans, led by General Aideed, Somalia had already disintegrated into its traditional clan segments. The situation now was exactly as Burton and other nineteenth-century explorers had described it – a land of clan republics where the traveller had to secure protection from each group whose territory he traversed. The only difference was that the volatile relationships between these clan units had been raised to fever pitch by the experience of Darod hegemony, and the bitter fighting with modern weapons which wrought death and suffering on a scale never experienced in the past. The scale of the ensuing clan-cleansing in Mogadishu and elsewhere

[16] I. M. Lewis (ed.), *Blueprint for a Socio-Demographic Survey and Re-enumeration of the Refugee Camp Population in the Somali Democratic Republic* (Geneva: UNHCR, 1986).

was unprecedented. Siyad's huge arsenals which had largely fallen into the hands of the various clan militia were supplemented by equipment from Mengistu's hastily demobilised army in Ethiopia, where tanks were almost as cheap as second-hand cars, and by continuing imports of arms across the Kenyan border and along the coast.

### The trigger to international intervention

Having ousted Siyad, the USC Hawiye leaders, General Aideed (who had links with the Isaqi SNM in the north) and Ali Mahdi (a prominent businessman) could not agree on how to share power. Ali Mahdi, who represented the original Hawiye inhabitants of Mogadishu in contrast to the recent invaders of Aideed's clan, had provocatively already set up an elaborate 'government'. This conflict, which split Mogadishu into two armed camps, polarised along clan lines, quickly engulfing what was left of the city in a protracted blood-bath, killing an estimated 14,000 people and wounding 30,000.[17]

Ferocious fighting outside Mogadishu spread devastation and starvation throughout southern Somalia. The USC Hawiye outlawed or drove out of Mogadishu those Darod clansmen who remained there. The Darod, especially those related to Siyad's clan, regrouped under the leadership of one of his sons-in-law, a general with a particularly brutal record in north-western Somalia (Somaliland). Each side devastated the agricultural region between the rivers which is Somalia's bread basket, killing and terrorising the local cultivators who are less aggressive than the nomadic Somali. As the conflict widened, Aideed allied with Colonel Umar Jess's militia against Morgan who, in turn, joined forces loosely with another of Siyad's former generals, Adan Gabio, and his militia. These and the two factions in Mogadishu were the most heavily armed and dangerous militia fighting for control of what was left of southern Somalia. All were based primarily on traditional clan groupings manipulated by a powerful figure and held together by the attractions of the spoils of war. The so-called warlords who led them were all far from illustrious figures from the Siyad regime. Amplifying, on a smaller scale, this relatively organised violence, qat-chewing[18] young gangsters, whose role model was Rambo, spread mayhem, looting and killing in

---

[17] *Somalia Beyond the Warlords*, Africa Watch occasional report, March 1993, p. 5.
[18] Resembling the leaves of the English privet shrub, *qat* leaves are chewed raw, traditionally on religious or social occasions. Today, they are chewed more widely and frequently by individuals during the day and produce a strong craving for this stimulant which contains benzedrine-type compounds. See Roland Marchal, 'Le *mooryaan* de Mogadiscio. Formes de la violence et de son contrôle dans un espèce urbain en guerre', *Cahiers d'Etudes Africaines*, vol. 130, no. 33 (1993), pp. 295–320.

Mogadishu.[19] With agricultural and livestock production devastated, famine spread, especially in the arable areas between the rivers. The UN estimated that as many as 300,000 people perished from famine and 700,000 became refugees in Kenya, Ethiopia and to a lesser extent in Yemen, Europe, Scandinavia and North America.

The political and economic magnetism of the capital, Mogadishu, as a spur to conflict is highlighted by the contrasting situation in the north-east and north-west of the country. The north-east is dominated by the Mijerteyn (Darod) clan and, once it was liberated by the clan-based SSDF, remained at peace with a local administration which is a synthesis of the SSDF and the traditional local clan leaders. The only serious threat to order so far has been from militant Islamic fundamentalist groups. In the north-west, which is more heterogeneous in clan composition, the record is even more impressive. While the victorious SNM guerrillas set up a government and distanced themselves from the chronic conflict in the south by declaring unilateral independence in May 1991, clan rivalries within the Isaq federation prevented the 'modern' political leaders from exercising effective authority. Leadership reverted to the clan elders who, employing traditional diplomacy, inaugurated a remarkable series of peace conferences which slowly but surely restored a surprising degree of peace throughout the region – despite the continuing security problems posed by 'freelance' armed gangs. Finally, in June 1993 a new government was formed by a national council of clan elders which elected the former premier of Somalia (1966–9), Mohamad Haji Ibrahim Egal as president. This reassuring demonstration of the positive side of clanship and the successful potential of genuinely locally based peace initiatives contrasted markedly with the high-profile, extremely expensive and much less successful peacemaking by the UN and other outside bodies in southern Somalia. It indicated also the negative effect of the power-hungry southern warlords and of inequitably distributed foreign aid.[20]

### International intervention

In the successive blood-baths into which Mogadishu descended after Siyad's defeat, foreign embassies and most agencies, including the UN, abandoned southern Somalia to its gruesome fate. In March 1992 a

[19] See L. V. Cassanelli, 'Qat: Changes in the Production and Consumption of a Quasi-legal Commodity', in A. Appadurai (ed.), *The Social Life of Things* (Cambridge: Cambridge University Press, 1986), pp. 236–60.

[20] See A. Y. Farah and I. M. Lewis, *Somalia: The Roots of Reconciliation* (London: Actionaid, 1993).

ceasefire between Ali Mahdi and Aideed made possible the resumption of humanitarian relief. However, fighting and looting by various factions seeking to control ports and distribution routes became an important factor in the political economy of the militia and greatly reduced the effectiveness of aid deliveries. Factions levied heavy taxes on cargoes, took direct cuts of 10 per cent to 20 per cent of incoming aid, and charged exorbitantly for providing relief agencies with armed escorts to 'protect' food deliveries which they frequently also looted. Foreign NGOs were thus trapped in a web of protection rackets to an extent that they often failed to appreciate. Clearly, security was a critical issue in what had become Africa's latest famine, widely publicised in the media.[21] The question was how it was to be alleviated in a country where central government had lapsed.

The international community did not immediately conclude that large-scale humanitarian intervention was the appropriate response. On 24 April 1992, the Security Council adopted a resolution (Resolution 751) requesting the Secretary-General to deploy a group of 50 UN observers to monitor the ceasefire in Mogadishu. This had been negotiated in New York in February under the auspices of the Organisation of African Unity (OAU), the Arab League and the Islamic Conference. Although the resolution also indicated that the Council had agreed, in principle, to establish a UN peacekeeping force once the necessary conditions existed, no one seemed anxious to see Somalia move rapidly up the international agenda. Indeed, so reluctant were the Americans to face Congress on the issue that they had to be persuaded by the other members of the Council to allow the observer mission to be paid for out of assessed rather than voluntary contributions over which they had discretionary control. A few days later, the Secretary-General appointed an Algerian diplomat, Mohammed Sahnoun, as his special representative in Somalia. Sahnoun energetically set about the task of restoring the UN's credibility in Mogadishu and winning the confidence of faction leaders, donor governments and relief agencies alike. He was less successful in his dealing with the UN itself, a fact which eventually forced his resignation in October after he had repeatedly and publicly criticised the performance of UN agencies in Somalia.[22]

The underlying political and security problems remained as intractable as ever. Sahnoun's primary task was to secure effective food distri-

---

[21] See 'Misunderstanding the Somali Crisis', *Anthropology Today*, vol. 9 (1993), pp. 1–3.

[22] Mohammed Sahnoun has written his own account of these events: *Somalia: The Missed Opportunities* (Washington, D. C.: United States Institute of Peace, 1994). See also I. M. Lewis, *Making History in Somalia: Humanitarian Intervention in a Stateless Society*, Discussion Paper 6 (London: The Centre for the Study of Global Governance, LSE, 1993).

bution to stave off the impending humanitarian disaster – in August he reported that 1.5 million people or one-quarter of the Somali population were at risk – but the UN was not equipped to undertake the required level of armed protection to carry out this task. Following his report, the Secretary-General agreed to deploy 500 United Nations troops to Somalia and under a subsequent resolution, the Security Council authorised an additional 3,500 men to protect food convoys. Implementation did not quickly follow this authorisation. It was not until mid-September that the first contingent of Pakistani troops was flown in on a US aircraft and it was not until the second week of November that they were able to take control of Mogadishu airport.

There is no single explanation for the long delay in organising the international response to the Somali crisis. In part, it was undoubtedly the bureaucratic rigidity of which Ambassador Sahnoun complained so bitterly. In part, it was a consequence of logistical and financial constraints which prevented some countries from responding rapidly, even when they had taken the political decision to do so.[23] But it was also because the situation lay so far beyond the experience of UN peacekeeping that had developed over the previous forty years – there were simply no precedents for deploying UN forces on a humanitarian rather than a peacekeeping mission when there was no government with which to negotiate and where the practical decision, therefore, was always going to be whether to appease those with the power on the ground or oppose them by force.

By mid-summer it had become clear that, without strong support from the United States, the UN lacked the organisational resources and its members the political interest or will to fashion a coherent strategy for Somalia. The trouble was that those elements of the administration which were in favour of intervention and strong US leadership – the

[23] The nature of the problems involved is illustrated by the Canadian experience. The total lack of modern infrastructure over much of Somalia meant that even a battalion could not be deployed without an off-shore supply ship. The Canadians, who were assigned to the north-east, chartered their own ship which had to be in position by the time they arrived. However, even then they lacked the air transport capability to deploy a battalion quickly, which was obviously desirable if the UN was to take the initiative. Other countries with the capacity were not prepared to meet the cost – by air, US $14m, compared with US $1m if they were sent by sea. This meant that the Canadians could not move until the UN Secretariat had chartered two transport ships. This in turn caused further delays as, under the strict procurement rules which the Secretariat operates to avoid charges of profligacy, the UN can only charter vessels after an open international tender. The ships eventually arrived in Montreal on the day that President Bush offered the UN a task force. Once the agreement had been reached with the Americans, the Canadians, like the Pakistanis, were shipped to Somalia in US transports, where they were deployed not to the north-east as originally intended, but to an area west of Mogadishu (interview with David Mallone, deputy head of the Canadian Mission to the United Nations, 16 April 1993).

Office for Disaster Relief and the Africa Bureau in the State Department – had few cards to play in Washington's game of bureaucratic politics, particularly in an election year. Thus, even after the president had ordered a food air-lift on 14 August, the White House and the political divisions of the State Department and the Pentagon remained adamantly opposed to any escalation in American involvement. The election was being fought primarily on domestic issues and the administration was above all concerned to protect the president from a damaging and open-ended foreign entanglement.

There were even persistent rumours of tension between the UN Secretary-General and the US administration over the size and composition of UNOSOM I. The Americans were well aware that the air-lift was not working but they had estimated that at least 30,000 heavily armed troops would be needed. Neither the numbers of troops available – they were angered by Boutros-Ghali's plucking the number 3,500 out of a hat at random – nor the mandate were designed to do the job.[24] On the other hand, at this stage they were as reluctant as the other western governments to see Somalia used as a test case in the reinterpretation (and effective extension) of Chapter VII of the Charter.

By all accounts the change in the American position owed much to George Bush himself. Once he had lost the election, he was, in any case, no longer constrained by domestic considerations. Moreover, as the architect of the 'new world order' he evidently felt it incumbent on him to 'do something'. His speech to the General Assembly on 21 September had contained the first indications that the end of the Cold War was changing traditional American attitudes to UN peacekeeping, which had always been considered off-limits by the US military. The speech evidently 'rang bells' in the Department of Defense with the result that when the president began taking a personal interest in Somalia, they were ready 'to turn on a dime', the Pentagon's opposition to intervention transforming itself into measured support. On 21 November the Deputies' Committee of the National Security Council reconsidered the options on Somalia and on the basis of a recommendation from the chief of staff, Colin Powell, decided in favour of intervention.

---

[24] This announcement also infuriated Sahnoun, who was not informed in advance and was therefore unable to allay Somali suspicions of UN motives. '[It] was made without informing the UNOSOM delegation in Mogadishu, or the leaders of the neighbouring countries who had previously been informed by me of every intended move. Worse, the announcement was made without consulting the Somali leaders and community elders': Sahnoun, *Somalia*, p. 39.

Powell's conversion was conditional on the operation being limited in three important respects: its function was to be confined to securing the effective distribution of food to those in need; its geographical scope was to be limited to the most devastated parts of the country in and around Mogadishu, Berbera and Baidoa; and the mission was to be completed preferably before or very soon after the inauguration of the new president in January 1993. Providing these conditions were met, he favoured intervening with sufficient force and fire-power to overawe any Somali opposition and minimise casualties.

The die was now cast. It remained to secure authorisation from the UN Security Council and to arrange a division of labour with UNOSOM I. While the Americans were prepared to act unilaterally, they were understandably anxious to have international support on the ground as well as in the Security Council. The United Nations turned down the American offer that they should serve in blue berets, i.e. as a UN force, as they had done during the Korean War in the early 1950s, since they were not prepared to countenance any weakening in their national chain of command, however nominal. Nonetheless, as one diplomat who witnessed the negotiations remarked, 'The UN gave an almost audible sigh of relief when the Americans made their offer.'

The empowering resolution, Resolution 794 of 3 December 1992, was not only the first to establish an humanitarian operation under Chapter VII of the Charter, and without an explicit invitation from the parties to the conflict, but it also gained the unanimous support of the Council, including China and a number of African members who in the aftermath of Operation Desert Storm had expressed their suspicions that the West might use humanitarian arguments to mask their interference in the domestic affairs of other states. In addition to the Pakistani forces that were already committed to UNOSOM, support for the Americans within UNITAF was provided by sizeable contingents from France (Foreign Legion), Italy, Belgium, Saudi Arabia, Egypt and Morocco. More than 20 other contingents of various sizes and specialised functions were either provided or promised (not always the same thing).[25] As in the Gulf in 1990, so in Somalia in 1992: the UN was able to organise broad international support, and so legitimise the operation, but it was left to the Americans to impose peace on the warring

[25] The full list at the beginning of February 1993 consisted of the USA, Canada, France, Belgium, Italy, Australia, Egypt, Pakistan, Norway, Saudi Arabia, Mauritania, Nigeria, Kenya, Argentina, Germany, Sweden, Kuwait, the UAE, Morocco, Turkey, Zimbabwe, Tunisia, Botswana, Algeria, Malaysia, Eire, India, Uganda, Greece, Namibia, Indonesia, Jordan, Zambia, New Zealand and the Republic of Korea. The total deployment was 33,656, of which the United States provided 28,100.

factions and foster the new interventionist role for which the United Nations had opted.

Empowered by Resolution 794 to employ 'all necessary means to establish . . . a secure environment for humanitarian relief operations in Somalia', Operation Restore Hope provided force feeding for Somalia, and paved the way for the unique UN peacemaking military administration, UNOSOM II, which followed in May 1993. In line with the Pentagon's original plan, the Americans saw their primary objective as being to distribute food and humanitarian supplies securely to the worst affected areas of southern Somalia. They were, understandably, anxious to avoid casualties (especially in the run-up to Christmas) and thus proceeded cautiously and with maximum, even if often ill-conceived, publicity,[26] relying on their sheer numbers and technical superiority to overawe the Somali population.

The operation was directed by an experienced diplomat, Robert Oakley, who had served as ambassador in Mogadishu and knew some of the protagonists personally. He had also the delicate task of coordinating the work of his Unified Task Force (UNITAF) with UNOSOM, which was now led by the Iraqi diplomat, Ismat Kittani, who had replaced Mohammed Sahnoun as Boutros-Ghali's special representative. One of the main tensions arose from UN pressure for UNITAF to enlarge its role to include disarmament, and thus aid the process of negotiation and reconciliation among the main armed groups. The Americans for their part were apt to raise the spectre of Vietnam and stress the limited and short-term character of their intervention. Oakley apparently felt that, despite the formidable force at his disposal, the Somali protagonists were not seriously overawed and believed that they could successfully manipulate the Americans to their advantage.[27] Events were to prove him right.

Most observers concluded after a few weeks, with a minimum of incidents, that UNITAF had succeeded in opening up the supply routes and getting food through to most of the needy areas in southern Somalia.[28] This entailed establishing military garrisons in key regions to quell oppressive militia, impose peace and control conflict – not always com-

---

[26] For assessments, see I. M. Lewis, 'Restoring Hope in a Future of Peace', *Cooperazione*, Rome, March 1993; *Somalia – Operation Restore Hope: A Preliminary Assessment*, Africa Rights occasional report, May 1993.

[27] From a personal conversation between Oakley's deputy, John Hirsch, and I. M. Lewis; the Americans were, of course, aware of the irony of their enforcing disarmament on an African people.

[28] Cf. Robert G. Patman, 'The UN Operation in Somalia', in Ramesh Thakur and Carlyle Thayer (eds.), *UN Peacekeeping in the 1990s* (Boulder, Colo.: Westview Press, 1995), p. 94.

pletely successfully. It also meant trying to re-establish a Somali police force in Mogadishu, where relations between the two local warlords, Ali Mahdi and Aideed, remained tense despite the truce negotiated by Ambassador Oakley prior to the American intervention.

When they realised that it was inevitable, both sides had welcomed the powerful new force and attempted to extract as much advantage as possible from it for themselves. Heavy weapons and military trucks ('technicals') disappeared from the streets; some were hidden locally, others moved to the interior. While many of the citizens of Mogadishu and elsewhere unrealistically saw the Americans as saviours who would restore normal life and rebuild their country, others felt that the tyranny of the warlords was now sufficiently curtailed to allow them to voice independent views. Outside Mogadishu also, the US military presence enabled local elders, previously terrorised by the rival militia, to regain some of their traditional authority as community leaders.

The policy of re-empowering traditional community leaders, which had been consistently urged on UNOSOM by the Uppsala advisory group[29] had been initiated by Mohammed Sahnoun, but was pursued only in a token fashion by his successor. The UN leadership in Mogadishu was more inclined to concentrate on the high-profile warlords who had gained in legitimacy through their extensive dealings with Ambassador Oakley, despite his efforts to prevent it and despite the fact that their military strength was held in check.

Taking advantage of the precarious lull in the fighting, which had been produced by the huge American military presence, Boutros-Ghali pressed ahead with his own conception of the reconciliation process. Despite a hostile reception when he briefly visited Mogadishu, he succeeded in opening a peace conference of the faction leaders in Addis Ababa in early January 1993. Agreement in principle of a ceasefire was reached, although the terms remained to be settled. Aideed and his allies wanted an immediate ceasefire to consolidate their territorial gains, with reconciliation postponed to a later date. The other groups wanted the militia to return to their traditional clan areas and then proceed immediately to reconciliation. Eventually, formal ceasefire and disarmament agreements were signed, providing for the handing over of heavy weaponry to a 'ceasefire monitoring group' to be completed by March when a further reconciliation conference would be held.

Clearly, the expectation was that UNITAF would now be involved

[29] Based at the Horn of Africa Centre of the Life and Peace Institute of Uppsala, this small group consists of social scientists with specialist expertise on Somalia drawn from a number of countries. The group has consistently advised UNOSOM to follow a 'bottom-up' regionalist approach with as much decentralisation as possible.

in disarmament in one way or another, and despite the American unease at what they perceived as 'mission creep'. In fact, the uneasy calm which had initially followed their intervention had already begun to break down in the face of renewed outbreaks of fighting in Mogadishu and the southern port of Kismayu. The deteriorating security situation jolted the UNITAF troops into patrolling more aggressively, disarming townsmen who openly carried weapons, and raiding one of the most notorious arms markets in Mogadishu. One of Aideed's encampments was destroyed and a contingent of General Morgan's attacked to prevent it gaining control of Kismayu. Given the vast quantities of weapons in the country and their constant replenishment from Kenya and Ethiopia, such action hardly constituted disarmament, although it was vividly described by Ambassador Oakley as 'bird-plucking' disarmament – feather by feather. There were similar erratic shifts in dealing with the tricky question of the employment by NGOs of privately recruited armed guards; theoretically these freelance security agents were supposed to be unnecessary once UNITAF was established. In practice, arms permits were issued to various categories of guards, as well as to NGO personnel, but the rules kept changing.

Thus, although Somalia was far from fully sanitised, UNITAF and UNOSOM acting together had established an unprecedented level of UN intervention in a previously sovereign state. The terms 'peacemaking' and 'peacekeeping' no longer adequately covered the range of activities undertaken. Efforts were being made, especially by UNITAF, to involve the elders – i.e. local traditional community leaders – in aid distribution and preparations at the local level for reconstruction. Embryonic police forces were being recruited and in the run-up to the March Addis Ababa meeting of warlords some disarmament took place. Simultaneously, in the United States, preparations were begun for the establishment of UNOSOM II which was due to take over from UNITAF in May 1993.

On the Somali political front, the UN continued to maintain its pressure on the leaders of the movement. The third UN coordination meeting in Addis Ababa in March on humanitarian assistance received donor pledges of US $142m for relief and rehabilitation. The meeting was attended by a wide range of Somali peace groups who stressed the upsurge of violence in Somalia and the urgent need for improved security. This was highlighted by the brazen incursion of Morgan's forces into Kismayu, which occurred during the Addis Ababa reconciliation conference and under the noses of the UN peacekeepers.

The agreement signed on 27 March by the leading warlords and representatives of sundry clan movements (some of dubious status) evoked local custom in its preamble. 'The serenity and shade of a tree, which according to our Somali tradition is a place of reverence and rapprochement, has been replaced by the conference hall. Yet the promises made here are no less sacred or binding'. It is tempting to conclude from what subsequently occurred that the change of venue was in fact interpreted as having qualified the pledge. Nonetheless, the signatories committed their organisations to 'complete' disarmament and urged that UNITAF/ UNOSOM should apply 'strong and effective sanctions against those responsible for an violation of the ceasefire agreement of January 1993'.[30]

In a new departure, which was in line with the UN's understandable but misguided desire to cobble together a Somali government as soon as possible, the agreement also provided for the establishment over two years of a 'transitional system of governance'. This included a Transitional National Council (TNC) with representatives from the 18 regions where Regional and District Councils would be established – a concession to the 'bottom-up' strategy advocated by the Uppsala advisory group and others. The TNC was also to be 'a repository of Somali sovereignty', a particularly unfortunate reference, since the delegation from the self-proclaimed Somaliland Republic in the relatively untroubled north-west had left the Addis Ababa conference before the agreement was signed. It subsequently dissociated itself from these provisions. This insensitive approach to the achievements and aspirations of the people of the north-west was unfortunately characteristic of UN policy following Sahnoun's departure.

UNOSOM II took over formally from UNITAF/UNOSOM I on 4 May 1993, not as early as Colin Powell had originally hoped, but soon enough to satisfy the new administration whose primary concern was to limit the president's vulnerability in a foreign commitment which he had inherited from his predecessor. But, although they may have hoped to engineer, if not a solution to Somalia's political crisis, at least a situation of sufficient stability to allow them 'to tip toe away', American prestige was now invested in the United Nations operation whether they liked it or not. In these circumstances, both the transition to a United Nations command, and its organisation and leadership, were of considerable importance to the Americans. In the early summer of 1993 the official view was that, having broken new ground with Resolution 794, the United States could not afford to have the Somali operation fail.

For their part, the UN Secretariat was fully aware that support for

---

[30] *Somalia News Update*, Uppsala, vol. 2, no. 12 (30 March 1993), p. 2.

UNOSOM would be likely to wither on the vine if it was perceived that the United States were 'dumping' an insoluble problem onto the UN as a way of extricating itself. Boutros-Ghali accurately calculated that if the operation was headed by an American this would guarantee strong US support. It would also be necessary, if as planned a US force was to serve for the first time in their history under a foreign, albeit UN, command.

The arrangement that was reached gave the military command to Lieutenant-General Levik Bir, a Turk who had worked closely with the Americans in NATO, and replaced Ambassador Kittani, the Secretary-General's special representative, with Admiral Howe, who had served as security advisor to President Bush. His appointment thus represented continuity between the two administrations. Resolution 814 of 26 March 1993 provided for a multinational force of 20,000 peacekeeping troops, 8,000 logistical support staff and some 3,000 civilian personnel. In addition, the Americans undertook to provide a tactical 'quick reaction' force, as required. With the prominence of US logistical support and special forces, this inevitably gave UNOSOM II a strongly American orientation which, when UN forces became embroiled in actual fighting, made it difficult to decide whether the Pentagon or Boutros-Ghali was calling the shots.

### The price of intervention, 'new world order'-style

It was not long before the new UN dispensation received a fierce test of its resolve and competence. On 5 June 1993, without any substantial progress toward disarmament, and with new supplies of weapons, forces – presumed to be under Aideed's command – attacked a party of Pakistani blue berets, near Aideed's radio station, killing over twenty. Instead of holding an independent legal enquiry and seeking to marginalise Aideed politically, Admiral Howe's forces reacted with injudicious force causing very considerable Somali casualties – not necessarily all supporters of Aideed.[31] The Security Council denounced Aideed, accusing him and the other warlords of committing war crimes. Admiral Howe, behaving as though he were the sheriff of Mogadishu, proclaimed Aideed an outlaw, offering a reward of US $20,000 for his

[31] At the request of the UN Secretary-General, an independent judicial investigation into the 5 June incident (and further incidents on 12/13 June) was carried out by Professor Tom Farer, a legal specialist at the American University in Washington, who had been an advisor to the Somali police in the 1960s. The report submitted on 12 August convincingly implicates Aideed in masterminding a deliberate and carefully staged ambush which targeted the Pakistani blue berets.

capture. Aideed responded in the same idiom, and both sides were launched on collision course with the UN reacting increasingly aggressively with helicopter gunship strikes and remarkably clumsy and unsuccessful attempts by US special forces to seize Aideed and his henchmen.

Aideed had lured Howe and the unwieldy UN/US war machine into a bitter confrontation in which every raid on southern Mogadishu earned him more support. Indeed, with the aid of simplistic media reporting, he quickly gained an international reputation as an oppressed national hero bravely struggling against overwhelming 'imperialist' forces. He had also managed to distort UN operations into concentrating far too much of their efforts on attempting to deal with him.[32] The inevitable denouement occurred at the beginning of October when his forces succeeded in shooting down a number of helicopters, capturing an American airman and inflicting serious casualties on US personnel. US/UN forces could not win in the back streets of Mogadishu without inflicting and sustaining unacceptable levels of casualties. Thus Aideed succeeded in cocking a snook at the mighty United States. The American public, horrified by grisly television pictures from Mogadishu and haunted by memories of Vietnam, clamoured for withdrawal.

The joint US/UN plan for a smooth transition had gone well, but the aftermath confirmed the worst fears of the operation's critics. What had gone wrong? Inevitably, it was the Americans who bore the brunt of the criticisms. And no doubt the complexities of the dual command structure had much to do with it. Nonetheless, much of the responsibility lies with the UN Organisation itself, although it is difficult to know whether the rapid deterioration of the situation should be laid at the door of the Secretary-General and his representatives, who mounted the vendetta against General Aideed, or rather should be understood as an unintended outcome which flowed with tragic necessity from the Security Council's reaction to the events of 5 June.

Understandably, the Americans themselves were drawn to the first of these explanations, and administration spokesmen were openly critical of Howe's policies and actions. No doubt he could have interpreted his mandate with more caution and subtlety – in particular the UN seemed insensitive to the fact that their attempts to capture Aideed would inevitably be interpreted as an attack on his clan group with the deliberate intention of favouring their rivals. But Howe had acted under Resolution 837 which had been passed *unanimously* on 6 June. This resolution called on UNOSOM 'to arrest and detain for trial and punishment the

---

[32] See I. M. Lewis, 'Ambush in Somalia', *Guardian*, 7 October 1993.

Somalis responsible for the slaying of a ... Pakistani unit of the UN peacekeeping force'. The resolution also condemned the USC/SNA broadcasts inciting attacks against the UN, and recalled a statement by their president – Aideed – promising to take action against anyone found guilty of violent attacks on UN personnel. What lay behind this strong and explicit resolution was, of course, the need to shore up the authority of the UN in general and to reassure the Pakistan government in particular.[33]

That such a reassurance would be needed became abundantly clear on 7 October when public outcry forced President Clinton to announce that all US forces would leave Somalia by 31 March 1994 and to state publicly that they were all under American command.[34] Withdrawing with honour, the Americans evidently believed, would require short-run military reinforcements and a change in political direction. To meet the first requirement, President Clinton announced that he was sending an additional 1,700 army troops and 104 army vehicles plus an aircraft carrier and two amphibious groups of Marines, offshore; while to secure the second, he reappointed Ambassador Oakley to go out to Somalia once more, ostensibly to lend American support to new Ethiopian and Eritrean efforts to broker a political settlement, in reality to secure the release of the prisoners taken by Aideed's forces. Probably hurt by US media coverage depicting his forces as barbarians, and delighted with this new attention, Aideed welcomed Oakley's return and released the prisoners on terms which were not made public but evidently involved the holding of a further enquiry into the notorious incident of 5 June. Aideed was also brought back into the unfolding political discussions. How this might affect Resolution 837 of 6 June remained unclear. There was, in any event, serious doubt about whether UNOSOM would be able to continue in the absence of active involvement of any of the major industrial countries with the capacity to provide the logistical support

---

[33] Cf. Ken Menkhaus, 'Getting Out v. Getting Through: US and UN Policies in Somalia', *Middle East Policy*, vol. 3, no. 1 (1994), p. 157.

[34] The issue of the command of American forces within UNOSOM II had been a sensitive one from the start. In a report submitted to Congress on 13 October 1993 the command structure was described as follows: 'all US military personnel are under US command. In addition, all US combat forces are under US operational control. The logistic units that support the overall UN military presence are assigned to the UN commander for operational control through the UNOSOM deputy commander, Major-General Thomas Montgomery, US Army. That means that for purposes explicitly agreed in writing between the United States and the United Nations, the UN commander may provide them direction in their logistic mission of supporting UN units. These units do not have any combat role': Official text, United States Information Service, London, 15 October 1993.

on which the operation depended. By the end of the year the Belgians, French and Italians had all announced that they too would withdraw all their forces in early 1994.

The projected US withdrawal in March 1994 was not entirely out of gear with the existing UN timetable for organising District and Regional Councils with a view to establishing the Transitional National Council envisaged in the Addis Ababa agreements. Criticism of Howe's obsessive, but not impressively successful, pursuit of Aideed encouraged more attention being given to this process of setting up local Councils. In the absence of any informed, independent assessment, however, it was difficult to decide how well this was proceeding and whether there was a realistic prospect of establishing a genuinely representative National Council which was not dominated by the power-hungry warlords.

The announcement of the US and other withdrawals inevitably had a further destabilising effect in Somalia and led on 24 October to a brief clash in Mogadishu between Ali Mahdi's and Aideed's supporters. There was obvious anxiety that Aideed (who still seemed to possess plenty of weapons) would attempt to seize power when the Americans left, and Ali Mahdi publicly threatened to 'rearm' his own followers. To demonstrate the UN's continuing commitment to Somalia, Boutros-Ghali, against US advice, made a brief visit to Somalia on 22 October and opened a flurry of negotiations with OAU and Arab League leaders, with the Ethiopian president Meles Zenawi playing a prominent role. Although Aideed was now back in the unwieldy negotiations, they proceeded at a snail's pace, taxing the patience of all the major negotiators – especially the Americans, who naturally wanted to leave behind at least an impression of achievement.

By the end of March 1994, following hectic meetings in Addis Ababa, Cairo and Nairobi, involving the original Addis Ababa signatories and other Somali dignitaries arbitrarily assembled by the UN, an agreement was finally signed by Aideed and Ali Mahdi ostensibly on behalf of their allies as well as themselves. The 60 participants whose hotel bills were reported to run to US $150,000 per day were apparently informed that UNOSOM was not prepared to incur further expenses and the junkets would have to end on a positive note. The resulting agreement issued the usual ritual declarations forswearing violence and urging the implementation of general disarmament as a precondition for reconstruction. It also set a date three weeks later for the signatories to establish rules and procedures for voting and participation in a national reconciliation conference, which was scheduled for 15 May 1994 when an interim government was to be formed. These rather vague and certainly extremely optimistic developments were foreshadowed by Resolution

897 which revised UNOSOM's mandate from peace-enforcement to peacekeeping and envisaged a reduced military establishment of 22,000 at best and drawn exclusively from the Third World after the impending departure of the US, French, Belgian and Italian contingents. Admiral Howe and the head of UNOSOM's political section had already left Mogadishu, leaving the acting special envoy in charge. The latter had already been promoted to a senior position in the UN hierarchy in New York which he was due to take up at the end of May, on the assumption that his assiduous negotiations with the warlords would by then have led to the actual formation of a Somali government, or something that might be represented as one. The UN had by now reverted to its earlier tactic of dealing primarily with the military leaders and their henchmen, and had given up its never-convincing efforts to 'empower' local leaders, which it had neither the resources nor the local knowledge to do effectively.

No real progress was made toward disarmament or the division of power in an interim Somali administration. The leading protagonists were unwilling to make any substantial concessions and, with mounting uncertainty about the future after the US withdrawal, busily rearmed their militias.

All these negative trends continued to gather momentum throughout the remainder of 1994. Inter-clan violence and attacks on UN personnel increased as the reduced UN force withdrew its garrisons from the hinterland to concentrate in Mogadishu and prepare for the final UN withdrawal from Somalia by the end of March 1995. The new UN special representative and his colleagues redoubled their efforts to cajole the Somali 'faction-leaders' to form a government, any government would do, to enable the residual international forces to pull out in as orderly a fashion as possible, leaving some equipment behind and taking such heavy equipment as they could with them. Money for 'expenses' was lavished on these 'leaders', adding to the substantial benefits they had already derived from careless UN largesse and such memorable unofficial hand-outs as the 'theft' of almost US $4 million in dollar bills stored overnight in a UNOSOM filing cabinet.[35]

Following a litany of ever-less-credible reports from UNOSOM via the Secretary-General to the Security Council, whose members were losing patience at the deteriorating situation in Somalia and the faction-leaders' manifest inability to reach any workable agreement, the UN finally announced in September 1994 that the Somali operation would

[35] Patman, 'UN Operation in Somalia', p. 100.

be wound down as soon as possible.[36] One current of opinion in the mounting chaos of Mogadishu believed, apparently, that the Americans would return again to rescue Somalia. In fact, the final UN evacuation was carried out under the protection of US Marines and with the aid of a small multinational flotilla in which even Britain, reluctant to the last, played a minor role. Since so much also went wrong with the UN's operation in Somalia, it is worth recording that the secure and orderly withdrawal for which the Security Council had called in Resolution 953 was accomplished in time and without serious mishap.

### Assessment

While Ambassador Sahnoun, who initiated UNOSOM I, and Oakley, who led Operation Restore Hope, were both relatively well informed about Somali politics, the same cannot be said for their successors, nor does UNOSOM seem to have been well served by various ad hoc advisors. The UN headquarters were located in southern Mogadishu, dominated by Aideed's Habar Gaddir clansmen who, in the main, had invaded Mogadishu during and after the guerrilla operations which overthrew the Darod dictator, Mohammed Siyad Barre, in 1991. Without adequate consideration of the consequences, large numbers of Somali ancillary staff were recruited from this clan which helped to finance Aideed's operations while at the same time supplying him with vital intelligence. Very few adequately representative Somali advisors were recruited, and UN officials generally could hardly have been more inadequately briefed about Somali society and culture. The huge gap between traditional Somali methods of dealing with foreigners and American high-tech put most of the UN staff at a great disadvantage in their local dealings. This is perhaps most graphically illustrated by US helicopters dropping leaflets on a population with a primarily oral tradition whose sensitivity to radio broadcasting is famous in Africa.

While both Sahnoun and Oakley negotiated directly with the various Somali figures and had some awareness of the partisan interests involved, their successors relied on indirect contacts through various deputies and aids, a style of diplomacy calculated to sow suspicion in the minds of their interlocutors. The demanding Somali situation, in which each group vigorously sought to influence UN activity to its own advantage, required skilful, shrewd diplomacy of a high order, making

[36] *Report by the Secretary-General Concerning the Situation in Somalia*, S/1994/1968, 17 September 1994, paras. 17–21. In Resolution 953 of 31 October 1994, the Security Council called for withdrawal by 31 March 1995.

the job of UN special envoy exceedingly difficult and taxing. The distance between the fortified UN bureaucracy in Mogadishu and the local population was further magnified by the failure of the UN to employ a range of Somali professionals spanning the different clans, and this was greatly intensified as Admiral Howe became increasingly embattled in the feud with Aideed. In addition, with the cumbersome UN bureaucracy and the multinational military force, logistically linked to Washington rather than New York, with an ineffective command structure and national components like the Italians with their own agenda, the possibilities for misunderstanding and confusion were enormous. Put at its simplest, this vast, unwieldy UN organisation was ill adapted to the Somali environment and poorly equipped to encourage the grass-roots political initiatives that were developing so notably in the north.[37]

This was, perhaps, to some extent an unfortunate unintended effect of the overconcentration of resources in Mogadishu (despite Sahnoun's earlier plans for decentralisation) which, of course, stimulated conflict between rival Somali groups. Indeed, three weeks after the American departure, Aideed's forces seized the area adjoining Mogadishu airport, routing the previous inhabitants, and were clearly poised at some future opportunity to assume control of the airport itself. While Aideed, who had benefited so much from the shifts of US policy toward him, remained outside Somalia, posturing like a head of state in Nairobi, Addis Ababa and other African capitals, his forces steadily extended his conquests at home. Outside and to the south of Mogadishu, they had captured the port of Merca, heavily defeating the local militias, and menacing the more important and repeatedly contested port of Kismayu. UN forces continued to control Mogadishu airport itself and to provide aid convoy protection while prudently turning a blind eye to the engagements which were becoming more and more frequent between rival Somali factions. Thus, the political situation, despite the much-publicised formal peace agreements, remained extremely fluid and unstable and, with the new pattern of UN action or inaction, came to resemble Bosnia ever more closely. These were not circumstances which suggested that the UN-brokered negotiations could have any positive outcome. Indeed, any viable future government that could be realistically envisaged would almost certainly have to be minimalist with a much higher degree of regional decentralisation than the UN officials contemplated.

Here, as we have repeatedly seen, there is a recurrent problem in the UN's dealings in Somalia, namely their reliance on the warlords and

---

[37] See Farah and Lewis, *Roots of Reconciliation.*

other so-called Somali 'leaders'. These figures have been consistently endowed with a degree of power and authority which they would like to, but do not actually, have, as has been demonstrated time and again by their failure to deliver on their various promises. This approach simply fails to grasp the shifting and situationally focused character of political groupings and leadership in this profoundly uncentralised but not literally anarchic society. The Somali political economy was, moreover, grossly overheated by the protracted clan wars in which modern weapons had produced casualties on an unprecedented scale. This is not a setting conducive to the 'quick-fix' solutions purveyed by the UN and other international organisations.

The most that might be said for this inordinately expensive, poorly led and coordinated, and incredibly cumbersome UN operation is that with all its glaring inadequacies, it offered something for everyone.[38] In the short run, the inter-riverine agro-pastoralists who had earlier been driven to starvation by the ravages of Aideed's and Morgan's marauding forces, had been rescued and protected. Aideed's henchmen who had invaded and seized control of part of Mogadishu when Siyad Barre was overthrown, quickly developed a monopoly in supplying local services and housing at exorbitant cost to UNOSOM. The blue berets themselves earned for their governments almost US $1,000 per month per soldier, as well as generous allowances for work which was extremely dangerous. Supplying troops was thus a profitable business, especially for Third World countries short of hard currency. Foreign contractors providing international transport and other services also did very well out of UNOSOM. At the same time despite the exigencies of life in Somalia, UN careerism flourished and even quite junior officials, few if any adequately trained or briefed, made quite significant financial gains. In stark contrast to the money lavished on the construction of the UN headquarters compound, with its modern services, shops, bowling alleys and other US home comforts, no serious humanitarian development of benefit to the Somali public has been accomplished, despite an inordinate outpouring of rhetoric. Of US $1.6 billion allocated for UNOSOM's military operations in the period up to the end of 1993, it is estimated that only 4 per cent will work its way into the Somali economy, mostly into the hands of the warlords and other operators

[38] If humanitarian assistance and UN assessments are included with expenditures by the Department of Defense, the cost to the United States government alone of all Somali operations amounted to nearly US $2.3 billion between April 1992 and July 1994. See John G. Sommer, *Hope Restored? Humanitarian Aid in Somalia 1990–1994* (Washington, D. C.: Refugee Policy Group, Center for Policy Analysis and Research on Refugee Issues, November 1994).

whose financial activities, subsidised by UNOSOM, have distorted, perhaps irrevocably, the Somali economy.[39] It would require quite remarkable ignorance to consider all this a UN success.

[39] These figures are quoted from Rick Atkinson, 'For UN Force in Mogadishu, the Comforts of Home', *International Herald Tribune*, 25 March 1994, p. 1.

# Appendixes

*Appendix A*
# Cambodia

## CHRONOLOGY

| | |
|---|---|
| November 1953 | Cambodia wins limited independence from France |
| July 1954 | Independence confirmed by Geneva Conference on Indochina |
| 18 March 1970 | Prince Sihanouk deposed by Lon Nol, Sirik Matak and Chang Heng |
| 23 March 1970 | Prince Sihanouk announces the formation of the National United Front of Kampuchea, including Khmer Rouge, to oppose Lon Nol regime |
| 30 April 1970 | US and South Vietnamese troops invade Cambodia, attacking communist bases |
| 9 October 1970 | Khmer Republic is declared |
| 27 January 1973 | Paris Agreement to end war in Vietnam calls on all parties to end military activities in Cambodia |
| 17 April 1975 | Khmer Rouge orders evacuation of Phnom Penh |
| 9 September 1975 | Sihanouk becomes head of state of Democratic Kampuchea |
| 4 April 1976 | Prince Sihanouk resigns as head of state and is put under house arrest |
| November 1978 | Vietnam signs 25-year friendship treaty with USSR |
| 25 December 1978 | Vietnam invades Kampuchea |
| 1979–81 | Democratic Kampuchea occupies a seat at UN |
| June 1982 | Khmer Rouge, Son Sann and Prince Sihanouk form Coalition Government of Democratic Kampuchea which is seated in UN |
| 7 May 1987 | Prince Sihanouk steps down for a year as president of UN-recognised Coalition Government of Democratic Kampuchea in protest of Khmer Rouge attacks on his supporters |
| 26 May 1988 | Vietnam announces it will withdraw 50,000 troops from Cambodia by end of 1988 |
| 1 July 1988 | Chinese foreign ministry proposes a four-point peace plan, offering to act as guarantor of a Cambodian settlement |
| 25 July 1988 | Warring factions meet in Bogor, Indonesia for four-day informal meeting; Premier Hun of Vietnamese-backed Cambodian regime offers a peace plan |

| | |
|---|---|
| 28 July 1988 | Prince Sihanouk's representatives at Bogor talks introduce alternative peace plan; talks end without agreement on final communiqué |
| 6 January 1989 | Cambodian president Heng Samrin announces Vietnamese troop withdrawal by September 1989 if Cambodian peace settlement is reached by that time |
| 21 March 1989 | Talks are suspended |
| 5 April 1989 | Cambodian premier Hun Sen announces Vietnam will withdraw all 70,000 troops by 30 September |
| 2 May 1989 | Premier Hun Sen and Prince Sihanouk begin two-day meeting in Jakarta |
| 3 May 1989 | In Jakarta, Prince Sihanouk announces he is willing to return to Cambodia as head of state if Hun agrees to a multiparty system and a coalition government |
| 6 July 1989 | US secretary of state James Baker announces US backing of the Hun–Sihanouk negotiations, effectively shifting US position regarding Hun's government as illegitimate |
| 30 July 1989 | Cambodian peace conference begins in Paris with representatives of warring factions and 19 states attending |
| 27 August 1989 | Prince Sihanouk resigns as head of guerrilla faction, but remains president of resistance coalition |
| 30 August 1989 | Paris peace talks end, failing to reach any agreements |
| 21 September 1989 | Vietnam begins final withdrawal of troops |
| 24 November 1989 | Australian foreign minister, Gareth Evans, proposes UN administration of Cambodia to ensure Vietnamese withdrawal and a ceasefire, and to organise elections |
| 14 December 1989 | Prime Minister Hun Sen announces he will disband his government and allow UN supervision for the purpose of elections and in return asks that Cambodian UN seat be vacated |
| 15 January 1990 | UN permanent members meet in Paris, agreeing to enhanced UN role to end conflict |
| 24 January 1990 | Prince Sihanouk resigns as head of Cambodian resistance coalition |
| 27 February 1990 | Peace talks are held in Jakarta; Cambodian government refuses to disband or allow UN administration before elections |
| 12 March 1990 | UN permanent members meet in Paris, agreeing that UN should be responsible for elections and government of Cambodia through UN Transitional Authority in Cambodia (UNTAC) |
| 10 April 1990 | Prince Sihanouk proposes nine-point peace plan |
| 26 May 1990 | Four factions sign ceasefire to begin 4 June |
| 4 June 1990 | Tokyo peace talks end due to Khmer Rouge boycott |
| 5 June 1990 | Vietnamese-backed government and non-communist resistance sign ceasefire agreement to begin 31 July |

| | |
|---|---|
| August 1990 | UN permanent members dilute original provision for UN administration in light of Phnom Penh government objections |
| 27 August 1990 | UN Security Council agree on comprehensive peace plan |
| 29 August 1990 | Khmer Rouge accepts UN peace plan |
| 31 August 1990 | Cambodian government backs UN peace plans with reservations |
| 10 September 1990 | Meeting in Jakarta, all four factions endorse UN peace plan and agree to form Supreme National Council (SNC) |
| 20 September 1990 | Resolution 688 endorses the framework set out at Paris conference for comprehensive political settlement of conflict |
| 23 September 1990 | Prime Minister Hun Sen accepts Prince Sihanouk's power-sharing deal to establish SNC |
| 24 November 1990 | Meeting in Paris, UN Security Council agrees to final draft of peace settlement |
| 7 February 1991 | Cambodian government postpones scheduled 1991 elections in hope of encouraging peace negotiations |
| 9 April 1991 | United States offers to lift trade embargo on Vietnam in exchange for Vietnamese cooperation with UN-sponsored peace plan for Cambodia |
| 23 April 1991 | Prince Sihanouk's forces accept temporary ceasefire |
| 26 April 1991 | Khmer Rouge accepts UN-backed ceasefire |
| 2 June 1991 | Cambodian premier Hun Sen accepts Prince Sihanouk as chairman of the Cambodian coalition SNC |
| 3 June 1991 | Khmer Rouge objects to Prince Sihanouk as SNC chairman |
| 4 June 1991 | Three-day peace talks collapse |
| 7 June 1991 | Sihanouk joins SNC |
| 23 June 1991 | Factions agree to indefinite ceasefire beginning 24 June |
| 16–17 July 1991 | Cambodian peace talks begin in Beijing; Prince Sihanouk is unanimously elected president of SNC |
| 29 August 1991 | Five-day peace talks end with only post-war electoral system left to be decided |
| 16 October 1991 | Resolution 717 establishes a UN Advance Mission in Cambodia (UNAMIC) after signing agreements for political settlement |
| 23 October 1991 | Paris Agreement: peace treaty installing Prince Sihanouk as provisional leader of Cambodia and calling for transition to democracy with UN supervision |
| 31 October 1991 | Resolution 718 expresses support for 23 October peace treaty and authorises Secretary-General to designate special representative for Cambodia |
| 9 November 1991 | UNAMIC establishes headquarters in Phnom Penh |
| 10 November 1991 | Prince Sihanouk returns after 13 years in exile |
| 17 November 1991 | Khmer Rouge delegation returns |

| | |
|---|---|
| 17 December 1991 | Government closes universities in capital as demonstrations continue |
| 30 December 1991 | Cambodian factions hold talks in Phnom Penh and request immediate deployment of UN peacekeeping troops |
| 8 January 1992 | Resolution 728 expands UNAMIC's mandate to include training in mine clearance |
| 19–21 January 1992 | Government forces attack Khmer Rouge and are repelled in Kompong Thom province |
| 26 February 1992 | Khmer Rouge shoots down UN helicopter |
| 28 February 1992 | Resolution 745 authorises 22,000 peacekeeping force of military and civilian personnel to establish UNTAC |
| 11 March 1992 | UNTAC's first military contingent arrives |
| 15 March 1992 | Yasushi Akashi, Secretary-General's special representative, arrives in Phnom Penh |
| 29 March 1992 | Cambodian troops launch offensive against Khmer Rouge in north |
| 30 March 1992 | UN-sponsored programme to repatriate exiles begins |
| 31 March 1992 | Army and Khmer Rouge open talks in Phnom Penh |
| 1 April 1992 | SNC decides to sign two UN charters that form part of International Bill of Rights |
| 20 April 1992 | Khmer Rouge and other Cambodian factions sign UN convention on human rights; invites UN to inspect limited areas in Khmer Rouge zones |
| 9 May 1992 | UNTAC announces that Phase I of ceasefire will be followed by Phase II beginning 13 June to regroup the military forces of four factions |
| 10 June 1992 | Khmer Rouge refuses to participate in demobilisation of four factions outlined by Cambodian peace accord due by 13 June |
| 22 June 1992 | Ministerial Conference on the Rehabilitation and Reconstruction of Cambodia meets in Tokyo, pledging US $880m to assist reconstruction |
| 2 July 1992 | Khmer Rouge places conditions on its compliance with the Paris peace accords at SNC meeting |
| 21 July 1992 | Resolution 766 deplores continuing ceasefire violations and urges all parties to cooperate with UNTAC |
| 26 July 1992 | At Manila meeting, the EC, the United States, Japan, South Korea, Canada, Australia, New Zealand, Indonesia, Malaysia, the Philippines, Singapore, Thailand and Brunei agree to back UN sanctions against Khmer Rouge |
| 7 September 1992 | Khmer Rouge drops demand for UN verification of Vietnamese troop withdrawals |
| 17 September 1992 | Khmer Rouge ends three-month boycott of Mixed Military Working Group chaired by UNTAC military commander |

| | |
|---|---|
| 20 September 1992 | Japanese troops join peacekeeping forces, deployed for first time overseas since World War II |
| 13 October 1992 | Resolution 783 maintains that elections should continue as scheduled despite Khmer Rouge opposition |
| 21 October 1992 | Yasushi Akashi, head of UNTAC, announces temporary freeze in effort to disarm due to Khmer Rouge refusal to participate |
| 6–8 November 1992 | Representatives of four Cambodian factions and ten states meet in Beijing for talks aimed at saving Cambodian peace efforts, but fail to reach agreement |
| 30 November 1992 | Resolution 792 confirms elections for constituent assembly will not be held later than May 1993 |
| 8 December 1992 | Khmer Rouge boycotts SNC meeting |
| 27 December 1992 | Khmer Rouge kills 13 Vietnamese civilians |
| 28 December 1992 | Khmer Rouge refuses UN peace plan |
| 31 December 1992 | Khmer Rouge shells UN troops |
| 4 January 1993 | Prince Sihanouk announces cessation of cooperation with UN peacekeepers |
| 6 January 1993 | UNTAC announces it will form Special Prosecutors' Office and courts to try political crimes in Cambodia |
| 29 January 1993 | Government launches offensive against Khmer Rouge |
| 2 February 1993 | Government halts offensive against Khmer Rouge |
| 8 March 1993 | Resolution 810 confirms dates of Cambodian elections, 23–27 May 1993 |
| 11 March 1993 | Khmer Rouge kills 33 Vietnamese civilians near Siem Reap |
| 30 March 1993 | UN High Commissioner for Refugees, Sadako Ogata, closes last remaining Cambodian refugee camp |
| 2 April 1993 | Khmer Rouge kills three UN peacekeepers |
| 7–8 April 1993 | Secretary-General Boutros-Ghali visits Cambodia, announcing UN troop withdrawal on 22 August 1993 |
| 8 April 1993 | Japanese UN volunteer is killed |
| 13 April 1993 | Khmer Rouge officials withdraw from Phnom Penh |
| 19 April 1993 | Khmer Rouge kills UN peacekeeper |
| 20 April 1993 | UN removes military observers from Kompong Thom |
| 24 April 1993 | 20 states condemn killings of UN troops |
| 3 May 1993 | Khmer Rouge attacks Siem Reap |
| 4 May 1993 | A Japanese policeman serving with UN is killed |
| 16 May 1993 | Khmer Rouge shell UN-controlled Siem Reap airport |
| 20 May 1993 | Resolution 826 demands that all parties abide by Paris Agreement and cooperate with UNTAC |
| 23–27 May 1993 | Legislative elections held under UNTAC supervision; Funcinpec finishes ahead of ruling CPP |
| 2 June 1993 | Resolution 835 expresses intention to support 'duly elected constituent assembly' and urges parties to respect election results |
| 3 June 1993 | Prince Sihanouk proclaims himself president, prime minister and military commander of transitional |

|                     | government of Funcinpec and CPP |
|---------------------|--------------------------------|
| 4 June 1993         | Transitional government coalition breaks down |
| 9 June 1993         | UN declares Cambodian vote fair |
| 12 June 1993        | CPP leader Prince Sihanouk announces secession of seven eastern provinces; Funcinpec leader Prince Norodom Ranariddh says he will retake provinces |
| 14 June 1993        | Prince Sihanouk is chosen head of state by new constituent assembly |
| 15 June 1993        | Resolution 840 endorses election results, certifying them as 'free and fair'; State of Cambodia deputy prime minister Chakrapong flees to Vietnam |
| 16 June 1993        | Funcinpec and CPP agree to form interim government |
| 21 June 1993        | CPP accepts election results |
| 24 June 1993        | Khmer Rouge offers to act as advisors to interim government |
| 1 July 1993         | New constituent assembly approves interim government |
| 18 August 1993      | Three interim government factions launch attack on Khmer Rouge |
| 15 September 1993   | Constituent assembly votes to reinstate monarchy |
| 21 September 1993   | New constitution passed by constituent assembly |
| 24 September 1993   | Prince Sihanouk signs constitution and becomes king |
| 26 September 1993   | UN ends peacekeeping mission |
| 28 September 1993   | Constitutional assembly transforms itself into national assembly |
| 1 October 1993      | Samphan announces support for King Sihanouk |
| 4 October 1993      | King Sihanouk offers Khmer Rouge advisory role in government |
| 11 October 1993     | Fighting erupts between Khmer Rouge and government forces in north-west |
| 4 November 1993     | Resolution 880 extends deployment of military police and medical elements of UNTAC to 31 December 1993 |
| 27 November 1993    | King Sihanouk threatens to take away Khmer Rouge advisory role in government if they do not agree to ceasefire |
| 17 December 1993    | Prime Minister Prince Ranariddh holds talks with Khmer Rouge in Bangkok |
| 22 December 1993    | Government forces launch offence against Khmer Rouge |
| 29 December 1993    | King Sihanouk revokes offer of Khmer Rouge advisory role in government |
| 10–11 March 1994    | Second meeting of International Committee on Reconstruction of Cambodia is held in Tokyo |
| 19 March 1994       | Government forces capture Pailin, Khmer Rouge headquarters |
| 9 April 1994        | Khmer Rouge kills 13 ethnic Vietnamese in Kandal Province |
| 19 April 1994       | Khmer Rouge recaptures its headquarters in Pailin |

# SELECTED RESOLUTIONS OF THE UN SECURITY COUNCIL AND PROGRESS REPORTS OF THE SECRETARY-GENERAL ON THE UN TRANSITIONAL AUTHORITY IN CAMBODIA

SC Resolution 668, 20 September 1990; Security Council 'endorses the framework for a comprehensive political settlement of the Cambodia conflict'

SC Resolution 717, 16 October 1991; Security Council establishes UN Advance Mission in Cambodia (UNAMIC)

SC Resolution 718, 31 October 1991; Security Council expresses its 'full support for the agreements on a comprehensive political settlement of the Cambodia conflict, signed in Paris on 23 October 1991' and 'authorises the Secretary-General to designate a Special Representative to act on his behalf' (for text of agreement, see pp. 134–65 in this appendix)

S/23613, Report of the Secretary-General on Cambodia, 19 February 1992; contains the Secretary-General's proposed implementation plan, including an estimate of the cost of UNTAC

SC Resolution 745, 28 February 1992; Security Council approves the Report of the Secretary-General containing his plan for implementing the mandate envisaged in the Paris Agreement and establishes UNTAC for a period of 18 months

S/24286, Second Special Report of the Secretary-General on the United Nations Transitional Authority in Cambodia, 14 July 1992

S/24578, Second Progress Report of the Secretary-General on the United Nations Transitional Authority in Cambodia, 21 September 1992

SC Resolution 783, 13 October 1992; Security Council 'deplores' failure of PDK to abide by obligations under the Paris Agreement, especially as regards the application of Phase II of the ceasefire

S/25124, Third Progress Report of the Secretary-General on the United Nations Transitional Authority in Cambodia, 25 January 1993

SC Resolution 810, 8 March 1993; 'deplores' ceasefire violations by PDK and SOC and expresses 'full confidence in the ability of UNTAC to conduct an election that is free and fair'

S/25719, Fourth Progress Report of the Secretary-General on the United Nations Transitional Authority in Cambodia, 3 May 1993

SC Resolution 826, 20 May 1993; Security Council 'fully supports decision of the Secretary-General that elections be held as scheduled in accordance with decision by Supreme National Council endorsed by Security Council in its Resolution 810'

SC Resolution 835, 2 June 1993; 'endorses' declaration of the Special Representative of the Secretary-General that 'the conduct of the election had been free and fair'

SC Resolution 840, 15 June 1993; 'endorse[s] the results of the elections, which has been certified free and fair by the United Nations', and calls upon parties to 'stand by their obligation to respect the results of the election'

S/26090, Report of the Secretary-General Pursuant to Paragraph 7 of Resolution 84 (1993), 16 July; reports on developments since the election

S/1994/645, Final Report of the Secretary-General on the United Nations Military Liaison team in Cambodia, 31 May 1994

# AGREEMENT
## ON A COMPREHENSIVE POLITICAL SETTLEMENT OF THE CAMBODIA CONFLICT; AGREEMENT CONCERNING THE SOVEREIGNTY, INDEPENDENCE, TERRITORIAL INTEGRITY AND INVIOLABILITY, NEUTRALITY AND NATIONAL UNITY OF CAMBODIA; A DECLARATION ON THE REHABILITATION AND RECONSTRUCTION OF CAMBODIA AND THE FINAL ACT OF THE PARIS CONFERENCE ON CAMBODIA

## AGREEMENT ON A COMPREHENSIVE POLITICAL SETTLEMENT OF THE CAMBODIA CONFLICT

The States participating in the Paris Conference on Cambodia, namely Australia, Brunei Darussalam, Cambodia, Canada, the People's Republic of China, the French Republic, the Republic of India, the Republic of Indonesia, Japan, the Lao People's Democratic Republic, Malaysia, the Republic of the Philippines, the Republic of Singapore, the Kingdom of Thailand, the Union of Soviet Socialist Republics, the United Kingdom of Great Britain and Northern Ireland, the United States of America, the Socialist Republic of Vietnam and the Socialist Federal Republic of Yugoslavia,

In the presence of the Secretary-General of the United Nations,

In order to maintain, preserve and defend the sovereignty, independence, territorial integrity and inviolability, neutrality and national unity of Cambodia,

*Desiring* to restore and maintain peace in Cambodia, to promote national reconciliation and to ensure the exercise of the right to self-determination of the Cambodian people through free and fair elections,

*Convinced* that only a comprehensive political settlement to the Cambodia conflict will be just and durable and will contribute to regional and international peace and security,

*Welcoming* the Framework document of 28 August 1990, which was accepted by the Cambodian Parties in its entirety as the basis for settling the Cambodia conflict, and which was subsequently unanimously endorsed by Security Council resolution 668 (1990) of 20 September 1990 and General Assembly resolution 45/3 of 15 October 1990,

*Noting* the formation in Jakarta on 10 September 1990 of the Supreme National Council of Cambodia as the unique legitimate body and source of authority in Cambodia in which, throughout the transitional period, national sovereignty and unity are enshrined, and which represents Cambodia externally,

*Welcoming* the unanimous election, in Beijing on 17 July 1991, of H. R. H. Prince NORODOM SIHANOUK as the President of the Supreme National Council,

*Recognizing* that an enhanced United Nations role requires the establishment of a United Nations Transitional Authority in Cambodia (UNTAC) with civilian and military components, which will act with full respect for the national sovereignty of Cambodia externally,

*Noting* the statements made at the conclusion of the meetings held in Jakarta on 9–10 September 1990, in Paris on 21–23 December 1990, in Pattaya on 24–26 June 1991, in Beijing on 16–17 July 1991, in Pattaya on 26–29 August 1991, and also the meetings held in Jakarta on 4–6 June 1991 and in New York on 19 September 1991,

*Welcoming* United Nations Security Council resolution 717 (1991) of 16 October 1991 on Cambodia,

*Recognizing* that Cambodia's tragic recent history requires special measures to assure protection of human rights, and the non-return to the policies and practices of the past,

Have agreed as follows:

## PART I
### Arrangements During the Transitional Period
#### SECTION I
#### Transitional period
##### ARTICLE 1

For the purposes of this Agreement, the transitional period shall commence with the entry into force of this Agreement and terminate when the constituent assembly elected through free and fair elections, organized and certified by the United Nations, has approved the constitution and transformed itself into a legislative assembly, and thereafter a new goverment has been created.

#### SECTION II
#### United Nations Transitional Authority in Cambodia
##### ARTICLE 2

1. The Signatories invite the United Nations Security Council to establish a United Nations Transitional Authority in Cambodia (hereinafter referred to as "UNTAC") with civilian and military components under the direct responsibility of the Secretary-General of the United Nations. For this purpose the Secretary-General will designate a Special Representative to act on his behalf.

2. The Signatories further invite the United Nations Security Council to provide UNTAC with the mandate set forth in this Agreement and to keep its implementation under continuing review through periodic reports submitted by the Secretary-General.

SECTION III
Supreme National Council
ARTICLE 3

The Supreme National Council (hereinafter referred to as "the SNC") is the unique legitimate body and source of authority in which, throughout the transitional period, the sovereignty, independence and unity of Cambodia are enshrined.

ARTICLE 4

The members of the SNC shall be committed to the holding of free and fair elections organized and conducted by the United Nations as the basis for forming a new and legitimate Government.

ARTICLE 5

The SNC shall, throughout the transitional period, represent Cambodia externally and occupy the seat of Cambodia at the United Nations, in the United Nations specialized agencies, and in other international institutions and international conferences.

ARTICLE 6

The SNC hereby delegates to the United Nations all powers necessary to ensure the implementation of this Agreement, as described in annex 1.

In order to ensure a neutral political environment conducive to free and fair general elections, administrative agencies, bodies and offices which could directly influence the outcome of elections will be placed under direct United Nations supervision or control. In that context, special attention will be given to foreign affairs, national defence, finance, public security and information. To reflect the importance of these subjects, UNTAC needs to exercise such control as is necessary to ensure the strict neutrality of the bodies responsible for them. The United Nations, in consultation with the SNC, will identify which agencies, bodies and offices could continue to operate in order to ensure normal day-to-day life in the country.

ARTICLE 7

The relationship between the SNC, UNTAC and existing administrative structures is set forth in annex 1.

SECTION IV
Withdrawal of foreign forces and its verification
ARTICLE 8

Immediately upon entry into force of this Agreement, any foreign forces, advisers, and military personnel remaining in Cambodia, together with their weapons, ammunition, and equipment, shall be withdrawn from Cambodia and not be returned. Such withdrawal and non-return will be subject to UNTAC verification in accordance with annex 2.

## Section V
### Cease-fire and cessation of outside military assistance
### Article 9

The cease-fire shall take effect at the time this Agreement enters into force. All forces shall immediately disengage and refrain from all hostilities and from any deployment, movement or action which would extend the territory they control or which might lead to renewed fighting.

The Signatories hereby invite the Security Council of the United Nations to request the Secretary-General to provide good offices to assist in this process until such time as the military component of UNTAC is in position to supervise, monitor and verify it.

### Article 10

Upon entry into force of this Agreement, there shall be an immediate cessation of all outside military assistance to all Cambodian Parties.

### Article 11

The objectives of military arrangements during the transitional period shall be to stabilize the security situation and build confidence among the parties to the conflict, so as to reinforce the purposes of this Agreement and to prevent the risks of a return to warfare.

Detailed provisions regarding UNTAC's supervision, monitoring, and verification of the cease-fire and related measures, including verification of the withdrawal of foreign forces and the regrouping, cantonment and ultimate disposition of all Cambodian forces and their weapons during the transitional period are set forth in annex 1, section C, and annex 2.

## PART II
### Elections
### Article 12

The Cambodian people shall have the right to determine their own political future through the free and fair election of a constituent assembly, which will draft and approve a new Cambodian Constitution in accordance with Article 23 and transform itself into a legislative assembly, which will create the new Cambodian Government. This election will be held under United Nations auspices in a neutral political environment with full respect for the national sovereignty of Cambodia.

### Article 13

UNTAC shall be responsible for the organization and conduct of these elections based on the provisions of annex 1, section D, and annex 3.

### Article 14

All Signatories commit themselves to respect the results of these elections once certified as free and fair by the United Nations.

## PART III
### Human Rights
#### ARTICLE 15

1. All persons in Cambodia and all Cambodian refugees and displaced persons shall enjoy the rights and freedoms embodied in the Universal Declaration of Human Rights and other relevant international human rights instruments.

2. To this end,
(a) Cambodia undertakes:
   – to ensure respect for and observance of human rights and fundamental freedoms in Cambodia;
   – to support the right of all Cambodian citizens to undertake activities which would promote and protect human rights and fundamental freedoms;
   – to take effective measures to ensure that the policies and practices of the past shall never be allowed to return;
   – to adhere to relevant international human rights instruments;
(b) the other Signatories to this Agreement undertake to promote and encourage respect for and observance of human rights and fundamental freedoms in Cambodia as embodied in the relevant international instruments and the relevant resolutions of the United Nations General Assembly, in order, in particular, to prevent the recurrence of human rights abuses.

#### ARTICLE 16

UNTAC shall be responsible during the transitional period for fostering an environment in which respect for human rights shall be ensured, based on the provisions of annex 1, section E.

#### ARTICLE 17

After the end of the transitional period, the United Nations Commission on Human Rights should continue to monitor closely the human rights situation in Cambodia, including, if necessary, by the appointment of a Special Rapporteur who would report his findings annually to the Commission and to the General Assembly.

## PART IV
### International Guarantees
#### ARTICLE 18

Cambodia undertakes to maintain, preserve and defend, and the other Signatories undertake to recognize and respect, the sovereignty, independence, territorial integrity and inviolability, neutrality and national unity of Cambodia, as set forth in a separate Agreement.

## PART V
### Refugees and Displaced Persons
#### ARTICLE 19

Upon entry into force of this Agreement, every effort will be made to create in Cambodia political, economic and social conditions conducive to the voluntary return and harmonious integration of Cambodian refugees and displaced persons.

## ARTICLE 20

1. Cambodian refugees and displaced persons, located outside Cambodia, shall have the right to return to Cambodia and to live in safety, security and dignity, free from intimidation or coercion of any kind.

2. The Signatories request the Secretary-General of the United Nations to facilitate the repatriation in safety and dignity of Cambodian refugees and displaced persons, as an integral part of the comprehensive political settlement and under the overall authority of the Special Representative of the Secretary-General, in accordance with the guidelines and principles on the repatriation of refugees and displaced persons as set forth in annex 4.

## PART VI
### Release of Prisoners of War and Civilian Internees
### ARTICLE 21

The release of all prisoners of war and civilian internees shall be accomplished at the earliest possible date under the direction of the International Committee of the Red Cross (ICRC) in co-ordination with the Special Representative of the Secretary-General, with the assistance, as necessary, of other appropriate international humanitarian organizations and the Signatories.

### ARTICLE 22

The expression "civilian internees" refers to all persons who are not prisoners of war and who, having contributed in any way whatsoever to the armed or political struggle, have been arrested or detained by any of the parties by virtue of their contribution thereto.

## PART VII
### Principles for a New Constitution for Cambodia
### ARTICLE 23

Basic principles, including those regarding human rights and fundamental freedoms as well as regarding Cambodia's status of neutrality, which the new Cambodian Constitution will incorporate, are set forth in annex 5.

## PART VIII
### Rehabilitation and Reconstruction
### ARTICLE 24

The Signatories urge the international community to provide economic and financial support for the rehabilitation and reconstruction of Cambodia, as provided in a separate declaration.

## PART IX
### Final Provisions
### ARTICLE 25

The Signatories shall, in good faith and in a spirit of co-operation, resolve through peaceful means any disputes with respect to the implementation of this Agreement.

## ARTICLE 26
The Signatories request other States, international organizations and other bodies to co-operate and assist in the implementation of this Agreement and in the fulfilment by UNTAC of its mandate.

## ARTICLE 27
The Signatories shall provide their full co-operation to the United Nations to ensure the implementation of its mandate, including by the provision of privileges and immunities, and by facilitating freedom of movement and communication within and through their respective territories.

In carrying out its mandate, UNTAC shall exercise due respect for the sovereignty of all States neighbouring Cambodia.

## ARTICLE 28
1. The Signatories shall comply in good faith with all obligations undertaken in this Agreement and shall extend full co-operation to the United Nations, including the provision of the information which UNTAC requires in the fulfilment of its mandate.

2. The signature on behalf of Cambodia by the members of the SNC shall commit all Cambodian parties and armed forces to the provisions of this Agreement.

## ARTICLE 29
Without prejudice to the prerogatives of the Security Council of the United Nations, and upon the request of the Secretary-General, the two Co-Chairmen of the Paris Conference on Cambodia, in the event of a violation or threat of violation of this Agreement, will immediately undertake appropriate consultations, including with members of the Paris Conference on Cambodia, with a view to taking appropriate steps to ensure respect for these commitments.

## ARTICLE 30
This Agreement shall enter into force upon signature.

## ARTICLE 31
This Agreement shall remain open for accession by all States. The instruments of accession shall be deposited with the Governments of the French Republic and the Republic of Indonesia. For each State acceding to the Agreement it shall enter into force on the date of deposit of its instruments of accession. Acceding States shall be bound by the same obligations as the Signatories.

## ARTICLE 32
The originals of this Agreement, of which the Chinese, English, French, Khmer and Russian texts are equally authentic, shall be deposited with the Governments of the French Republic and the Republic of Indonesia, which shall transmit certified true copies to the Governments of the other States partic-

ipating in the Paris Conference on Cambodia, as well as the Secretary-General of the United Nations.

In witness whereof the undersigned Plenipotentiaries, being duly authorized thereto, have signed this Agreement.

Done at Paris this twenty-third day of October, one thousand nine hundred and ninety-one.

## ANNEX 1
### UNTAC mandate

Section A *General procedures*

1. In accordance with Article 6 of the Agreement, UNTAC will exercise the powers necessary to ensure the implementation of this Agreement, including those relating to the organization and conduct of free and fair elections and the relevant aspects of the administration of Cambodia.

2. The following mechanism will be used to resolve all issues relating to the implementation of this Agreement which may arise between the Secretary-General's Special Representative and the Supreme National Council (SNC):

(a) The SNC offers advice to UNTAC, which will comply with this advice provided there is a consensus among the members of the SNC and provided this advice is consistent with the objectives of the present Agreement;

(b) If there is no consensus among the members of the SNC despite every endeavour of its President, H. R. H. Samdech NORODOM SIHANOUK, the President will be entitled to make the decision on what advice to offer to UNTAC, taking fully into account the views expressed in the SNC. UNTAC will comply with the advice provided it is consistent with the objectives of the present Agreement;

(c) If H. R. H. Samdech NORODOM SIHANOUK, President of the SNC, the legitimate representative of Cambodian sovereignty, is not, for whatever reason, in a position to make such a decision, his power of decision will transfer to the Secretary-General's Special Representative. The Special Representative will make the final decision, taking fully into account the views expressed in the SNC;

(d) Any power to act regarding the implementation of this Agreement conferred upon the SNC by the Agreement will be exercised by consensus or, failing such consensus, by its President in accordance with the procedure set out above. In the event that H. R. H. Samdech NORODOM SIHANOUK, President of the SNC, the legitimate representative of Cambodian sovereignty, is not, for whatever reason, in a position to act, his power to act will transfer to the Secretary-General's Special Representative who may take the necessary action;

(e) In all cases, the Secretary-General's Special Representative will determine whether advice or action of the SNC is consistent with the present Agreement.

3. The Secretary-General's Special Representative or his delegate will attend the meetings of the SNC and of any subsidiary body which might be established by it and give its members all necessary information on the decisions taken by UNTAC.

### Section B *Civil administration*

1. In accordance with Article 6 of the Agreement, all administrative agencies, bodies and offices acting in the field of foreign affairs, national defence, finance, public security and information will be placed under the direct control of UNTAC, which will exercise it as necessary to ensure strict neutrality. In this respect, the Secretary-General's Special Representative will determine what is necessary and may issue directives to the above-mentioned administrative agencies, bodies and offices. Such directives may be issued to and will bind all Cambodian Parties.

2. In accordance with Article 6 of the Agreement, the Secretary-General's Special Representative, in consultation with the SNC, will determine which other administrative agencies, bodies and offices could directly influence the outcome of elections. These administrative agencies, bodies and offices will be placed under direct supervision or control of UNTAC and will comply with any guidance provided by it.

3. In accordance with Article 6 of the Agreement, the Secretary-General's Special Representative, in consultation with the SNC, will identify which administrative agencies, bodies and offices could continue to operate in order to ensure normal day-to-day life in Cambodia, if necessary, under such supervision by UNTAC as it considers necessary.

4. In accordance with Article 6 of the Agreement, the authority of the Secretary-General's Special Representative will include the power to:

(a) Install in administrative agencies, bodies and offices of all the Cambodian Parties, United Nations personnel who will have unrestricted access to all administrative operations and information;

(b) Require the reassignment or removal of any personnel of such administrative agencies, bodies and offices.

5. (a) On the basis of the information provided in Article 1, paragraph 3, of annex 2, the Special Representative of the Secretary-General will determine, after consultation with the Cambodian Parties, those civil police necessary to perform law enforcement in Cambodia. All Cambodian Parties hereby undertake to comply with the determination made by the Special Representative in this regard.

(b) All civil police will operate under UNTAC supervision or control, in order to ensure that law and order are maintained effectively and impartially, and that human rights and fundamental freedoms are fully protected. In consultation with the SNC, UNTAC will supervise other law enforcement and judicial processes throughout Cambodia to the extent necessary to ensure the attainment of these objects.

6. If the Secretary-General's Special Representative deems it necessary, UNTAC, in consultation with the SNC, will undertake investigations of complaints and allegations regarding actions by the existing administrative structures in Cambodia that are inconsistent with or work against the objectives of this comprehensive political settlement. UNTAC will also be empowered to undertake such investigation on its own initiative. UNTAC will take, when necessary, appropriate corrective steps.

Section C *Military functions*
1. UNTAC will supervise, monitor and verify the withdrawal of foreign forces, the cease-fire and related measures in accordance with annex 2, including:

(a) Verification of the withdrawal from Cambodia of all categories of foreign forces, advisers and military personnel and their weapons, ammunition and equipment, and their non-return to Cambodia;

(b) Liaison with neighbouring Governments over any developments in or near their territory that could endanger the implementation of this Agreement;

(c) Monitoring the cessation of outside military assistance to all Cambodian Parties;

(d) Locating and confiscating caches of weapons and military supplies throughout the country;

(e) Assisting with clearing mines and undertaking training programmes in mine clearance and a mine awareness programme among the Cambodian people.

2. UNTAC will supervise the regrouping and relocating of all forces to specifically designated cantonment areas on the basis of an operational time-table to be agreed upon, in accordance with annex 2.

3. As the forces enter the cantonments, UNTAC will initiate the process of arms control and reduction specified in annex 2.

4. UNTAC will take necessary steps regarding the phased process of demobilization of the military forces of the Parties, in accordance with annex 2.

5. UNTAC will assist, as necessary, the International Committee of the Red Cross in the release of all prisoners of war and civilian internees.

Section D  *Elections*

1. UNTAC will organize and conduct the election referred to in Part II of this Agreement in accordance with this section and annex 3.

2. UNTAC may consult with the SNC regarding the organization and conduct of the electoral process.

3. In the exercise of its responsibilities in relation to the electoral process, the specific authority of UNTAC will include the following:

(a) The establishment, in consultation with the SNC, of a system of laws, procedures and administrative measures necessary for the holding of a free and fair election in Cambodia, including the adoption of an electoral law and of a code of conduct regulating participation in the election in a manner consistent with respect for human rights and prohibiting coercion or financial inducement in order to influence voter preference;

(b) The suspension or abrogation, in consultation with the SNC, of provisions of existing laws which could defeat the objects and purposes of this Agreement;

(c) The design and implementation of a voter education programme, covering all aspects of the election, to support the election process;

(d) The design and implementation of a system of voter registration, as a first phase of the electoral process, to ensure that eligible voters have the opportunity to register, and the subsequent preparation of verified voter registration lists;

(e) The design and implementation of a system of registration of political parties and lists of candidates;

(f) Ensuring fair access to the media, including press, television and radio, for all political parties contesting in the election;

(g) The adoption and implementation of measures to monitor and facilitate the participation of Cambodians in the elections, the political campaign, and the balloting procedures;

(h) The design and implementation of a system of balloting and polling, to ensure that registered voters have the opportunity to vote;

(i) The establishment, in consultation with the SNC, of co-ordinated arrangements to facilitate the presence of foreign observers wishing to observe the campaign and voting;

(j) Overall direction of polling and the vote count;

(k) The identification and investigation of complaints of electoral irregularities, and the taking of appropriate corrective action;

(l)  Determining whether or not the election was free and fair and, if so, certification of the list of persons duly elected.

4. In carrying out its responsibilities under the present section, UNTAC will establish a system of safeguards to assist it in ensuring the absence of fraud during the electoral process, including arrangements for Cambodian representatives to observe the registration and polling procedures and the provision of an UNTAC mechanism for hearing and deciding complaints.

5. The time-table for the various phases of the electoral process will be determined by UNTAC, in consultation with the SNC as provided in paragraph 2 of this section. The duration of the electoral process will not exceed nine months from the commencement of voter registration.

6. In organizing and conducting the electoral process, UNTAC will make every effort to ensure that the system and procedures adopted are absolutely impartial, while the operational arrangements are as administratively simple and efficient as possible.

Section E *Human rights*
   In accordance with article 16, UNTAC will make provisions for:

(a)  The development and implementation of a programme of human rights education to promote respect for and understanding of human rights;

(b)  General human rights oversight during the transitional period;

(c)  The investigation of human rights complaints, and, where appropriate, corrective action.

## ANNEX 2
### Withdrawal, cease-fire and related measures
#### ARTICLE I
#### Cease-fire

1. All Cambodian Parties (hereinafter referred to as "the Parties") agree to observe a comprehensive cease-fire on land and water and in the air. This cease-fire will be implemented in two phases. During the first phase, the cease-fire will be observed with the assistance of the Secretary-General of the United Nations through his good offices. During the second phase, which should commence as soon as possible, the cease-fire will be supervised, monitored and verified by UNTAC. The Commander of the military component of UNTAC, in consultation with the Parties, shall determine the exact time and date at which the second phase will commence. This date will be set at least four weeks in advance of its coming into effect.

2. The Parties undertake that, upon the signing of this Agreement, they will observe a cease-fire and will order their armed forces immediately to discharge and refrain from all hostilities and any deployment, movement or action that

would extend the territory they control or that might lead to a resumption of fighting, pending the commencement of the second phase. "Forces" are agreed to include all regular, provincial, district, paramilitary, and other auxiliary forces. During the first phase, the Secretary-General of the United Nations will provide his good offices to the Parties to assist them in its observance. The Parties undertake to co-operate with the Secretary-General or his representatives in the exercise of his good offices in this regard.

3. The Parties agree that, immediately upon the signing of this Agreement, the following information will be provided to the United Nations:
(a)  Total strength of their forces, organization, precise number and location of deployments inside and outside Cambodia. The deployment will be depicted on a map marked with locations of all troop positions, occupied or unoccupied, including staging camps, supply bases and supply routes;
(b)  Comprehensive lists of arms, ammunition and equipment held by their forces, and the exact locations at which those arms, ammunition and equipment are deployed;
(c)  Detailed record of their mine-fields, including types and characteristics of mines laid and information of booby traps used by them together with any information available to them about mine-fields laid or booby traps used by the other Parties;
(d)  Total strength of their police forces, organization, precise numbers and locations of deployments, as well as comprehensive lists of their arms, ammunition and equipment, and the exact locations at which those arms, ammunition and equipment are deployed.

4. Immediately upon his arrival in Cambodia, and not later than four weeks before the beginning of the second phase, the Commander of the military component of UNTAC will, in consultation with the Parties, finalize UNTAC's plan for the regroupment and cantonment of the forces of the Parties and for the storage of their arms, ammunition and equipment, in accordance with Article III of this annex. This plan will include the designation of regroupment and cantonment areas, as well as an agreed time-table. The cantonment areas will be established at battalion size or larger.

5. The Parties agree to take steps to inform their forces at least two weeks before the beginning of the second phase, using all possible means of communication, about the agreed date and time of the beginning of the second phase, about the agreed plan for the regroupment and cantonment of their forces and for the storage of their arms, ammunition and equipment and, in particular, about the exact locations of the regroupment areas to which their forces are to report. Such information will continue to be disseminated for a period of four weeks after the beginning of the second phase.

6. The Parties shall scrupulously observe the cease-fire and will not resume any hostilities by land, water or air. The commanders of their armed forces will ensure that all troops under their command remain on their respective positions, pending their movement to the designated regroupment areas, and refrain from

all hostilities and from any deployment or movement or action which would extend the territory they control or which might lead to a resumption of fighting.

ARTICLE II

Liaison system and Mixed Military Working Group

A Mixed Military Working group (MMWG) will be established with a view to resolving any problems that may arise in the observance of the cease-fire. It will be chaired by the most senior United Nations military officer in Cambodia or his representative. Each Party agrees to designate an officer of the rank of brigadier or equivalent to serve on the MMWG. Its composition, method of operation and meeting places will be determined by the most senior United Nations military officer, in consultation with the Parties. Similar liaison arrangements will be made at lower military command levels to resolve practical problems on the ground.

ARTICLE III

Regroupment and cantonment of the forces of the Parties and storage of their arms, ammunition and equipment

1. In accordance with the operational time-table referred to in paragraph 4 of Article I of the present annex, all forces of the Parties that are not already in designated cantonment areas will report to designated regroupment areas, which will be established and operated by the military component of UNTAC. These regroupment areas will be established and operational not later than one week prior to the date of the beginning of the second phase. The Parties agree to arrange for all their forces, with all their arms, ammunition and equipment, to report to regroupment areas within two weeks after the beginning of the second phase. All personnel who have reported to the regroupment areas will thereafter be escorted by personnel of the military component of UNTAC, with their arms, ammunition and equipment, to designated cantonment areas. All Parties agree to ensure that personnel reporting to the regroupment areas will be able to do so in full safety and without any hindrance.

2. On the basis of the information provided in accordance with paragraph 3 of Article I of the present annex, UNTAC will confirm that the regroupment and cantonment processes have been completed in accordance with the plan referred to in paragraph 4 of Article I of this annex. UNTAC will endeavour to complete these processes within four weeks from the date of the beginning of the second phase. On the completion of regroupment of all forces and of their movement to cantonment areas, respectively, the Commander of the military component of UNTAC will so inform each of the four Parties.

3. The Parties agree that, as their forces enter the designated cantonment areas, their personnel will be instructed by their commanders to immediately hand over all their arms, ammunition and equipment to UNTAC for storage in the custody of UNTAC.

4. UNTAC will check the arms, ammunition and equipment handed over to it against the lists referred to in paragraph 3 (b) of article I of this annex, in

order to verify that all the arms, ammunition and equipment in the possession of the Parties have been placed under its custody.

## ARTICLE IV
### Resupply of forces during cantonment

The military component of UNTAC will supervise the resupply of all forces of the Parties during the regroupment and cantonment processes. Such resupply will be confined to items of a non-lethal nature such as food, water, clothing and medical supplies as well as provision of medical care.

## ARTICLE V
### Ultimate disposition of the forces of the Parties and of their arms, ammunition and equipment

1. In order to reinforce the objectives of a comprehensive political settlement, minimize the risks of a return to warfare, stabilize the security situation and build confidence among the Parties to the conflict, all Parties agree to undertake a phased and balanced process of demobilization of at least 70 per cent of their military forces. This process of shall be undertaken in accordance with a detailed plan to be drawn up by UNTAC on the basis of the information provided under Article 1 of this annex and in consultation with the Parties. It should be completed prior to the end of the process of registration for the elections and on a date to be determined by the Special Representative of the Secretary-General.

2. The Cambodian Parties hereby commit themselves to demobilize all their remaining forces before or shortly after the elections and, to the extent that full demobilization is unattainable, to respect and abide by whatever decision the newly elected government that emerges in accordance with Article 12 of this Agreement takes with regard to the incorporation of parts or all of those forces into a new national army. Upon completion of the demobilization referred to in paragraph 1, the Cambodian Parties and the Special Representative of the Secretary-General shall undertake a review regarding the final disposition of the forces remaining in the cantonments, with a view to determining which of the following shall apply.

(a) If the Parties agree to proceed with the demobilization of all or some of the forces remaining in the cantonments, preferably prior to or otherwise shortly after the elections, the Special Representative shall prepare a time-table for so doing, in consultation with them.

(b) Should total demobilization of all of the residual forces before or shortly after the elections not be possible, the Parties hereby undertake to make available all of their forces remaining in cantonments to the newly elected government that emerges in accordance with Article 12 of this Agreement, for consideration for incorporation into a new national army. They further agree that any such forces which are not incorporated into the new national army will be demobilized forthwith according to a plan to be prepared by the Special Representative. With regard to the ultimate disposition of the remaining forces and all the arms, ammunition and equipment, UNTAC, as it withdraws from Cambodia, shall retain such authority as is necessary to ensure an orderly transfer to the newly elected government of those responsibilities it has exercised during the transitional period.

3. UNTAC will assist, as required, with the reintegration into civilian life of the forces demobilized prior to the elections.

4. (a) UNTAC will control and guard all the arms, ammunition and equipment of the Parties throughout the transitional period;

(b) As the cantoned forces are demobilized in accordance with pargraph 1 above, there will be a parallel reduction by UNTAC of the arms, ammunition and equipment stored on site in the cantonment areas. For the forces remaining in the cantonment areas, access to their arms, ammunition and equipment shall only be on the basis of the explicit authorization of the Special Representative of the Secretary-General;

(c) If there is a further demobilization of the military forces in accordance with paragraph 2 (a) above, there will be a commensurate reduction by UNTAC of the arms, ammunition and equipment stored on site in the cantonment areas;

(d) The ultimate disposition of all arms, ammunition and equipment will be determined by the government that emerges through the free and fair elections in accordance with Article 12 of this Agreement.

ARTICLE VI
Verification of withdrawal from Cambodia and non-return of all categories of foreign forces

1. UNTAC shall be provided, no later than two weeks before the commencement of the second phase of the cease-fire, with detailed information in writing regarding the withdrawal of foreign forces. This information shall include the following elements:

(a) Total strength of these forces and their organization and deployment;

(b) Comprehensive lists of arms, ammunition and equipment held by these forces, and their exact locations;

(c) Withdrawal plan (already implemented or to be implemented), including withdrawal routes, border crossing points and time of departure from Cambodia.

2. On the basis of the information provided in accordance with paragraph 1 above, UNTAC will undertake an investigation in the manner it deems appropriate. The Party providing the information will be required to make personnel available to accompany UNTAC investigators.

3. Upon confirmation of the presence of any foreign forces, UNTAC will immediately deploy military personnel with the foreign forces and accompany them until they have withdrawn from Cambodian territory. UNTAC will also establish checkpoints on withdrawal routes, border crossing points and airfields to verify the withdrawal and ensure the non-return of all categories of foreign forces.

4. The Mixed Military Working Group (MMWG) provided for in Article II of this annex will assist UNTAC in fulfilling the above-mentioned tasks.

ARTICLE VII
Cessation of outside military assistance to all Cambodian Parties
1. All Parties undertake, from the time of the signing of this Agreement, not to obtain or seek any outside military assistance, including weapons, ammunition and military equipment from outside sources.

2. The Signatories whose territory is adjacent to Cambodia, namely, the Governments of the Lao People's Democratic Republic, the Kingdom of Thailand and the Socialist Republic of Vietnam, undertake to:

(a) Prevent the territories of their respective States, including land territory, territorial sea and air space, from being used for the purpose of providing any form of military assistance to any of the Cambodian Parties. Resupply of such items as food, water, clothing and medical supplies through their territories will be allowed, but shall, without prejudice to the provisions of sub-paragraph (c) below, be subject to UNTAC supervision upon arrival in Cambodia;

(b) Provide written confirmation to the Commander of the military component of UNTAC, not later than four weeks after the second phase of the cease-fire begins, that no forces, arms, ammunition or military equipment of any of the Cambodian Parties are present on their territories;

(c) Receive an UNTAC liaison officer in each of their capitals and designate an officer of the rank of colonel or equivalent, not later than four weeks after the beginning of the second phase of the cease-fire, in order to assist UNTAC in investigating, with due respect for their sovereignty, any complaints that activities are taking place on their territories that are contrary to the provisions of the comprehensive political settlement.

3. To enable UNTAC to monitor the cessation of outside assistance to all Cambodian Parties, the Parties agree that, upon signature of this Agreement, they will provide to UNTAC any information available to them about the routes and means by which military assistance, including weapons, ammunition and military equipment, have been supplied to any of the Parties. Immediately after the second phase of the cease-fire begins, UNTAC will take the following practical measures:

(a) Establish check-points along the routes and at selected locations along the Cambodian side of the border and at airfields inside Cambodia;

(b) Patrol the coastal and inland waterways of Cambodia;

(c) Maintain mobile teams at strategic locations within Cambodia to patrol and investigate allegations of supply of arms to any of the Parties.

ARTICLE VIII

Caches of weapons and military supplies

1. In order to stabilize the security situation, build confidence and reduce arms and military supplies throughout Cambodia, each Party agrees to provide to the Commander of the military component of UNTAC, before a date to be determined by him, all information at its disposal, including marked maps, about known or suspected caches of weapons and military supplies throughout Cambodia.

2. On the basis of information received, the military component of UNTAC shall, after the date referred to in paragraph 1, deploy verification teams to investigate each report and destroy each cache found.

ARTICLE IX

Unexploded ordnance devices

1. Soon after arrival in Cambodia, the military component of UNTAC shall ensure, as a first step, that all known minefields are clearly marked.

2. The Parties agree that, after completion of the regroupment and cantonment processes in accordance with Article III of the present annex, they will make available mine-clearing teams which, under the supervision and control of UNTAC military personnel, will leave the cantonment areas in order to assist in removing, disarming or deactivating remaining unexploded ordnance devices. Those mines or objects which cannot be removed, disarmed or deactivated will be clearly marked in accordance with a system to be devised by the military component of UNTAC.

3. UNTAC shall:

(a) Conduct a mass public education programme in the recognition and avoidance of explosive devices;

(b) Train Cambodian volunteers to dispose of unexploded ordnance devices;

(c) Provide emergency first-aid training to Cambodian volunteers.

ARTICLE X

Investigation of violations

1. After the beginning of the second phase, upon receipt of any information or complaint from one of the Parties relating to a possible case of non-compliance

with any of the provisions of the present annex or related provisions, UNTAC will undertake an investigation in the manner which it deems appropriate. Where the investigation takes place in response to a complaint by one of the Parties, that Party will be required to make personnel available to accompany the UNTAC investigators. The results of such investigation will be conveyed by UNTAC to the complaining Party and the Party complained against, and if necessary to the SNC.

2. UNTAC will also carry out investigations on its own initiative in other cases when it has reason to believe or suspect that a violation of this annex or related provisions may be taking place.

## ARTICLE XI
### Release of prisoners of war

The military component of UNTAC will provide assistance as required to the International Committee of the Red Cross in the latter's discharge of its functions relating to the release of prisoners of war.

## ARTICLE XII
### Repatriation and resettlement of displaced Cambodians

The military component of UNTAC will provide assistance as necessary in the repatriation of Cambodian refugees and displaced persons carried out in accordance with articles 19 and 20 of this Agreement, in particular in the clearing of mines from repatriation routes, reception centres and resettlement areas, as well as in the protection of the reception centres.

## ANNEX 3
### Elections

1. The constituent assembly referred to in Article 12 of the Agreement shall consist of 120 members. Within three months from the date of the election, it shall complete its tasks of drafting and adopting a new Cambodian Constitution and transform itself into a legislative assembly which will form a new Cambodian Government.

2. The election referred to in Article 12 of the Agreement will be held throughout Cambodia on a provincial basis in accordance with a system of proportional representation on the basis of lists of candidates put forward by political parties.

3. All Cambodians, including those who at the time of signature of this Agreement are Cambodian refugees and displaced persons, will have the same rights, freedoms and opportunities to take part in the electoral process.

4. Every person who has reached the age of eighteen at the time of application to register, or who turns eighteen during the registration period, and who either was born in Cambodia or is the child of a person born in Cambodia, will be eligible to vote in the election.

5. Political parties may be formed by any group of five thousand registered voters. Party platforms shall be consistent with the principles and objectives of the Agreement on a comprehensive political settlement.

6. Party affiliation will be required in order to stand for election to the constituent assembly. Political parties will present lists of candidates standing for election on their behalf, who will be registered voters.

7. Political parties and candidates will be registered in order to stand for election. UNTAC will confirm that political parties and candidates meet the established criteria in order to qualify for participation in the election. Adherence to a Code of Conduct established by UNTAC in consultation with the SNC will be a condition for such participation.

8. Voting will be by secret ballot, with provision made to assist those who are disabled or who cannot read or write.

9. The freedoms of speech, assembly and movement will be fully respected. All registered political parties will enjoy fair access to the media, including the press, television and radio.

## ANNEX 4
### Repatriation of Cambodian refugees and displaced persons
#### PART I
#### Introduction

1. As part of the comprehensive political settlement, every assistance will need to be given to Cambodian refugees and displaced persons as well as to countries of temporary refuge and the country of origin in order to facilitate the voluntary return of all Cambodian refugees and displaced persons in a peaceful and orderly manner. It must also be ensured that there would be no residual problems for the countries of temporary refuge. The country of origin with responsibility towards its own people will accept their return as conditions become conducive.

#### PART II
#### Conditions conducive to the return of refugees and displaced persons

2. The task of rebuilding the Cambodian nation will require the harnessing of all its human and natural resources. To this end, the return to the place of their choice of Cambodians from their temporary refuge and elsewhere outside their country of origin will make a major contribution.

3. Every effort should be made to ensure that the conditions which have led to a large number of Cambodian refugees and displaced persons seeking refuge in other countries should not recur. Nevertheless, some Cambodian refugees and displaced persons will wish and be able to return spontaneously to their homeland.

4. There must be full respect for the human rights and fundamental freedoms of all Cambodians, including those of the repatriated refugees and displaced

persons, in recognition of their entitlement to live in peace and security, free from intimidation and coercion of any kind. These rights would include, inter alia, freedom of movement within Cambodia, the choice of domicile and employment, and the right to property.

5. In accordance with the comprehensive political settlement, every effort should be made to create concurrently in Cambodia political, economic and social conditions conducive to the return and harmonious integration of the Cambodian refugees and displaced persons.

6. With a view to ensuring that refugees and displaced persons participate in the elections, mass repatriation should commence and be completed as soon as possible taking into account all the political, humanitarian, logistical, technical and socio-economic factors involved, and with the co-operation of the SNC.

7. Repatriation of Cambodian refugees and displaced persons should be voluntary and their decision should be taken in full possession of the facts. Choice of destination within Cambodia should be that of the individual. The unity of the family must be preserved.

PART III
Operational factors

8. Consistent with respect for principles of national sovereignty in the countries of temporary refuge and origin, and in close co-operation with the countries of temporary refuge and origin, full access by the Office of the United Nations High Commissioner for Refugees (UNHCR), ICRC and other relevant international agencies should be guaranteed to all Cambodian refugees and displaced persons, with a view to the agencies undertaking the census, tracing, medical assistance, food distribution and other activities vital to the discharge of their mandate and operational responsibilities; such access should also be provided in Cambodia to enable the relevant international organizations to carry out their traditional monitoring as well as operational responsibilities.

9. In the context of the comprehensive political settlement, the signatories note with satisfaction that the Secretary-General of the United Nations has entrusted UNHCR with the role of leadership and co-ordination among intergovernmental agencies assisting with the repatriation and relief of Cambodian refugees and displaced persons. The Signatories look to all non-governmental organizations to co-ordinate as much as possible their work for the Cambodian refugees and displaced persons with that of UNHCR.

10. The SNC, the Governments of the countries in which the Cambodian refugees and displaced persons have sought temporary refuge, and the countries which contribute to the repatriation and integration effort, will wish to monitor closely and facilitate the repatriation of the returnees. An ad hoc consultative body should be established for a limited term for these purposes. The UNHCR, the ICRC and other international agencies as appropriate, as well as UNTAC, would be invited to join as full participants.

11. Adequately monitored short-term repatriation assistance should be provided on an impartial basis to enable the families and individuals returning to Cambodia to establish their lives and livelihoods harmoniously in their society. These interim measures would be phased out and replaced in the longer term by the reconstruction programme.

12. Those responsible for organizing and supervising the repatriation operation will need to ensure that conditions of security are created for the movement of the refugees and displaced persons. In this respect, it is imperative that appropriate border crossing points and routes be designated and cleared of mines and other hazards.

13. The international community should contribute generously to the financial requirements of the repatriation operation.

ANNEX 5
Principles for a new constitution for Cambodia

1. The constitution will be the supreme law of the land. It may be amended only by a designated process involving legislative approval, popular referendum, or both.

2. Cambodia's tragic recent history requires special measures to assure protection of human rights. Therefore, the constitution will contain a declaration of fundamental rights, including the rights to life, personal liberty, security, freedom of movement, freedom of religion, assembly and association including political parties and trade unions, due process and equality before the law, protection from arbitrary deprivation of property or deprivation of private property without just compensation, and freedom from racial, ethnic, religious or sexual discrimination. It will prohibit the retroactive application of criminal law. The declaration will be consistent with the provisions of the Universal Declaration of Human Rights and other relevant international instruments. Aggrieved individuals will be entitled to have the courts adjudicate and enforce these rights.

3. The constitution will declare Cambodia's status as a sovereign, independent and neutral State, and the national unity of the Cambodian people.

4. The constitution will state that Cambodia will follow a system of liberal democracy, on the basis of pluralism. It will provide for periodic and genuine elections. It will provide for the right to vote and to be elected by universal and equal suffrage. It will provide for voting by secret ballot, with a requirement that electoral procedures provide a full and fair opportunity to organize and participate in the electoral process.

5. An independent judiciary will be established, empowered to enforce the rights provided under the constitution.

6. The constitution will be adopted by a two-thirds majority of the members of the constituent assembly.

## AGREEMENT
## CONCERNING THE SOVEREIGNTY, INDEPENDENCE, TERRITORIAL
## INTEGRITY AND INVIOLABILITY, NEUTRALITY AND NATIONAL UNITY OF CAMBODIA

Australia, Brunei Darussalam, Cambodia, Canada, the People's Republic of China, the French Republic, the Republic of India, the Republic of Indonesia, Japan, the Lao People's Democratic Republic, Malaysia, the Republic of the Philippines, the Republic of Singapore, the Kingdom of Thailand, the Union of Soviet Socialist Republics, the United Kingdom of Great Britain and Northern Ireland, the United States of America, the Socialist Republic of Vietnam and the Socialist Federal Republic of Yugoslavia,

In the presence of the Secretary-General of the United Nations,

*Convinced* that a comprehensive political settlement for Cambodia is essential for the long-term objective of maintaining peace and security in South-East Asia,

*Recalling* their obligations under the Charter of the United Nations and other rules of international law,

*Considering* that full observance of the principles of non-interference and non-intervention in the internal and external affairs of States is of the greatest importance for the maintenance of international peace and security,

*Reaffirming* the inalienable right of States freely to determine their own political, economic, cultural and social systems in accordance with the will of their peoples, without outside interference, subversion, coercion or threat in any form whatsoever,

*Desiring* to promote respect for and observance of human rights and fundamental freedoms in conformity with the Charter of the United Nations and other relevant international instruments,

Have agreed as follows:

### ARTICLE 1

1. Cambodia hereby solemnly undertakes to maintain, preserve and defend its sovereignty, independence, territorial integrity and inviolability, neutrality, and national unity; the perpetual neutrality of Cambodia shall be proclaimed and enshrined in the Cambodian constitution to be adopted after free and fair elections.

2. To this end, Cambodia undertakes:

(a) To refrain from any action that might impair the sovereignty, independence and territorial integrity and inviolability of other States;

(b) To refrain from entering into any military alliances or other military agreements with other States that would be inconsistent with its neutrality, without prejudice to Cambodia's right to acquire the necessary military equipment, arms, munitions and assistance to enable it to exercise its inherent right of self-defence and to maintain law and order;

(c) To refrain from interference in any form whatsoever, whether direct or indirect, in the internal affairs of other States;

(d) To terminate treaties and agreements that are imcompatible with its sovereignty, independence, territorial integrity and inviolability, neutrality, and national unity;

(e) To refrain from the threat or use of force against the territorial integrity or political independence of any State, or in any other manner inconsistent with the purposes of the United Nations;

(f) To settle all disputes with other States by peaceful means;

(g) To refrain from using its territory or the territories of other States to impair the sovereignty, independence, and territorial integrity and inviolability of other States;

(h) To refrain from permitting the introduction or stationing of foreign forces, including military personnel, in any form whatsoever, in Cambodia, and to prevent the establishment or maintenance of foreign military bases, strong points or facilities in Cambodia, except pursuant to United Nations authorization for the implementation of the comprehensive political settlement.

## Article 2

1. The other parties to this Agreement hereby solemnly undertake to recognize and to respect in every way the sovereignty, independence, territorial integrity and inviolability, neutrality and national unity of Cambodia.

2. To this end, they undertake:

(a) To refrain from entering into any military alliances or other military agreements with Cambodia that would be inconsistent with Cambodia's neutrality, without prejudice to Cambodia's right to acquire the necessary miltary equipment, arms, munitions and assistance to enable it to exercise its inherent right of self-defence and to maintain law and order;

(b) To refrain from interference in any form whatsoever, whether direct or indirect, in the internal affairs of Cambodia;

(c) To refrain from the threat or use of force against the territorial integrity or political independence of Cambodia, or in any other manner inconsistent with the purposes of the United Nations;

(d)  To settle all disputes with Cambodia by peaceful means;

(e)  To refrain from using their territories or the territories of other States to impair the sovereignty, independence, territorial integrity and inviolability, neutrality and national unity of Cambodia;

(f)  To refrain from using the territory of Cambodia to impair the sovereignty, independence and territorial integrity and inviolability of other States;

(g)  To refrain from the introduction or stationing of foreign forces, including military personnel, in any form whatsoever, in Cambodia and from establishing or maintaining military bases, strong points or facilities in Cambodia, except pursuant to United Nations authorization for the implementation of the comprehensive political settlement.

### ARTICLE 3

1. All persons in Cambodia shall enjoy the rights and freedoms embodied in the Universal Declaration of Human Rights and other relevant international human rights instruments.

2. To this end,

(a)  Cambodia undertakes:

– to ensure respect for and observance of human rights and fundamental freedoms in Cambodia;

– to support the right of all Cambodian citizens to undertake activities that would promote and protect human rights and fundamental freedoms;

– to take effective measures to ensure that the policies and practices of the past shall never be allowed to return;

– to adhere to relevant international human rights instruments;

(b)  The other parties to this Agreement undertake to promote and encourage respect for and observance of human rights and fundamental freedoms in Cambodia as embodied in the relevant international instruments in order, in particular, to prevent the recurrence of human rights abuses.

3. The United Nations Commission on Human Rights should continue to monitor closely the human rights situation in Cambodia, including, if necessary, by the appointment of a Special Rapporteur who would report his findings annually to the Commission and to the General Assembly.

### ARTICLE 4

The parties to this Agreement call upon all other States to recognize and respect in every way the sovereignty, independence, territorial integrity and inviolability, neutrality and national unity of Cambodia and to refrain from any action inconsistent with these principles or with other provisions of this Agreement.

## ARTICLE 5

1. In the event of a violation or threat of violation of the sovereignty, independence, territorial integrity and inviolability, neutrality or national unity of Cambodia, or of any of the other commitments herein, the parties to this Agreement undertake to consult immediately with a view to adopting all appropriate steps to ensure respect for these commitments and resolving any such violations through peaceful means.

2. Such steps may include, inter alia, reference of the matter to the Security Council of the United Nations or recourse to the means for the peaceful settlement of disputes referred to in Article 33 of the Charter of the United Nations.

3. The parties to this Agreement may also call upon the assistance of the co-chairmen of the Paris Conference on Cambodia.

4. In the event of serious violations of human rights in Cambodia, they will call upon the competent organs of the United Nations to take such other steps as are appropriate for the prevention and suppression of such violations in accordance with the relevant international instruments.

## ARTICLE 6

This Agreement shall enter into force upon signature.

## ARTICLE 7

This Agreement shall remain open for accession by all States. The instruments of accession shall be deposited with the Governments of the French Republic and the Republic of Indonesia. For each State acceding to this Agreement, it shall enter into force on the date of deposit of its instrument of accession.

## ARTICLE 8

The original of this Agreement, of which the Chinese, English, Khmer and Russian texts are equally authentic, shall be deposited with the Governments of the French Republic and the Republic of Indonesia, which shall transmit certified true copies to the Governments of the other States participating in the Paris Conference on Cambodia and to the Secretary-General of the United Nations.

In witness whereof the undersigned plenipotentiaries, being duly authorized thereto, have signed this Agreement.

Done at Paris this twenty-third day of October, one thousand nine hundred and ninety-one.

## DECLARATION ON THE REHABILITATION AND RECONSTRUCTION OF CAMBODIA

1. The primary objective of the reconstruction of Cambodia should be the advancement of the Cambodian nation and people, without discrimination or prejudice, and with full respect for human rights and fundamental freedom for all. The achievement of this objective requires the full implementation of the comprehensive political settlement.

2. The main responsibility for deciding Cambodia's reconstruction needs and plans should rest with the Cambodian people and the government formed after free and fair elections. No attempt should be made to impose a development strategy on Cambodia from any outside source or deter potential donors from contributing to the reconstruction of Cambodia.

3. International, regional and bilateral assistance to Cambodia should be co-ordinated as much as possible, complement and supplement local resources and be made available impartially with full regard for Cambodia's sovereignty, priorities, institutional means and absorptive capacity.

4. In the context of the reconstruction effort, economic aid should benefit all areas of Cambodia, especially the more disadvantaged, and reach all levels of society.

5. The implementation of an international aid effort would have to be phased in over a period that realistically acknowledges both political and technical imperatives. It would also necessitate a significant degree of co-operation between the future Cambodian Government and bilateral, regional and international contributors.

6. An important role will be played in rehabilitation and reconstruction by the United Nations system. The launching of an international reconstruction plan and an appeal for contributions should take place at an appropriate time, so as to ensure its success.

7. No effective programme of national reconstruction can be initiated without detailed assessments of Cambodia's human, natural and other economic assets. It will be necessary for a census to be conducted, developmental priorities identified, and the availability of resources, internal and external, determined.

To this end there will be scope for sending to Cambodia fact-finding missions from the United Nations system, international financial institutions and other agencies, with the consent of the future Cambodian Government.

8. With the achievement of the comprehensive political settlement, it is now possible and desirable to initiate a process of rehabilitation, addressing immediate needs, and to lay the groundwork for the preparation of medium- and long-term reconstruction plans.

9. For this period of rehabilitation, the United Nations Secretary-General is requested to help co-ordinate the programme guided by a person appointed for this purpose.

10. In this rehabilitation phase, particular attention will need to be given to food security, health, housing, training, education, the transport network and the restoration of Cambodia's existing basic infrastructure and public utilities.

11. The implementation of a longer-term international development plan for reconstruction should await the formation of a government following the elections and the determination and adoption of its own policies and priorities.

12. This reconstruction phase should promote Cambodian entrepreneurship and make use of the private sector, among other sectors, to help advance self-sustaining economic growth. It would also benefit from regional approaches, involving, inter alia, institutions such as the Economic and Social Commission for Asia and the Pacific (ESCAP) and the Mekong Committee, and Governments within the region; and from participation by non-governmental organizations.

13. In order to harmonize and monitor the contributions that will be made by the international community to the reconstruction of Cambodia after the formation of a government following the elections, a consultative body, to be called the International Committee on the Reconstruction of Cambodia (ICORC), should be set up at an appropriate time and be open to potential donors and other relevant parties. The United Nations Secretary-General is requested to make special arrangements for the United Nations system to support ICORC in its work, notably in ensuring a smooth transition from the rehabilitation to reconstruction phases.


## ANNEX
### Final act of the Paris Conference on Cambodia
1. Concerned by the tragic conflict and continuing bloodshed in Cambodia, the Paris Conference on Cambodia was convened, at the invitation of the Government of the French Republic, in order to achieve an internationally guaranteed comprehensive settlement which would restore peace to that country. The Conference was held in two sessions, the first from 30 July to 30 August 1989, and the second from 21 to 23 October 1991.

2. The Co-Presidents of the Conference were H. E. Mr. Roland DUMAS, Minister for Foreign Affairs of the French Republic, and H. E. Mr. Ali ALATAS, Minister for Foreign Affairs of the Republic of Indonesia.

3. The following States participated in the Conference: Australia, Brunei Darussalam, Cambodia, Canada, the People's Republic of China, the French Republic, the Republic of India, the Republic of Indonesia, Japan, the Lao People's Democratic Republic, Malaysia, the Republic of the Philippines, the Republic of Singapore, the Kingdom of Thailand, the Union of Soviet Socialist Repub-

lics, the United Kingdom of Great Britain and Northern Ireland, the United States of America and the Socialist Republic of Vietnam.

In addition, the Non-Aligned Movement was represented at the Conference by its current Chairman at each session, namely Zimbabwe at the first session and Yugoslavia at the second session.

4. At the first session of the Conference, Cambodia was represented by the four Cambodian parties. The Supreme National Council of Cambodia, under the leadership of its President, H. R. H. Prince NORODOM SIHANOUK, represented Cambodia at the second session of the Conference.

5. The Secretary-General of the United Nations, H. E. M. Javier PEREZ DE CUELLAR, and his Special Representative, M. Rafeeuddin AHMED, also participated in the Conference.

6. The Conference organized itself into three working committees of the whole, which met throughout the first session of the Conference. The First Committee dealt with military matters, the Second Committee dealt with the question of international guarantees, and the Third Committee with the repatriation of refugees and displaced persons and the eventual reconstruction of Cambodia.

The officers of each committee were as follows:

*First Committee*
| | |
|---|---|
| Co-Chairmen: | Mr. C. R. GHAREKHAN (India) |
| | Mr. Alain SULLIVAN (Canada) |
| Rapporteur: | Ms. Victoria SISANTE-BATACLAN |
| | (Philippines) |

*Second Committee*
| | |
|---|---|
| Co-Chairmen: | Mr. Soulivong PHRASITHIDETH (Laos) |
| | Dato ZAINAL ABIDIN IBRAHIM |
| | (Malaysia) |
| Rapporteur: | Mr. Hervé DEJEAN de la BATIE (France) |

*Third Committee*
| | |
|---|---|
| Co-Chairmen: | Mr. Yukio IMAGAWA (Japan) |
| | Mr. Robert MERRILLEES (Australia) |
| Rapporteur: | Colonel Ronachuck SWASDIKIAT |
| | (Thailand) |

The Conference also established an Ad Hoc Committee, composed of the representatives of the four Cambodian Parties and chaired by the representatives of the two Co-Presidents of the Conference, whose mandate involved matters related to national reconciliation among the Cambodian Parties. The Ad Hoc Committee held several meetings during the first session of the Conference.

The Co-ordination Committee of the Conference, chaired by the representatives of the two Co-Presidents, was established and given responsibility for general co-ordination of the work of the other four committees. The Co-ordination

Committee met at both the first and second sessions of the Conference. An informal meeting of the Co-ordination Committee was also held in New York on 21 September 1991.

7. At the conclusion of the first session, the Conference had achieved progress in elaborating a wide variety of elements necessary for the achievement of a comprehensive settlement of the conflict in Cambodia. The Conference noted, however, that it was not yet possible to achieve a comprehensive settlement. It was therefore decided to suspend the Conference on 30 August 1989. However, in doing so, the Conference urged all parties concerned to intensify their efforts to achieve a comprehensive settlement, and asked the Co-Presidents to lend their good offices to facilitate these efforts.

8. Following the suspension of the first session of the Conference, the Co-Presidents and the Secretary-General of the United Nations undertook extensive consultations, in particular with the five permanent members of the United Nations Security Council, with the Supreme National Council of Cambodia, and with other participants in the Paris Conference. The object of these consultations was to forge agreement on all aspects of a settlement, to ensure that all initiatives to this end were compatible and to enhance the prospects of ending the bloodshed in Cambodia at the earliest possible date. The efforts of the Co-Presidents and the Secretary-General paved the way for the reconvening of the Paris Conference on Cambodia.

9. At the inaugural portion of the final meeting of the Paris Conference, on 23 October 1991, the Conference was addressed by H. E. Mr. François MITTERRAND, President of the French Republic, H. R. H. Prince NORODOM SIHANOUK, President of the Supreme National Council of Cambodia, and H. E. Mr. Javier PEREZ DE CUELLAR, Secretary-General of the United Nations.

10. At the second session, the Conference adopted the following instruments:

1. AGREEMENT ON A COMPREHENSIVE POLITICAL SETTLEMENT OF THE CAMBODIA CONFLICT, with annexes on the mandate for UNTAC, military matters, elections, repatriation of Cambodian refugees and displaced persons, and the principles for a new Cambodian constitution;

2. AGREEMENT CONCERNING THE SOVEREIGNTY, INDEPENDENCE, TERRITORIAL INTEGRITY AND INVIOLABILITY, NEUTRALITY AND NATIONAL UNITY OF CAMBODIA; and

3. DECLARATION ON THE REHABILITATION AND RECONSTRUCTION OF CAMBODIA.

These instruments represent an elaboration of the "Framework for a Comprehensive Political Settlement of the Cambodia Confict" adopted by the five permanent members of the United Nations Security Council on 28 August 1990, and of elements of the work accomplished at the first session of the Conference. They entail a continuing process of national reconciliation and an enhanced role for the United Nations, thus enabling the Cambodian people to determine their own political future through free and fair elections organized and conducted by the United Nations in a neutral political environment with full respect for the national sovereignty of Cambodia.

11. These instruments, which together form the comprehensive settlement the achievement of which was the objective of the Paris Conference, are being presented for signature to the States participating in the Paris Conference. On behalf of Cambodia, the instruments will be signed by the twelve members of the Supreme National Council of Cambodia, which is the unique legitimate body and source of authority enshrining the sovereignty, independence and unity of Cambodia.

12. The States participating in the Conference call upon the Co-Presidents of the conference to transmit an authentic copy of the comprehensive political settlement instruments to the Secretary-General of the United Nations. The States participating in the Conference request the Secretary-General to take the appropriate steps in order to enable consideration of the comprehensive settlement by the United Nations Security Council at the earliest opportunity. They pledge their full co-operation in the fulfilment of this comprehensive settlement and their assistance in its implementation.

Above all, in view of the recent tragic history of Cambodia, the States participating in the Conference commit themselves to promote and encourage respect for and observance of human rights and fundamental freedoms in Cambodia, as embodied in the relevant international instruments to which they are party.

13. The States participating in the Conference request the International Committee of the Red Cross to facilitate, in accordance with its principles, the release of prisoners of war and civilian internees. They express their readiness to assist the ICRC in this task.

14. The States participating in the Conference invite other States to accede to the Agreement on a Comprehensive Political Settlement of the Cambodia Conflict and to the Agreement concerning the Sovereignty, Independence, Territorial Integrity and Inviolability, Neutrality and National Unity of Cambodia.

15. Further recognizing the need for a concerted international effort to assist Cambodia in the tasks of rehabilitation and reconstruction, the States participating in the Conference urge the international community to provide generous economic and financial support for the measures set forth in the Declaration of the Rehabilitation and Reconstruction of Cambodia.

In witness whereof the representatives have signed this Final Act.

Done at Paris this twenty-third day of October one thousand nine hundred and ninety-one, in two copies in the Chinese, English, French, Khmer and Russian languages, each text being equally authentic. The originals of this Final Act shall be deposited with the governments of the French Republic and of the Republic of Indonesia.

*Appendix B*
# Former Yugoslavia

CHRONOLOGY

| | |
|---|---|
| 25 June 1991 | Croatia and Slovenia declare independence |
| 3 July 1991 | Conference on Security and Cooperation in Europe (CSCE) Committee of Senior Officials meets for first time in emergency session in Prague; they back EC mission and agree to send a CSCE 'good offices' mission to assist peace dialogue |
| 5 July 1991 | EC arms embargo and freeze on aid imposed on Yugoslavia; fighting on the Croatian–Serbian border ensues |
| 6 August 1991 | EC foreign ministers meet at The Hague, agreeing to extend European observer mission and to consider unblocking loans to republics which accept mediation |
| 5 September 1991 | Yugoslav army forces now control one-third of Croatia; first of 200 ceasefire monitors arrive in Zagreb |
| 12 September 1991 | Second session of The Hague Peace Conference chaired by Lord Carrington issues declaration establishing that internal borders cannot be changed by force, that rights of minorities must be guaranteed and that differences not resolvable through negotiation will be submitted to arbitration commission |
| 25 September 1991 | Resolution 713 calls for complete arms embargo on Yugoslavia, for immediate end to hostilities and for UN Secretary-General to assist with mediation |
| 15 October 1991 | Parliament of Bosnia-Herzegovina declares sovereignty |
| 17 November 1991 | Vukovar reported to have fallen to Yugoslav army forces after 86-day siege |
| 23 November 1991 | First UN-negotiated ceasefire takes effect |
| 27 November 1991 | Resolution 721 authorises peacekeeping forces provided 23 November ceasefire agreement holds |
| 28 November 1991 | Ceasefire appears successful as Yugoslav army troops begin withdrawal from Zagreb |
| 15 December 1991 | Resolution 724 agrees to send small team of monitors to prepare for deployment of peacekeeping troops |

166

| | |
|---|---|
| 23 December 1991 | Germany recognises independence of Croatia and Slovenia |
| 24 December 1991 | Bosnia-Herzegovina, Croatia, Macedonia and Slovenia request EC recognition |
| 5 January 1992 | Leader of the Republic of Serbian Krajina (SRK), Milan Babic, rejects proposals to station UN troops in Serb areas of Croatia |
| 8 January 1992 | Resolution 727 condemns situation in former Yugoslavia and approves deployment of advance force, UN Military Liaison Officers' force |
| 15 January 1992 | Presidency of EC announces that EC will recognise Croatia and Slovenia as independent |
| 7 February 1992 | Resolution 740 calls on Serbian leaders to accept UN peace plan |
| 13 February 1992 | Secretary-General Boutros-Ghali recommends to Security Council deployment of UN forces in Krajina and eastern and western Slavonia |
| 21 February 1992 | Resolution 743 approves dispatch of peacekeeping troops in former Yugoslavia |
| 29 February– 1 March 1992 | Referendum held in Bosnia-Herzegovina, boycotted by majority of Serbs; 99 per cent vote for full independence |
| 3 March 1992 | Izetbegovic proclaims independence of Bosnia-Herzegovina |
| 27 March 1992 | Serb leaders proclaim 'Serbian Republic of Bosnia-Herzegovina' |
| 6 April 1992 | EC foreign ministers agree to recognise independence of Bosnia-Herzegovina from 7 April |
| 7 April 1992 | Resolution 749 establishes deployment of United Nations Protection Force in Yugoslavia (UNPROFOR); United States recognises independence of Croatia, Slovenia and Bosnia-Herzegovina |
| 27 April 1992 | Federal Assembly in Belgrade adopts constitution of new federation formed by Serbia and Montenegro, Federal Republic of Yugoslavia (FRY) |
| 22 May 1992 | General Assembly accepts Croatia, Slovenia and Bosnia-Herzegovina as UN members |
| 30 May 1992 | Resolution 757 imposes sanctions on FRY |
| 29 June 1992 | Resolution 761 redeploys 1,000 Canadian troops from Croatia to secure Sarajevo airport |
| 10 July 1992 | WEU and NATO agree to police UN sanctions against Yugoslavia by air and sea operations in Adriatic |
| 7 August 1992 | Resolution 769 authorises enlargement of UNPROFOR mandate and strength |
| 13 August 1992 | Resolution 770 authorises 'all measures necessary' to ensure delivery of humanitarian aid |
| 26–28 August 1992 | London Conference is held with representatives from |

|  | 20 countries, six republics in former Yugoslavia, EC and five permanent members of UN Security Council |
|---|---|
| 27 August 1992 | Lord Owen named successor to Carrington as EC special envoy |
| 3 September 1992 | Permanent conference on Yugoslavia opens in Geneva, co-chaired by Owen of EC and Vance of UN |
| 14 September 1992 | Resolution 776 enlarges mandate of UNPROFOR to facilitate delivery of humanitarian aid in Bosnia-Herzegovina; Resolution 780 establishes that war crimes commission will be formed |
| 9 October 1992 | Resolution 781 establishes ban on military flights over Bosnian airspace |
| 11 December 1992 | Resolution 795 authorises the deployment of 700 UNPROFOR troops to Macedonia (FYROM) |
| 2–4 January 1993 | Geneva peace talks resume, bringing together leaders of three warring factions in Bosnia-Herzegovina for first time; Owen and Vance present new proposals for peace, providing for reorganisation of Bosnia-Herzegovina into ten provinces, constitutional principles within a decentralised state, ceasefire and demilitarisation arrangements |
| 12 February 1993 | Croatia agrees to extension of UNPROFOR mandate in Croatia until 31 March 1993 |
| 25 February 1993 | President Clinton announces US relief air-drop to areas cut off from UN operations |
| 27 March 1993 | Ceasefire signed by 3 parties in Bosnia-Herzegovina, to be in effect by noon, 28 March |
| 31 March 1993 | Resolution 816 authorises NATO aircraft to shoot down planes violating no-fly zone over Bosnian airspace |
| 2 April 1993 | NATO endorses Resolution 816 |
| 25–26 April 1993 | Bosnian Serb Assembly meets in emergency session, voting to reject Vance–Owen plan |
| 1–3 May 1993 | Greek prime minister Mitsotakis hosts emergency conference where Milosevic signs Vance–Owen plan |
| 6 May 1993 | Resolution 824 declares Sarajevo, Tuzla, Zepa, Gorazde, Bihac and Srebrenica 'safe areas' |
| 15–16 May 1993 | Bosnian Serb referendum held, rejecting Vance–Owen plan |
| 16 June 1993 | At Geneva conference, chaired by Owen and Stoltenberg, agreement is reached on establishment of a new Bosnia, comprising three ethnically based states with federal or confederal constitution |
| 30 July 1993 | At Geneva conference, Izetbegovic accepts three-part division of Bosnia-Herzegovina |
| 28 February 1994 | NATO enforces no-fly zone, shooting down four light attack aircraft |

| | |
|---|---|
| 3 March 1994 | Special envoy to former Yugoslavia, Yasushi Akashi, requests 10,650 more peacekeepers |
| 18 March 1994 | Clinton hosts ceremony where Izetbegovic and Tudjman sign accord on formation of federation of Bosnian Muslims and Croats |
| 10 April 1994 | Commander of UN forces in Bosnia, General Sir Michael Rose, requests NATO aircraft to bomb ground targets; Akashi gives approval; two US planes drop three bombs on Serbian artillery command post near Gorazde |
| 11 April 1994 | Renewed Serb bombing of Gorazde results in Rose making second request for air strikes; two US planes drop three bombs |
| 16 April 1994 | British plane shot down by Serbs |
| 24 April 1994 | Kozyrev signals Russian willingness to use force against Serb troops; withdrawal from Gorazde begins |
| 26 April 1994 | First meeting of Contact Group comprising France, Russia, the United Kingdom and the United States held in London to discuss plans for cessation of hostilities in former Yugoslavia |
| 27 April 1994 | Resolution 914 authorises increase in UNPROFOR personnel by 6,500 troops |
| 19 July 1994 | Karadzic rejects Contact Group plan for division of Bosnia-Herzegovina on a 51–49 per cent split between Croat–Bosnian confederation and Bosnian Serbs |
| 4 August 1994 | FRY announces closure of borders with Bosnia, isolating Bosnian Serbs |
| 5 August 1994 | Fourteen NATO jets attack Bosnian Serb positions after latter seize weaponry in UN collection depots |
| 11 August 1994 | United States threatens lifting of arms embargo on Bosnian government if Bosnian Serbs do not accept Contact Group plan by mid-October |
| 28 August 1994 | Contact Group plan rejected by Bosnian Serbs after referendum |
| 8 September 1994 | Bihac enclave attacked by Serbs from both Bosnia and Krajina |
| 11 September 1994 | EU rejects lifting of arms embargo against Bosnian government |
| 23 September 1994 | Security Council eases sanctions against FRY for 100-day probationary period |
| 28 October 1994 | United States introduces Security Council resolution calling for end of arms embargo against Bosnian government |
| 9 November 1994 | Bosnian Serbs attempt to retake Bihac enclave from Bosnian government troops |
| 19 November 1994 | Security Council grants authorisation for extension of 'air power' guarantee to include parts of Croatia |

| 21 November 1994 | NATO war planes attack Serb military airport in Croatia |
| 18 December 1994 | Former US president Jimmy Carter meets Croatian and Bosnian leaders in attempt to work out ceasefire |
| 19 December 1994 | Carter claims Bosnian Serbs have agreed to ceasefire |
| 24 December 1994 | Ceasefire agreement comes into operation for four-month period |

## SELECTED RESOLUTIONS OF THE UN SECURITY COUNCIL

SC Resolution 713, 25 September 1991; calls for a complete arms embargo on Yugoslavia, the immediate end of hostilities and UN Secretary-General to assist with mediation (for text, see pp. 173–5 in this appendix)

SC Resolution 721, 27 November 1991; promotes the recommendation for peacekeeping forces provided the 23 November ceasefire agreement holds

SC Resolution 724, 15 December 1991; agrees to send a small team of monitors to prepare for the deployment of peacekeeping troops

SC Resolution 727, 8 January 1992; condemns the situation in former Yugoslavia and approves the deployment of an advance force, the UN Military Liaison Officers' force

SC Resolution 740, 7 February 1992; calls on Serbian leaders to accept the UN peace plan

SC Resolution 743, 21 February 1992; approves the dispatch of a peacekeeping operation in former Yugoslavia (for text, see pp. 176–8 in this appendix)

SC Resolution 749, 7 April 1992; establishes the deployment of the United Nations Protection Force in Yugoslavia (UNPROFOR)

SC Resolution 752, 15 May 1992; contains first reference to the *former* Socialist Federal Republic of Yugoslavia, and demands the withdrawal of the Yugoslav National Army from republics other than Serbia and Montenegro

SC Resolution 757, 30 May 1992; imposes sanctions on FRY (for text, see pp. 179–84 in this appendix)

SC Resolution 758, 8 June 1992; calls for the reopening of Sarajevo airport

SC Resolution 761, 29 June 1992; redeploys 1,000 Canadian troops from Croatia to secure the Sarajevo airport and 'does not exclude other measures to secure aid' to Bosnia-Herzegovina

SC Resolution 769, 7 August 1992; authorises enlargement of UNPROFOR mandate and strength

SC Resolution 770, 13 August 1992; authorises 'all measures necessary' to ensure the delivery of humanitarian aid (for text, see pp. 185–6 in this appendix)

SC Resolution 771, 13 August 1992; calls for unimpeded access of the Red Cross to detention camps

SC Resolution 776, 14 September 1992; enlarges the mandate of UNPROFOR to facilitate the delivery of humanitarian aid in Bosnia-Herzegovina

SC Resolution 780, 6 October 1992; requests creation of Commission of Experts to investigate and report on breaches of international humanitarian law

SC Resolution 781, 9 October 1992; establishes a ban on military flights over Bosnian airspace

SC Resolution 786, 10 November 1992; authorises UNPROFOR strength increase to implement flight ban over Bosnia-Herzegovina

SC Resolution 787, 16 November 1992; authorises stop and search of vessels in the Adriatic to enforce UN sanctions

SC Resolution 795, 11 December 1992; authorises the deployment of 700 UNPROFOR troops to Macedonia

SC Resolution 802, 25 January 1993; demands withdrawal of Croatian forces from UN-protected areas

SC Resolution 808, 22 February 1993; decides to create 'international tribunal
... for the prosecution of persons responsible for serious violations of international humanitarian law'

SC Resolution 816, 31 March 1993; authorises NATO aircraft to shoot down
planes violating the no-fly zone over Bosnian airspace

SC Resolution 820, 17 April 1993; urges Serbs to accept Vance–Owen plan
and threatens to tighten sanctions

SC Resolution 824, 6 May 1993; declares Sarajevo, Tuzla, Zepa, Gorazde,
Bihac and Srebrenica to be 'safe areas'

SC Resolution 836, 4 June 1993; authorises UNPROFOR to use force, including air power, in the defence of 'safe areas'

SC Resolution 908, 31 March 1994; declares intention to increase number of
UNPROFOR personnel and reaffirms commitment to ensure the sovereignty
of Croatia and Bosnia-Herzegovina

SC Resolution 914, 27 April 1994; authorises an increase in UNPROFOR personnel by 6,500 troops

SC Resolution 941, 23 September 1994; condemns ethnic cleansing and
demands that Bosnian Serbs immediately cease campaign of ethnic cleansing

SC Resolution 942, 23 September 1994; condemns Bosnian Serb rejection of
Contact Group plan and declares UN readiness to take 'all measures necessary'
to assist in implementation of plan once agreed

SC Resolution 943, 23 September 1994; welcomes FRY's decision to close
borders with Bosnia and suspends UN sanctions on transport links with FRY
for 100 days

SC Resolution 947, 30 September 1994; extends UNPROFOR mandate until
end of March 1995

SC Resolution 958, 19 November 1994; extends 'air power' protection of 'safe
areas' in Bosnia to cover Croatia as well

SC Resolution 959, 19 November 1994; condemns attacks by Krajina Serbs
into the Bihac pocket

## RESOLUTION 713 (1991)

## ADOPTED BY THE SECURITY COUNCIL AT ITS 3009TH MEETING, ON 25 SEPTEMBER 1991

The Security Council,

*Conscious* of the fact that Yugoslavia has welcomed the convening of a Security Council meeting through a letter conveyed by the Permanent Representative of Yugoslavia to the President of the Security Council (S/23069),

*Having heard* the statement by the Foreign Minister of Yugoslavia,

*Deeply concerned* by the fighting in Yugoslavia which is causing a heavy loss of human life and material damage, and by the consequences for the countries of the region, in particular in the border areas of neighbouring countries,

*Concerned* that the continuation of this situation constitutes a threat to international peace and security,

*Recalling* its primary responsibility under the Charter of the United Nations for the maintenance of international peace and security,

*Recalling also* the provisions of Chapter VIII of the Charter of the United Nations,

*Commending* the efforts undertaken by the European Community and its Member States, with the support of the States participating in the Conference on Security and Cooperation in Europe, to restore peace and dialogue in Yugoslavia, through, inter alia, the implementation of a cease-fire including the sending of observers, the convening of a Conference on Yugoslavia, including the mechanisms set forth within it, and the suspension of the delivery of all weapons and military equipment to Yugoslavia,

*Recalling* the relevant principles enshrined in the Charter of the United Nations and, in this context, *noting* the Declaration of 3 September 1991 of the States participating in the Conference on Security and Cooperation in Europe that no territorial gains or changes within Yugoslavia brought about by violence are acceptable,

*Noting also* the agreement for a cease-fire concluded on 17 September 1991 in Igalo, and also that signed on 22 September 1991,

*Alarmed* by the violations of the cease-fire and the continuation of the fighting,

*Taking note* of the letter dated 19 September 1991 to the President of the Security Council from the Permanent Representative of Austria (S/23052),

*Taking note also* of the letters dated 19 September 1991 and 20 September 1991 to the President of the Security Council from respectively the Permanent Representative of Canada (S/23053) and the Permanent Representative of Hungary (S/23057),

*Taking note also* of the letters dated 5 July 1991 (S/22775), 12 July 1991 (S/22785), 22 July 1991 (S/22834), 6 August 1991 (S/22898), 7 August 1991 (S/22902), 7 August 1991 (S/22903), 21 August 1991 (S/22975), 29 August 1991 (S/22991), 4 September 1991 (S/23010), 19 September 1991 (S/23047), 20 September 1991 (S/23059) and 20 September 1991 (S/23060), from respectively the Permanent Representative of the Netherlands, the Permanent Representative of Czechoslovakia, the Permanent Representatives of Belgium, France and the United Kingdom of Great Britain and Northern Ireland, the Charge d'Affaires a.i. of Austria, and the Permanent Representative of Australia,

1. *Expresses* its full support for the collective efforts for peace and dialogue in Yugoslavia undertaken under the auspices of the Member States of the European Community with the support of the States participating in the Conference on Security and Cooperation in Europe consistent with the principles of that Conference;

2. *Supports fully* all arrangements and measures resulting from such collective efforts as those described above, in particular of assistance and support to the cease-fire observers, to consolidate an effective end to hostilities in Yugoslavia and the smooth functioning of the process instituted within the framework of the Conference on Yugoslavia;

3. *Invites* to this end the Secretary-General to offer his assistance without delay, in consultation with the Government of Yugoslavia and all those promoting the efforts referred to above, and to report as soon as possible to the Security Council;

4. *Strongly urges* all parties to abide strictly by the cease-fire agreements of 17 September 1991 and 22 September 1991;

5. *Appeals urgently to and encourages* all parties to settle their disputes peacefully and through negotiation at the Conference on Yugoslavia, including through the mechanisms set forth within it;

6. *Decides*, under Chapter VII of the Charter of the United Nations, that all States shall, for the purposes of establishing peace and stability in Yugoslavia, immediately implement a general and complete embargo on all deliveries of weapons and military equipment to Yugoslavia until the Security Council decides otherwise following consultation between the Secretary-General and the Government of Yugoslavia;

7. *Calls on* all States to refrain from any action which might contribute to increasing tension and to impeding or delaying a peaceful and negotiated out-

come to the conflict in Yugoslavia, which would permit all Yugoslavs to decide upon and to construct their future in peace;

8. *Decides* to remain seized of the matter until a peaceful solution is achieved.

## RESOLUTION 743 (1992)

## ADOPTED BY THE SECURITY COUNCIL AT ITS 3055TH MEETING, ON 21 FEBRUARY 1992

The Security Council,

*Reaffirming* its resolutions 713 (1991) of 25 September 1991, 721 (1991) of 27 November 1991, 724 (1991) of 15 December 1991, 727 (1992) of 8 January 1992 and 740 (1992) of 7 February 1992,

*Noting* the report of the Secretary-General of 15 February 1992 (S/23592) submitted pursuant to resolution 721 (1991), and the request of the Government of Yugoslavia (S/23240) for a peace-keeping operation referred to in that resolution,

*Noting* in particular that the Secretary-General considers that the conditions permitting the early deployment of a United Nations Protection Force (UNPROFOR) are met and welcoming his recommendation that this Force should be established with immediate effect,

*Expressing* its gratitude to the Secretary-General and his Personal Envoy for their contribution to the achievement of conditions facilitating the deployment of a United Nations Protection Force (UNPROFOR) and their continuing commitment to this effort,

*Concerned* that the situation in Yugoslavia continues to constitute a threat to international peace and security, as determined in resolution 713 (1991),

*Recalling* its primary responsibility under the Charter of the United Nations for the maintenance of international peace and security,

*Recalling also* the provisions of Article 25 Chapter VIII of the Charter of the United Nations,

*Commending* again the efforts undertaken by the European Community and its Member States, with the support of the States participating in the Conference on Security and Cooperation in Europe, through the convening of a Conference on Yugoslavia, including the mechanisms set forth within it, to ensure a peaceful political settlement,

*Convinced* that the implementation of the United Nations peace-keeping plan (S/23280, annex III) will assist the Conference on Yugoslavia in reaching a peaceful political settlement,

1. *Approves* the report of the Secretary-General of 15 February 1992 (S/23592);

2. *Decides* to establish, under its authority, a United Nations Protection Force (UNPROFOR) in accordance with the above-mentioned report and the United Nations peace-keeping plan and *requests* the Secretary-General to take the measures necessary to ensure its earliest possible deployment;

3. *Decides* that, in order to implement the recommendations in paragraph 30 of the report of the Secretary-General, the Force is established in accordance with paragraph 4 below, for an initial period of 12 months unless the Council subsequently decides otherwise;

4. *Requests* the Secretary-General immediately to deploy those elements of the Force which can assist in developing an implementation plan for the earliest possible full deployment of the force for approval by the Council and a budget which together will maximize the contribution of the Yugoslav parties to offsetting its costs and in all other ways secure the most efficient and cost-effective operation possible;

5. *Recalls* that, in accordance with paragraph 1 of the United Nations peace-keeping plan, the Force should be an interim arrangement to create the conditions of peace and security required for the negotiation of an overall settlement of the Yugoslav crisis;

6. *Invites* accordingly the Secretary-General to report as appropriate and not less than every six months on progress towards a peaceful political settlement and the situation on the ground, and to submit a first report on the establishment of the Force within two months of the adoption of this resolution;

7. *Undertakes*, in this connection, to examine without delay any recommendations that the Secretary-General may make in his reports concerning the Force, including the duration of its mission, and to adopt appropriate decisions;

8. *Urges* all parties and others concerned to comply strictly with the cease-fire arrangements signed at Geneva on 23 November 1991 and at Sarajevo on 2 January 1992, and to cooperate fully and unconditionally in the implementation of the peace-keeping plan;

9. *Demands* that all parties and others concerned take all the necessary measures to ensure the safety of the personnel sent by the United Nations and of the members of the European Community Monitoring Mission;

10. *Calls again upon* the Yugoslav parties to cooperate fully with the Conference on Yugoslavia in its aim of reaching a political settlement consistent with the principles of the Conference on Security and Cooperation in Europe and reaffirms that the United Nations peace-keeping plan and its implementation is in no way intended to prejudge the terms of a political settlement;

11. *Decides* within the same framework that the embargo imposed by paragraph 6 of Security Council resolution 713 (1991) shall not apply to weapons and military equipment destined for the sole use of UNPROFOR;

12. *Requests* all States to provide appropriate support to UNPROFOR, in particular to permit and facilitate the transit of its personnel and equipment;

13. *Decides* to remain actively seized of the matter until a peaceful solution is achieved.

## RESOLUTION 757 (1992)

## ADOPTED BY THE SECURITY COUNCIL AT ITS 3082ND MEETING, ON 30 MAY 1992

The Security Council,

*Reaffirming* its resolutions 713 (1991) of 25 September 1991, 721 (1991) of 27 November 1991, 724 (1991) of 15 December 1991, 727 (1992) of 8 January 1992, 740 (1992) of 7 February 1992, 743 (1992) of 21 February 1992, 749 (1992) of 7 April 1992 and 752 (1992) of 15 May,

*Noting* that in the very complex context of events in the former Socialist Federal Republic of Yugoslavia all parties bear some responsibility for the situation,

*Reaffirming* its support for the Conference on Yugoslavia, including the efforts undertaken by the European Community in the framework of the discussions on constitutional arrangements for Bosnia and Herzegovina, and *recalling* that no territorial gains or changes brought about by violence are acceptable and that the borders of Bosnia and Herzegovina are inviolable,

*Deploring* the fact that the demands in resolution 752 (1992) have not been complied with, including its demands:
– that all parties and others concerned in Bosnia and Herzegovina stop the fighting immediately,
– that all forms of interference from outside Bosnia and Herzegovina cease immediately,
– that Bosnia and Herzegovina's neighbours take swift action to end all interference and respect the territorial integrity of Bosnia and Herzegovina,
– that action be taken as regards units of the Yugoslav People's Army (JNA) in Bosnia and Herzegovina, including the disbanding and disarming with weapons placed under effective international monitoring of any units that are neither withdrawn nor placed under the authority of the Government of Bosnia and Herzegovina,
– that all irregular forces in Bosnia and Herzegovina be disbanded and disarmed,

*Deploring* further that its call for the immediate cessation of forcible expulsions and attempts to change the ethnic composition of that population has not been heeded, and *reaffirming* in this context the need for the effective protection of human rights and fundamental freedoms, including those of ethnic minorities,

*Dismayed* that conditions have not yet been established for the effective and unhindered delivery of humanitarian assistance, including safe and secure access to and from Sarajevo and other airports in Bosnia and Herzegovina,

*Deeply concerned* that those United Nations Protection Force (UNPROFOR) personnel remaining in Sarajevo have been subjected to deliberate mortar and small-arms fire, and the United Nations Military Observers deployed in the Mostar region have had to be withdrawn,

*Deeply concerned also* at developments in Croatia, including persistent cease-fire violations and the continued expulsion of non-Serb civilians, and at the obstruction of and lack of cooperation with UNPROFOR in other parts of Croatia,

*Deploring* the tragic incident on 18 May 1992 which caused the death of a member of the ICRC team in Bosnia and Herzegovina,

*Noting* that the claim by the Federal Republic of Yugoslavia (Serbia and Montenegro) to continue automatically the membership of the former Socialist Federal Republic of Yugoslavia in the United Nations has not been generally accepted,

*Expressing* its appreciation for the report of the Secretary-General of 26 May 1992 (S/24000) pursuant to resolution 752 (1992),

*Recalling* its primary responsibility under the Charter of the United Nations for the maintenance of international peace and security,

*Recalling also* the provisions of Chapter VIII of the Charter of the United Nations, and the continuing role that the European Community is playing in working for a peaceful solution in Bosnia and Herzegovina, as well as in other republics of the former Socialist Federal Republic of Yugoslavia,

*Recalling* its decision in resolution 752 (1992) to consider further steps to achieve a peaceful solution in conformity with relevant resolutions of the Council, and *affirming* its determination to take measures against any party or parties which fail to fulfil the requirements of resolution 752 (1992) and its other relevant resolutions,

*Determined* in this context to adopt certain measures with the sole objective of achieving a peaceful solution and encouraging the efforts undertaken by the European Community and its Member States,

*Recalling* the right of States, under Article 50 of the Charter, to consult the Security Council where they find themselves confronted with special economic problems arising from the carrying out of preventive or enforcement measures,

*Determining* that the situation in Bosnia and Herzegovina and in other parts of the Former Socialist Federal Republic of Yugoslavia constitutes a threat to international peace and security,

*Acting* under Chapter VII of the Charter of the United Nations,

1. *Condemns* the failure of the authorities in the Federal Republic of Yugoslavia (Serbia and Montenegro), including the Yugoslav People's Army (JNA), to take effective measures to fulfil the requirements of resolution 752 (1992);

2. *Demands* that any elements of the Croatian Army still present in Bosnia and Herzegovina act in accordance with paragraph 4 of resolution 752 (1992) without further delay;

3. *Decides* that all States shall adopt the measures set out below, which shall apply until the Security Council decides that the authorities in the Federal Republic of Yugoslavia (Serbia and Montenegro), including the Yugoslav People's Army (JNA), have taken effective measures to fulfil the requirements of resolution 752 (1992);

4. *Decides* that all States shall prevent:
(a) The import into their territories of all commodities and products originating in the Federal Republic of Yugoslavia (Serbia and Montenegro) exported therefrom after the date of the present resolution;

(b) Any activities by their nationals or in their territories which would promote or are calculated to promote the export or trans-shipment of any commodities or products originating in the Federal Republic of Yugoslavia (Serbia and Montenegro); and any dealings by their nationals or their flag vessels or aircraft or in their territories in any commodities or products originating in the Federal Republic of Yugoslavia (Serbia and Montenegro) and exported therefrom after the date of the present resolution, including in particular any transfer of funds to the Federal Republic of Yugoslavia (Serbia and Montenegro) for the purposes of such activities or dealings;

(c) The sale or supply by their nationals or from their territories or using their flag vessels or aircraft of any commodities or products, whether or not originating in their territories, but not including supplies intended strictly for medical purposes and foodstuffs notified to the Committee established pursuant to resolution 724 (991), to any person or body in the Federal Republic of Yugoslavia (Serbia and Montenegro) or to any person or body for the purposes of any business carried on in or operated from the Federal Republic of Yugoslavia (Serbia and Montenegro), and any activities by their nationals or in their territories which promote or are calculated to promote such sale or supply of such commodities or products;

5. *Decides* that all States shall not make available to the authorities in the Federal Republic of Yugoslavia (Serbia and Montenegro) or to any commercial, industrial or public utility undertaking in the Federal Republic of Yugoslavia (Serbia and Montenegro), any funds or any other financial or economic resources and shall prevent their nationals and any persons within their territories from removing from their territories or otherwise making available to those authorities or to any such undertaking any such funds or resources and from remitting any other funds to persons or bodies within the Federal Republic of

Yugoslavia (Serbia and Montenegro), except payments exclusively for strictly medical or humanitarian purposes and foodstuffs;

6. *Decides* that the prohibitions in paragraphs 4 and 5 above shall not apply to the trans-shipment through the Federal Republic of Yugoslavia (Serbia and Montenegro) of commodities and products originating outside the Federal Republic of Yugoslavia (Serbia and Montenegro) and temporarily present in the territory of the Federal Republic of Yugoslavia (Serbia and Montenegro) only for the purpose of such trans-shipment, in accordance with guidelines approved by the Committee established by resolution 724 (1991);

7. *Decides* that all States shall:
(a) Deny permission to any aircraft to take off from, land in or overfly their territory if it is destined to land in or had taken off from the territory of the Federal Republic of Yugoslavia (Serbia and Montenegro), unless the particular flight has been approved, for humanitarian or other purposes consistent with the relevant resolutions of the Council, by the Committee established by resolution 724 (1991);

(b) Prohibit, by their nationals or from their territory, the provision of engineering and maintenance servicing of aircraft registered in the Federal Republic of Yugoslavia (Serbia and Montenegro) or operated by or on behalf of entities in the Federal Republic of Yugoslavia (Serbia and Montenegro) or components for such aircraft, the certification of airworthiness for such aircraft, and the payment of new claims against existing insurance contracts and the provision of new direct insurance for such aircraft;

8. *Decides* that all States shall:
(a) Reduce the level of the staff at diplomatic missions and consular posts in the Federal Republic of Yugoslavia (Serbia and Montenegro);

(b) Take the necessary steps to prevent the participation in sporting events on their territory of persons or groups representing the Federal Republic of Yugoslavia (Serbia and Montenegro);

(c) Suspend scientific and technical cooperation and cultural exchanges and visits involving persons or groups officially sponsored by or representing the Federal Republic of Yugoslavia (Serbia and Montenegro).

9. *Decides* that all States, and the authorities in the Federal Republic of Yugoslavia (Serbia and Montenegro), shall take the necessary measures to ensure that no claim shall lie at the instance of the authorities in the Federal Republic of Yugoslavia (Serbia and Montenegro), or of any person or body in the Federal Republic of Yugoslavia (Serbia and Montenegro), or of any person claiming through or for the benefit of any such person or body, in connection with any contract or other transaction where its performance was affected by reason of the measures imposed by this resolution and related resolutions;

10. *Decides* that the measures imposed by this resolution shall not apply to activities related to UNPROFOR, to the Conference on Yugoslavia or to the European Community Monitor Mission, and that States, parties and others concerned shall cooperate fully with UNPROFOR, the Conference on Yugoslavia and the European Community Monitor Mission and respect fully their freedom of movement and the safety of their personnel;

11. *Calls upon* all States, including States not members of the United Nations, and all international organizations, to act strictly in accordance with the provisions of the present resolution, notwithstanding the existence of any rights or obligations conferred or imposed by any international agreement or any contract entered into or any licence or permit granted prior to the date of the present resolution;

12. *Requests* all States to report to the Secretary-General by 22 June 1992 on the measures they have instituted for meeting the obligations set out in paragraphs 4 to 9 above;

13. *Decides* that the Committee established by resolution 724 (1991) shall undertake the following tasks additional to those in respect of the arms embargo established by resolutions 713 (1991) and 727 (1992):

(a) To examine the reports submitted pursuant to paragraph 12 above;

(b) To seek from all States further information regarding the action taken by them concerning the effective implementation of the measures imposed by paragraphs 4 to 9 above;

(c) To consider any information brought to its attention by States concerning violations of the measures imposed by paragraphs 4 to 9 above and, in that context, to make recommendations to the Council on ways to increase their effectiveness;

(d) To recommend appropriate measures in response to violations of the measures imposed by paragraphs 4 to 9 above and provide information on a regular basis to the Secretary-General for general distribution to Member States;

(e) To consider and approve the guidelines referred to in paragraph 6 above;

(f) To consider and decide upon expeditiously any applications for the approval of flights for humanitarian or other purposes consistent with the relevant resolutions of the Council in accordance with paragraph 7 above;

14. *Calls upon* all States to cooperate fully with the Committee in the fulfilment of its tasks, including supplying such information as may be sought by the Committee in the pursuance of the present resolution;

15. *Requests* the Secretary-General to report to the Security Council, not later than 15 June 1992 and earlier if he considers it appropriate, on the implementation of resolution 752 (1992) by all parties and others concerned;

16. *Decides* to keep under continuous review the measures imposed by paragraphs 4 to 9 above with a view to considering whether such measures might be suspended or terminated following compliance with the requirements of resolution 752 (1992);

17. *Demands* that all parties and others concerned create immediately the necessary conditions for unimpeded delivery of humanitarian supplies to Sarajevo and other destinations in Bosnia and Herzegovina, including the establishment of a security zone encompassing Sarajevo and its airport and respecting the agreements signed in Geneva on 22 May 1992;

18. *Requests* the Secretary-General to continue to use his good offices in order to achieve the objectives contained in paragraph 17 above, and *invites* him to keep under continuous review any further measures that may become necessary to ensure unimpeded delivery of humanitarian supplies;

19. *Urges* all States to respond to the Revised Joint Appeal for humanitarian assistance of early May 1992 issued by the United Nations High Commissioner for Refugees, UNICEF and the World Health Organization;

20. *Reiterates* the call in paragraph 2 of resolution 752 (1992) that all parties continue their efforts in the framework of the Conference on Yugoslavia and that the three communities in Bosnia and Herzegovina resume their discussions on constitutional arrangements for Bosnia and Herzegovina;

21. *Decides* to remain actively seized of the matter and to consider immediately, whenever, necessary, further steps to achieve a peaceful solution in conformity with relevant resolutions of the Council.

## RESOLUTION 770 (1992)

### ADOPTED BY THE SECURITY COUNCIL AT ITS 3106TH MEETING, ON 13 AUGUST 1992

The Security Council,

*Reaffirming* its resolutions 713 (1991) of 25 September 1991, 721 (1991) of 27 November 1991, 724 (1991) of 15 December 1991, 727 (1992) of 8 January 1992, 740 (1992) of 7 February 1992, 743 (1992) of 21 February 1992, 749 (1992) of 7 April 1992, 752 (1992) of 15 May 1992, 757 (1992) of 30 May 1992, 758 (1992) of 8 June 1992, 760 (1992) of 18 June 1992, 761 (1992) of 29 June 1992 and 762 (1992) of 30 June 1992, 764 (1992) of 13 July 1992 and 769 (1992) of 7 August 1992,

*Noting* the letter dated 10 August 1992 from the Permanent Representative of the Republic of Bosnia and Herzegovina to the United Nations (S/24401),

*Underlining once again* the imperative need for an urgent negotiated political solution to the situation in the Republic of Bosnia and Herzegovina to enable that country to live in peace and security within its borders,

*Reaffirming* the need to respect the sovereignty, territorial integrity and political independence of the Republic of Bosnia and Herzegovina,

*Recognizing* that the situation in Bosnia and Herzegovina constitutes a threat to international peace and security and that the provision of humanitarian assistance in Bosnia and Herzegovina is an important element in the Council's effort to restore international peace and security in the area,

*Commending* the United Nations Protection Force (UNPROFOR) for its continuing action in support of the relief operation in Sarajevo and other parts of Bosnia and Herzegovina,

*Deeply disturbed* by the situation that now prevails in Sarajevo, which has severely complicated UNPROFOR's efforts to fulfil its mandate to ensure the security and functioning of Sarajevo airport and the delivery of humanitarian assistance in Sarajevo and other parts of Bosnia and Herzegovina pursuant to resolutions 743 (1992), 749 (1992), 761 (1992) and 764 (1992) and the reports of the Secretary-General cited therein,

*Dismayed* by the continuation of conditions that impede the delivery of humanitarian supplies to destinations within Bosnia and Herzegovina and the consequent suffering of the people of that country,

*Deeply concerned* by reports of abuses against civilians imprisoned in camps, prisons and detention centres,

*Determined* to establish as soon as possible the necessary conditions for the delivery of humanitarian assistance wherever needed in Bosnia and Herzegovina, in conformity with resolution 764 (1992),

*Acting* under Chapter VII of the Charter of the United Nations,

1. *Reaffirms* its demand that all parties and others concerned in Bosnia and Herzegovina stop the fighting immediately;

2. *Calls upon* States to take nationally or through regional agencies or arrangements all measures necessary to facilitate in coordination with the United Nations the delivery by relevant United Nations humanitarian organizations and others of humanitarian assistance to Sarajevo and wherever needed in other parts of Bosnia and Herzegovina;

3. *Demands* that unimpeded and continuous access to all camps, prisons and detention centres be granted immediately to the International Committee of the Red Cross and other relevant humanitarian organizations and that all detainees therein receive humane treatment, including adequate food, shelter and medical care;

4. *Calls upon* States to report to the Secretary-General on measures they are taking in coordination with the United Nations to carry out this resolution, and *invites* the Secretary-General to keep under continuous review any further measures that may be necessary to ensure unimpeded delivery of humanitarian supplies;

5. *Requests* all States to provide appropriate support for the actions undertaken in pursuance of this resolution;

6. *Demands* that all parties and others concerned take the necessary measures to ensure the safety of United Nations and other personnel engaged in the delivery of humanitarian assistance;

7. *Requests* the Secretary-General to report to the Council on a periodic basis on the implementation of this resolution;

8. *Decides* to remain actively seized of the matter.

*Appendix C*
# Somalia

## CHRONOLOGY

| | |
|---|---|
| 26 June 1960 | British Somaliland becomes independent |
| 1 July 1960 | British Somaliland joined with Somalia, trusteeship territory administered by Italy; becomes independent republic |
| 20 June 1961 | National referendum on provisional constitution joining two territories; boycotted by Somaliland National League (SNL) |
| October 1963 | Border incidents lead to open war in Ogaden |
| November 1963 | Somalia accepts US $11 million in military aid from Soviet Union |
| October 1967 | Somali and Ethiopian heads of state meet in Tanzania agreeing to normalise relations |
| 15 October 1969 | President of Somalia, 'Abd ar-Rashid' Ali Shirmarke, shot by his police guard |
| 1 November 1969 | Supreme Revolutionary Council named, appointing General Mohammed Siyad Barre president |
| February 1972 | Siyad signs military cooperation agreement with Soviet Union granting access to Somali military facilities in exchange for US $60 million in military aid |
| 12 September 1974 | Haile Selassie, emperor of Ethiopia, overthrown |
| March 1975 | Fidel Castro fails in negotiating socialist confederation including Ethiopia, Somalia and South Yemen under Soviet sponsorship |
| April 1977 | Mengistu closes US installations in Ethiopia and Eritrea |
| 26 June 1977 | Territory of Djibouti becomes independent republic |
| July 1977 | Western Somali Liberation Front (WSLF) revolts in Ogaden |
| September 1977 | Ethiopia breaks off diplomatic relations with Somalia |
| 13 November 1977 | Military facilities in Somalia withdrawn from Soviet use and 1974 Treaty of Friendship and Cooperation with Soviet Union renounced |
| December 1977 | Ethiopia executes series of air strikes in northern Somalia |

187

| | |
|---|---|
| February 1978 | Somalia officially enters war in Ogaden |
| early March 1978 | Russian and Cuban counter-offensive forces Somalis to vacate Jijiga |
| 9 March 1978 | In response to requests from United States, Siyad announces withdrawal of Somali forces from Ogaden |
| 9 April 1978 | Abortive military coup |
| 22 August 1980 | Somalia and United States sign ten-year military facilities and security assistance agreement |
| 19 August 1981 | Tripartite Pact between Ethiopia, Libya and South Yemen formed to coordinate destabilisation campaign against Somalia |
| end of June 1982 | 9,000 Ethiopian troops enter Somalia to support Somali Salvation Democratic Front (SSDF), Ethiopia-based Somali dissident force |
| 24 July 1982 | US State Department announces arms airlift into Somalia |
| 18–19 January 1986 | Ethiopian and Somali heads of state meet, agreeing to establish joint commission to normalise relations |
| February 1987 | Fighting between Somalia and Ethiopia breaks out as result of military campaign in northern Somalia launched by Somali National Movement (SNM), founded in London in 1981 |
| April 1988 | Soviet ambassador announces end of large-scale military shipments to Ethiopia when five-year agreement expires in 1991 |
| 3 April 1988 | Peace treaty between Somalia and Ethiopia signed, withdrawing troops from border areas and renouncing support for each other's dissidents |
| May 1988 | SNM begins new offensive in northern Somalia |
| September 1988 | Siyad's military response quashes SNM offensive |
| autumn 1988 | United States freezes aid to Somalia in response to severe repression and human rights abuses |
| January 1989 | United Somalia Congress (USC), anti-Siyad organisation, founded in Rome by Hawiye clan members who left SNM |
| March 1989 | Mutiny among Ogadeni troops occurs in response to demotion of Ogadeni defence minister |
| 29 August 1989 | Siyad agrees to creation of multiparty system and to February 1991 elections |
| September 1989 | Gersony report investigating human rights abuses in Somalia from May 1988 to March 1989 issued, confirming government forces killed thousands of Somalis during period |
| autumn 1989 | Somali Patriot Movement (SPM), anti-Siyad organisation, formed |
| December 1990 | Fighting erupts between forces of USC and Somali military units |
| 6 January 1991 | After being under armed fire for days, United States Embassy evacuated |

| | |
|---|---|
| 24 January 1991 | Siyad agrees to step down, nominating Omar Arteh Ghaleb as president if rebels agree to truce; truce rejected |
| 27 January 1991 | USC declares victory |
| 28 January 1991 | Ali Mahdi Mohammed sworn in as interim president |
| May 1991 | SNM declares Republic of Somaliland along administrative borders of former British Somaliland |
| July 1991 | USC's call for conference of unity rejected by SPM and SNM |
| 16 November–31 December 1991 | 4,000 killed and 20,000 wounded in chaotic fighting in Mogadishu between Abgal clan supporting interim president Ali Mahdi and Habar Gadir supporters of General Aideed |
| 3–5 January 1992 | UN Assistant Secretary-General James O. C. Jonah visits Mogadishu, failing in efforts to end fighting |
| 17 January 1992 | Aideed seizes control of Mogadishu's port from Achamou, the interim president's militia |
| 23 January 1992 | Resolution 733 urges all Somali parties to agree to ceasefire, imposes embargo on all weapons deliveries and requests that Secretary-General takes action to increase humanitarian assistance |
| 14 February 1992 | Two sides in civil war meet in New York under aegis of UN, OAU, Arab League and ICO, agreeing to end hostilities |
| 3 March 1992 | Jonah gets two sides to sign ceasefire document, yet it fails to end disruption to humanitarian aid deliveries |
| 17 March 1992 | Resolution 746 establishes UN technical mission to examine requirements for future peacekeeping operation and mechanisms for humanitarian aid to get through unhindered |
| 24 April 1992 | Resolution 751 establishes United Nations Operation in Somalia (UNOSOM) |
| 9 May 1992 | Mohammed Sahnoun, newly appointed UN special representative in Somalia, arrives; first permanent UN presence in Somalia since fall of Siyad Barre in 1991 |
| 6 June 1992 | Representatives of 11 Somali factions reach accord in Bahr Dar, Ethiopia, on ceasefire to be implemented with UN help |
| 5 July 1992 | First three UNOSOM military observers arrive in Somalia |
| 23 July 1992 | Remaining 47 UNOSOM military observers arrive in Somalia |
| 27 July 1992 | Resolution 767 adopts Boutros-Ghali's plan to create four operational zones in Somalia as part of UNOSOM, to organise air bridge for food aid, and send technical mission to examine possibility of monitoring ceasefire |
| 28 August 1992 | Resolution 775 authorises increase in strength of |

|                        | UNOSOM and invites Secretary-General to establish four-zone headquarters |
|------------------------|--------------------------------------------------------------------------|
| 5 September 1992       | UK foreign secretary Douglas Hurd, Danish foreign minister Uffe Ellemann-Jensen and Portugese state secretary Dura Barrosso visit Mogadishu, criticising international effort and pledging more EC humanitarian aid |
| 14–15 September 1992   | First group of 500 Pakistani soldiers arrive to guard aid supplies at Mogadishu airport |
| 16 September 1992      | US goverment orders four navy warships from Gulf to coast of Somalia |
| October 1992           | Mohammad Sahnoun resigns, bitterly critical of UN operations |
| 10 November 1992       | UN troops secure Mogadishu airport by agreement with clan controlling it |
| 22 November 1992       | Mogadishu airport closed; gunmen demand payment for relief aircraft to land |
| 23 November 1992       | In Kismayu, UN relief plane is boarded and robbed by gunmen |
| 27 November 1992       | US administration offers 30,000 troops to proposed UN military intervention force to protect food aid; US State Department announces offer to airlift 3,000 UN troops once UN approval for their deployment granted |
| 3 December 1992        | Resolution 794 establishes Unified Task Force (UNITAF) |
| 4 December 1992        | President Bush orders 28,000 US troops to Somalia in operation code-named Restore Hope, directed by Robert Oakley, former US ambassador to Somalia; France offers to send 1,500–2,000 troops to Somalia |
| 9 December 1992        | First US troops land on beaches of Mogadishu |
| 11 December 1992       | Two main Somali factions hold peace talks, agreeing to ceasefire and to remove weapons from Mogadishu |
| 17 December 1992       | Despite perceived constitutional ban, German chancellor Kohl offers to send 1,500 troops to Somalia |
| 18 December 1992       | Japan offers US $100m to UN trust fund to pay for relief effort |
| 27 December 1992       | In further talks brokered by US representative Robert Oakley, a reconcilation agreement between Aideed and Ali Mahdi announced |
| 28 December 1992       | Aideed and Ali Mahdi lead peace march across 'green line', which divides Mogadishu between their forces |
| 2 January 1993         | UN-sponsored peace talks, involving 14 Somali factions, begin in Addis Ababa |
| 3 January 1993         | Secretary-General Boutros-Ghali on visit to Mogadishu jeered by Aideed supporters and forced to take refuge in US Embassy |
| 13 January 1993        | First foreign military serviceman, a United States Marine, shot dead |
| 15 January 1993        | Agreement to immediate ceasefire and disarming of all |

|                      | factions reached in UN-sponsored peace talks; national reconciliation conference scheduled for 15 March in Addis Ababa |
|----------------------|---|
| 25 January 1993 | Forces loyal to former president Siyad advance on Kismayu with Belgian and US troops intervening |
| 23–25 February 1993 | Aideed supporters barricade streets in Mogadishu with burning tyres, fight with troops and attack US and French Embassies |
| 24 February 1993 | After fighting between General Aideed's Somali National Alliance (SNA) forces and pro-Morgan forces in Kismayu, Morgan's forces yield to US representative Robert Oakley's ultimatum and leave Kismayu |
| 5 March 1993 | Boutros-Ghali proposes 1 May as date for handover of operations to a 28,000-member UN force |
| 9 March 1993 | Retired US admiral Jonathan Howe replaces Ismat Kittani as Secretary-General's special representative in Somalia, to oversee transition to UNOSOM II |
| 15 March 1993 | National reconciliation conference held in Addis Ababa |
| 17 March 1993 | Aideed leaves peace talks in Addis Ababa, accusing international force of refusing to respond to fighting in Kismayu |
| 18 March 1993 | 500 US Marines arrive in Kismayu to restore order |
| 19 March 1993 | Aideed returns to peace talks |
| 26 March 1993 | Resolution 814 establishes UNOSOM II |
| 27 March 1993 | 1,300 more US Marines arrive in Kismayu after renewed fighting; compromise agreement reached, to form Transnational Council to be supreme authority, leading Somalia into elections within two years |
| 4 May 1993 | United States-led multinational Unified Task Force, UNITAF, formally hands over control to UN Operation in Somalia, UNOSOM II |
| 5 May 1993 | Mohamad Haji Ibrahim Egal elected president of Somaliland |
| 5 June 1993 | Over 20 Pakistani soldiers killed in fighting between UN forces and SNA |
| 6 June 1993 | Resolution 837 condemns 'unprovoked attack' of 5 June on UN forces and calls for arrest and punishment of those responsible |
| 12–16 June 1993 | US aircraft strike SNA targets in southern Mogadishu; UN ground troops follow after air strikes |
| 13 June 1993 | Pakistani troops fire on demonstrators protesting air strikes, killing at least 20, including women and children |
| 17 June 1993 | Security Council officially issues a warrant for arrest of Aideed |
| 2 July 1993 | 3 Italian paratroopers killed in Mogadishu |

| | |
|---|---|
| 5 July 1993 | Italian government demands more say in UNOSOM operations |
| 13 July 1993 | US helicopter gunship attack kills 54 Somalis, including Sheik Mohammed Iman; in response, crowds beat to death four foreign journalists |
| 12 August 1993 | Italian defence minister Fabbri announces withdrawal of Italian forces from UN operations in Mogadishu and their deployment elsewhere in Somalia |
| 27 August 1993 | US troops mistakenly capture UN and French aid workers in a raid in Mogadishu |
| 6 September 1993 | Italy announces delay in withdrawal of troops |
| 9 September 1993 | Crowds turn on UN troops engaged in fighting with Somali militia men, prompting US helicopter to fire on civilians, killing around 200 |
| 22 September 1993 | Resolution 865 states that it is important for UNOSOM II to be concluded by March 1995, handing over responsibility to an elected government |
| 3 October 1993 | Gun battle in Mogadishu results in deaths of 300 Somalis and 18 US soldiers, and capture of US helicopter pilot Michael Durant and Nigerian soldier Umar Shantali |
| October 1993 | Clinton announces removal of all US troops from Somalia by 31 March 1994 and sends Oakley back to negotiate |
| 9 October 1993 | Aideed announces unilateral ceasefire |
| 10–13 October 1993 | Robert Oakley meets with advisors of Aideed to secure release of Durant and Shantali |
| 17 October 1993 | Germany announces withdrawal of troops from Somalia by April 1994; Pakistan announces it will send another 5,000 troops to Somalia |
| 16 November 1993 | Resolution 885 suspends warrant of arrest Aideed and establishes Commission of Inquiry into attacks against UNOSOM II forces |
| 2 December 1993 | Aideed arrives in Addis Ababa to attend UN-sponsored peace conference |
| 4 February 1994 | Resolution 897 places new emphasis on peacemaking and reconstruction, returning to less reactive role |
| 11 February 1994 | Heavy fighting breaks out in Kismayu |
| 10 March 1994 | Howe ends tour of duty; Lansana Kouyate of Guinea takes over as acting UN special representative in Somalia |
| 24 March 1994 | Aideed and Ali Mahdi sign peace agreement repudiating violence for settling disputes |
| 25 March 1994 | Last units of US troops leave Somalia |
| 14 August 1994 | Boutros-Ghali reports troop reduction proposals to reduce UNOSOM forces to 17,000 and then to 15,000 |
| November 1994 | Resolution 954 extends UNOSOM mandate for final period until 31 March 1995 |

March 1995          Remaining UNOSOM forces finally withdraw under
                    protection of US Marines at beginning of March
                    1995

## SELECTED RESOLUTIONS OF THE UN SECURITY COUNCIL AND REPORT OF THE SECRETARY-GENERAL ON THE UN OPERATIONS IN SOMALIA

SC Resolution 733, 23 January 1992; requests Secretary-General to increase humanitarian aid to Somalia and calls for end to conflict; imposes arms embargo

SC Resolution 746, 17 March 1992; requests Secretary-General to pursue humanitarian effort in Somalia, and asks parties to respect security of UN technical team

SC Resolution 751, 24 April 1992; establishes UN Operation in Somalia (UNOSOM) and a committee to monitor arms embargo (for text, see pp. 195–7 in this appendix)

SC Resolution 767, 27 July 1992; requests Secretary-General to increase humanitarian assistance in Somalia, and calls on all parties to cooperate

SC Resolution 775, 28 August 1992; authorises further increase in UNOSOM strength as recommended by Secretary-General

SC Resolution 794, 3 December 1992; endorses Secretary-General's recommendation to take action under Chapter VII to ensure delivery of aid in Somalia (for text, see pp. 198–201 in this appendix)

SC Resolution 814, 26 March 1993; requests Secretary-General to ensure delivery of aid to Somalia, increases force size, and approves an expanded UNOSOM II with an extended mandate to 31 October 1993 (for text, see pp. 202–7 in this appendix)

SC Resolution 837, 6 June 1993; condemns attacks of 5 June 1993 on Pakistani soldiers serving with UNOSOM II (for text, see pp. 211–21 in this appendix)

S/26022 Report of the Secretary-General on the Implementation of Security Council Resolution 837, 1 July 1993; reports on action taken on those responsible, calls for the arrest of General Mohamed Aideed, regrets the loss of UN soldiers from Pakistan (for text, see pp. 000–0 in this appendix)

SC Resolution 865, 22 September 1993; condemns attacks on UNOSOM II personnel

SC Resolution 878, 29 October 1993; extends UNOSOM II to 18 November 1993

SC Resolution 885, 16 November 1993; establishes Commission of Inquiry to investigate armed attacks on UNOSOM II personnel

SC Resolution 886, 18 November 1993; extends UNOSOM II to 31 May 1994

SC Resolution 897, 4 February 1994; condemns continued violence in Somalia, especially against UN personnel, authorises reduction in forces to a level of 22,000

SC Resolution 923, 31 May 1994; welcomes Somali intentions to restore order and to convene a national reconciliation conference with the aim of appointing a prime minister, condemns continued violence, renews UNOSOM II until 30 September 1994

SC Resolution 946, 30 September 1994; extends mandate of UNOSOM II to 31 October 1994, prepares arrangements for possible withdrawal of UNOSOM II within a specified time frame

SC Resolution 954, 4 November 1994; extends the mandate of UNOSOM II for a final period until 31 March 1995 (for text, see pp. 222–5 in this appendix)

# RESOLUTION 751 (1992)

## ADOPTED BY THE SECURITY COUNCIL AT ITS 3069TH MEETING, ON 24 APRIL 1992

The Security Council,

*Considering* the request by Somalia for the Security Council to consider the situation in Somalia (S/23445),

*Reaffirming* its resolutions 733 (1992) of 23 January 1992 and 746 (1992) of 17 March 1992,

*Having considered* the report of the Secretary-General on the situation in Somalia (S/23829 and Add. 1 and Add. 2),

*Taking note* of the signing of the cease-fire agreements in Mogadishu on 3 March 1992, including agreements for the implementation of measures aimed at stabilizing the cease-fire through a United Nations monitoring mission,

*Taking note also* of the signing of letters of agreement in Mogadishu, Hargeisa and Kismayu on the mechanism for monitoring the cease-fire and arrangements for the equitable and effective distribution of humanitarian assistance in and around Mogadishu,

*Deeply disturbed* by the magnitude of the human suffering caused by the conflict and concerned that the continuation of the situation in Somalia constitutes a threat to international peace and security,

*Cognizant* of the importance of cooperation between the United Nations and regional organizations in the context of Chapter VIII of the Charter of the United Nations,

*Underlining* the importance which it attaches to the international, regional and non-governmental organizations, including the International Committee of the Red Cross, continuing to provide humanitarian and other relief assistance to the people of Somalia under difficult circumstances,

*Expressing* its appreciation to the regional organizations, including the Organization of African Unity, the League of Arab States and the Organization of the Islamic Conference, for their cooperation with the United Nations in the effort to resolve the Somali problem,

1. *Takes note with appreciation* of the report of the Secretary-General of 21 April 1992 (S/23829 and Add. 1 and Add. 2);

2. *Decides* to establish under its authority, and in support of the Secretary-General in accordance with paragraph 7 below, a United Nations Operation in Somalia (UNOSOM);

3. *Requests* the Secretary-General immediately to deploy a unit of 50 United Nations Observers to monitor the cease-fire in Mogadishu in accordance with paragraphs 24 to 26 of the Secretary-General's report (S/23829);

4. *Agrees*, in principle, also to establish under the overall direction of the Secretary-General's Special Representative a United Nations security force to be deployed as soon as possible to perform the functions described in paragraphs 27–29 of the Secretary-General's report (S/23829);

5. *Further requests* the Secretary-General to continue his consultations with the parties in Mogadishu regarding the proposed United Nations security force and, in light of those consultations, to submit his further recommendations to the Security Council for its decision as soon as possible;

6. *Welcomes* the intention expressed by the Secretary-General in paragraph 64 of his report (S/23829) to appoint a Special Representative for Somalia to provide overall direction of United Nations activities in Somalia and to assist him in his endeavours to reach a peaceful resolution of the conflict in Somalia;

7. *Requests* the Secretary-General as part of his continuing mission in Somalia to facilitate an immediate and effective cessation of hostilities and the maintenance of a cease-fire throughout the country in order to promote the process of reconciliation and political settlement in Somalia and to provide urgent humanitarian assistance;

8. *Welcomes* the cooperation between the United Nations and the League of Arab States, the Organization of African Unity and the Organization of the Islamic Conference in resolving the problem in Somalia;

9. *Calls upon* all parties, movements and factions in Somalia immediately to cease hostilities and to maintain a cease-fire throughout the country in order to promote the process of reconciliation and political settlement in Somalia;

10. *Requests* the Secretary-General to continue as a matter of priority his consultations with all Somali parties, movements and factions towards the convening of a conference on national reconciliation and unity in Somalia in close cooperation with the League of Arab States, the Organization of African Unity and the Organization of the Islamic Conference;

11. *Decides* to establish, in accordance with rule 28 of the provisional rules of procedure of the Security Council, a Committee of the Security Council consisting of all the members of the Council, to undertake the following tasks and to report on its work to the Council with its observations and recommendations:

(a) to seek from all States information regarding the action taken by them concerning the effective implementation of the embargo imposed by paragraph 5 of resolution 733 (1992);

(b) to consider any information brought to its attention by States concerning violations of the embargo, and in that context to make recommendations to the Council on ways of increasing the effectiveness of the embargo;

(c) to recommend appropriate measures in response to violations of the general and complete embargo on all deliveries of weapons and military equipment to Somalia and provide information on a regular basis to the Secretary-General for general distribution to Member States;

12. *Notes with appreciation* the ongoing efforts of the United Nations, its specialized agencies and humanitarian organizations to ensure delivery of humanitarian assistance to Somalia, particularly to Mogadishu;

13. *Calls upon* the international community to support, with financial and other resources, the implementation of the 90-day Plan of Action for Emergency Humanitarian Assistance to Somalia;

14. *Urges* all parties concerning in Somalia to facilitate the efforts of the United Nations, its specialized agencies and humanitarian organizations to provide urgent humanitarian assistance to the affected population in Somalia and reiterates its call for the full respect of the security and safety of the personnel of the humanitarian organizations and the guarantee of their complete freedom of movement in and around Mogadishu and other parts of Somalia;

15. *Calls upon* all Somali parties, movements and factions to cooperate fully with the Secretary-General in the implementation of this resolution;

16. *Decides* to remain seized of the matter until a peaceful solution is achieved.

# RESOLUTION 794 (1992)

## ADOPTED BY THE SECURITY COUNCIL AT ITS 3145TH MEETING, ON 3 DECEMBER 1992

The Security Council,

*Reaffirming* its resolutions 733 (1992) of 23 January 1992, 746 (1992) of 17 March 1992, 751 (1992) of 24 April 1992, 767 (1992) of 27 July 1992 and 775 (1992) of 28 August 1992,

*Recognizing* the unique character of the present situation in Somalia and mindful of its deteriorating, complex and extraordinary nature, requiring an immediate and exceptional response,

*Determining* that the magnitude of the human tragedy caused by the conflict in Somalia, further exacerbated by the obstacles being created to the distribution of humanitarian assistance, constitutes a threat to international peace and security,

*Gravely alarmed* by the deterioration of the humanitarian situation in Somalia and *underlining* the urgent need for the quick delivery of humanitarian assistance in the whole country,

*Noting* the efforts of the League of Arab States, the Organization of African Unity, and in particular the proposal made by its Chairman at the forty-seventh regular session of the General Assembly for the organization of an international conference in Somalia, and the Organization of Islamic Conference and other regional agencies and arrangements to promote reconciliation and political settlement in Somalia and to address the humanitarian needs of the people of that country,

*Commending* the ongoing efforts of the United Nations, its specialized agencies and humanitarian organizations and of non-governmental organizations and of States to ensure delivery of humanitarian assistance in Somalia,

*Responding to* the urgent calls from Somalia for the international community to take measures to ensure the delivery of humanitarian assistance in Somalia,

*Expressing grave alarm* at continuing reports of widespread violations of international humanitarian law occurring in Somalia, including reports of violence and threats of violence against personnel participating lawfully in impartial humanitarian relief activities; deliberate attacks on non-combatants, relief consignments and vehicles, and medical and relief facilities; and impeding the delivery of food and medical supplies essential for the survival of the civilian population,

*Dismayed* by the continuation of conditions that impede the delivery of humanitarian supplies to destinations within Somalia, and in particular reports of looting of relief supplies destined for starving people, attacks on aircraft and ships bringing in humanitarian relief supplies, and attacks on the Pakistani UNOSOM contingent in Mogadishu,

*Taking note* with appreciation of the letters of the Secretary-General of 24 November 1992 (S/24859) and of 29 November 1992 (S/24868),

*Sharing* the Secretary-General's assessment that the situation in Somalia is intolerable and that it has become necessary to review the basic premises and principles of the United Nations effort in Somalia, and that UNOSOM's existing course would not in present circumstances be an adequate response to the tragedy in Somalia,

*Determined* to establish as soon as possible the necessary conditions for the delivery of humanitarian assistance wherever needed in Somalia, in conformity with resolutions 751 (1992) and 767 (1992),

*Noting* the offer by Member States aimed at establishing a secure environment for humanitarian relief operations in Somalia as soon as possible,

*Determined further* to restore peace, stability and law and order with a view to facilitating the process of a political settlement under the auspices of the United Nations, aimed at national reconciliation in Somalia, and encouraging the Secretary-General and his Special Representative to continue and intensify their work at the national and regional levels to promote these objectives,

*Recognizing* that the people of Somalia bear ultimate responsibility for national reconciliation and the reconstruction of their own country,

1. *Reaffirms* its demand that all parties, movements and factions in Somalia immediately cease hostilities, maintain a cease-fire throughout the country, and cooperate with the Special Representative of the Secretary-General as well as with the military forces to be established pursuant to the authorization given in paragraph 10 below in order to promote the process of relief distribution, reconciliation and political settlement in Somalia;

2. *Demands* that all parties, movements and factions in Somalia take all measures necessary to facilitate the efforts of the United Nations, its specialized agencies and humanitarian organizations to provide urgent humanitarian assistance to the affected population in Somalia;

3. *Also demands* that all parties, movements and factions in Somalia take all measures necessary to ensure the safety of United Nations and all other personnel engaged in the delivery of humanitarian assistance, including the military forces to be established pursuant to the authorization given in paragraph 10 below;

4. *Further demands* that all parties, movements and factions in Somalia immediately cease and desist from all breaches of international humanitarian law including from actions such as those described above;

5. *Strongly condemns* all violations of international humanitarian law occurring in Somalia, including in particular the deliberate impeding of the delivery of food and medical supplies essential for the survival of the civilian population, and affirms that those who commit or order the commission of such acts will be held individually responsible in respect of such acts;

6. *Decides* that the operations and the further deployment of the 3,500 personnel of the United Nations Operation in Somalia (UNOSOM) authorized by paragraph 3 of resolution 775 (1992) should proceed at the discretion of the Secretary-General in the light of his assessment of conditions on the ground; and requests him to keep the Council informed and to make such recommendations as may be appropriate for the fulfilment of its mandate where conditions permit;

7. *Endorses* the recommendation by the Secretary-General in his letter of 29 November 1992 (S/24868) that action under Chapter VII of the Charter of the United Nations should be taken in order to establish a secure environment for humanitarian relief operations in Somalia as soon as possible;

8. *Welcomes* the offer by a Member State described in the Secretary-General's letter to the Council of 29 November 1992 (S/24868) concerning the establishment of an operation to create such a secure environment;

9. *Welcomes also* offers by other Member States to participate in that operation;

10. Acting under Chapter VII of the Charter of the United Nations, *authorizes* the Secretary-General and Member States cooperating to implement the offer referred to in paragraph 8 above to use all necessary means to establish as soon as possible a secure environment for humanitarian relief operations in Somalia;

11. *Calls on* all Member States which are in a position to do so to provide military forces and to make additional contributions, in cash or in kind, in accordance with paragraph 10 above and requests the Secretary-General to establish a fund through which the contributions, where appropriate, could be channelled to the States or operations concerned;

12. *Authorizes* the Secretary-General and the Member States concerned to make the necessary arrangements for the unified command and control of the forces involved, which will reflect the offer referred to in paragraph 8 above;

13. *Requests* the Secretary-General and the Member States acting under paragraph 10 above to establish appropriate mechanisms for coordination between the United Nations and their military forces;

14. *Decides* to appoint an ad hoc commission composed of members of the Security Council to report to the Council on the implementation of this resolution;

15. *Invites* the Secretary-General to attach a small UNOSOM liaison staff to the Field Headquarters of the unified command;

16. Acting under Chapters VII and VIII of the Charter, *calls upon* States, nationally or through regional agencies or arrangements, to use such measures as may be necessary to ensure strict implementation of paragraph 5 of the resolution 733 (1992);

17. *Requests* all States, in particular those in the region, to provide appropriate support for the actions undertaken by States, nationally or through regional agencies or arrangements, pursuant to this and other relevant resolutions;

18. *Requests* the Secretary-General and, as appropriate, the States concerned to report to the Council on a regular basis, the first such report to be made no later than fifteen days after the adoption of this resolution, on the implementation of this resolution and the attainment of the objective of establishing a secure environment so as to enable the Council to make the necessary decision for a prompt transition to continued peace-keeping operations;

19. *Requests* the Secretary-General to submit a plan to the Council initially within fifteen days after the adoption of this resolution to ensure that UNOSOM will be able to fulfil its mandate upon the withdrawal of the unified command;

20. *Invites* the Secretary-General and his Special Representative to continue their efforts to achieve a political settlement in Somalia;

21. *Decides* to remain actively seized of the matter.

## RESOLUTION 814 (1993)

## ADOPTED BY THE SECURITY COUNCIL AT ITS 3188TH MEETING, ON 26 MARCH 1993

The Security Council,

*Reaffirming* its resolutions 733 (1992) of 23 January 1992, 746 (1992) of 17 March 1992, 751 (1992) of 24 April 1992, 767 (1992) of 27 July 1992, 775 (1992) of 28 August 1992 and 794 (1992) of 3 December 1992,

*Bearing in mind* General Assembly resolution 47/167 of 18 December 1992,

*Commending* the efforts of Member States acting pursuant to resolution 794 (1992) to establish a secure environment for humanitarian relief operations in Somalia,

*Acknowledging* the need for a prompt, smooth and phased transition from the Unified Task Force (UNITAF) to the expanded United Nations Operation in Somalia (UNOSOM II),

*Regretting* the continuing incidents of violence in Somalia and the threat they pose to the reconciliation process,

*Deploring* the acts of violence against persons engaging in humanitarian efforts on behalf of the United Nations, States, and non-governmental organizations,

*Noting with deep regret and concern* the continuing reports of widespread violations of international humanitarian law and the general absence of the rule of law in Somalia,

*Recognizing* that the people of Somalia bear the ultimate responsibility for national reconciliation and reconstruction of their own country,

*Acknowledging* the fundamental importance of a comprehensive and effective programme for disarming Somali parties, including movements and factions,

*Noting* the need for continued humanitarian relief assistance and for the rehabilitation of Somalia's political institutions and economy,

*Concerned* that the crippling famine and drought in Somalia, compounded by the civil strife, have caused massive destruction to the means of production and the natural and human resources of that country,

*Expressing* its appreciation to the Organization of African Unity, the League of Arab States, the Organization of the Islamic Conference and the Non-Aligned Movement for their cooperation with, and support of, the efforts of the United Nations in Somalia,

*Further expressing* its appreciation to all Member States which have made contributions to the Fund established pursuant to paragraph 11 of resolution 794 (1992) and to all those who have provided humanitarian assistance to Somalia,

*Commending* the efforts, in difficult circumstances, of the initial United Nations Operation in Somalia (UNOSOM) established pursuant to resolution 751 (1992),

*Expressing* its appreciation for the invaluable assistance the neighbouring countries have been providing to the international community in its efforts to restore peace and security in Somalia and to host large numbers of refugees displaced by the conflict and taking note of the difficulties caused to them due to the presence of refugees in their territories,

*Convinced* that the restoration of law and order throughout Somalia would contribute to humanitarian relief operations, reconciliation and political settlement, as well as to the rehabilitation of Somalia's political institutions and economy,

*Convinced also* of the need for broad-based consultations and deliberations to achieve reconciliation, agreement on the setting up of transitional government institutions and consensus on basic principles and steps leading to the establishment of representative democratic institutions,

*Recognizing* that the re-establishment of local and regional administrative institutions is essential to the restoration of domestic tranquillity,

*Encouraging* the Secretary-General and his Special Representative to continue and intensify their work at the national, regional and local levels, including and encouraging broad participation by all sectors of Somali society, to promote the process of political settlement and national reconciliation and to assist the people of Somalia in rehabilitating their political institutions and economy,

*Expressing* its readiness to assist the people of Somalia, as appropriate, on a local, regional or national level, to participate in free and fair elections, with a view towards achieving and implementing a political settlement,

*Welcoming* the progress made at the United Nations-sponsored Informal Preparatory Meeting on Somali Political Reconciliation in Addis Ababa from 4 to 15 January 1993, in particular the conclusion at that meeting of three agreements by the Somali parties, including movements and factions, and welcoming also any progress made at the Conference on National Reconciliation which began in Addis Ababa on 15 March 1993,

*Emphasizing* the need for the Somali people, including movements and factions, to show the political will to achieve security, reconciliation and peace,

*Noting* the reports of States concerned of 17 December 1992 (S/24976) and 19 January 1993 (S/25126) and of the Secretary-General of 19 December 1992

(S/24992) and 26 January 1993 (S/25168) on the implementation of resolution 794 (1992),

*Having examined* the report of the Secretary-General of 3 March 1993 (S/25354 and Add. 1 and Add. 2),

*Welcoming* the intention of the Secretary-General to seek maximum economy and efficiency and to keep the size of the United Nations presence, both military and civilian, to the minimum necessary to fulfil its mandate,

*Determining* that the situation in Somalia continues to threaten peace and security in the region,

A

1. *Approves* the report of the Secretary-General of 3 March 1993;

2. *Expresses* its appreciation to the Secretary-General for convening the Conference on National Reconciliation for Somalia in accordance with the agreements reached during the Informal Preparatory Meeting on Somali Political Reconciliation in Addis Ababa in January 1993 and for the progress achieved towards political reconciliation in Somalia, and also for his efforts to ensure that, as appropriate, Somalis, including movements, factions, community leaders, women, professionals, intellectuals, elders and other representative groups are suitably represented at such conferences;

3. *Welcomes* the convening of the Third United Nations Coordination Meeting for Humanitarian Assistance for Somalia in Addis Ababa from 11 to 13 March 1993 and the willingness expressed by Governments through this process to contribute to relief and rehabilitation efforts in Somalia, where and when possible;

4. *Requests* the Secretary-General, through his Special Representative, and with assistance, as appropriate, from all relevant United Nations entities, offices and specialized agencies, to provide humanitarian and other assistance to the people of Somalia in rehabilitating their political institutions and economy and promoting political settlement and national reconciliation, in accordance with the recommendations contained in his report of 3 March 1993, including in particular:

(a) To assist in the provision of relief and in the economic rehabilitation of Somalia, based on an assessment of clear, prioritized needs, and taking into account, as appropriate, the 1993 Relief and Rehabilitation Programme for Somalia prepared by the United Nations Department of Humanitarian Affairs:

(b) To assist in the repatriation of refugees and displaced persons within Somalia;

(c) To assist the people of Somalia to promote and advance political reconciliation, through broad participation by all sectors of Somali society, and the re-establishment of national and regional institutions and civil administration in the entire country;

(d) To assist in the re-establishment of Somali police, as appropriate at the local, regional or national level, to assist in the restoration and maintenance of peace, stability and law and order, including in the investigation and facilitating the prosecution of serious violations of international humanitarian law;

(e) To assist the people of Somalia in the development of a coherent and integrated programme for the removal of mines throughout Somalia;

(f) To develop appropriate public information activities in support of the United Nations activities in Somalia;

(g) To create conditions under which Somali civil society may have a role, at every level, in the process of political reconciliation and in the formulation and realization of rehabilitation and reconstruction programmes;

B

*Acting* under Chapter VII of the Charter of the United Nations,

5. *Decides* to expand the size of the UNOSOM force and its mandate in accordance with the recommendations contained in paragraphs 56–88 of the report of the Secretary-General of 3 March 1992, and the provisions of this resolution;

6. *Authorizes* the mandate for the expanded UNOSOM (UNOSOM II) for an initial period through 31 October 1993, unless previously renewed by the Security Council;

7. *Emphasizes* the crucial importance of disarmament and the urgent need to build on the efforts of UNITAF in accordance with paragraphs 56–69 of the report of the Secretary-General of 3 March 1993;

8. *Demands* that all Somali parties, including movements and factions, comply fully with the commitments they have undertaken in the agreements they concluded at the Informal Preparatory Meeting on Somali Political Reconciliation in Addis Ababa, and in particular with their Agreement on Implementing the Cease-fire and on Modalities of Disarmament (S/25168, annex III);

9. *Further demands* that all Somali parties, including movements and factions, take all measures to ensure the safety of the personnel of the United Nations and its agencies as well as the staff of the International Committee of the Red Cross (ICRC), intergovernmental organizations and non-governmental organizations engaged in providing humanitarian and other assistance to the people of Somalia in rehabilitating their political institutions and economy and promoting political settlement and national reconciliation;

10. *Requests* the Secretary-General to support from within Somalia the implementation of the arms embargo established by resolution 733 (1992), utilizing as available and appropriate the UNOSOM II forces authorized by this resolution, and to report on this subject, with any recommendations regarding more effective measures if necessary, to the Security Council;

11. *Calls upon* all States, in particular neighbouring States, to cooperate in the implementation of the arms embargo established by resolution 733 (1992);

12. *Requests* the Secretary-General to provide security, as appropriate, to assist in the repatriation of refugees and the assisted resettlement of displaced persons, utilizing UNOSOM II forces, paying particular attention to those areas where major instability continues to threaten peace and security in the region;

13. *Reiterates its demand* that all Somali parties, including movements and factions, immediately cease and desist from all breaches of international humanitarian law and reaffirms that those responsible for such acts be held individually accountable;

14. *Requests* the Secretary-General, through his Special Representative, to direct the Force Commander of UNOSOM II to assume responsibility for the consolidation, expansion and maintenance of a secure environment throughout Somalia, taking account of the particular circumstances in each locality, on an expedited basis in accordance with the recommendations contained in his report of 3 March 1993, and in this regard to organize a prompt, smooth and phased transition from UNITAF to UNOSOM II;

15. *Requests* the Secretary-General to maintain the fund established pursuant to resolution 794 (1992) for the additional purpose of receiving contributions for maintenance of UNOSOM II forces following the departure of UNITAF forces and for the establishment of Somali police, and calls on Member States to make contributions to this fund, in addition to their assessed contributions;

16. *Expresses appreciation* to the United Nations agencies, intergovernmental and non-governmental organizations and the ICRC for their contributions and assistance and requests the Secretary-General to ask them to continue to extend financial, material and technical support to the Somali people in all regions of the country;

17. *Requests* the Secretary-General to seek, as appropriate, pledges and contributions from States and others to assist in financing the rehabilitation of the political institutions and economy of Somalia;

18. *Requests* the Secretary-General to keep the Security Council fully informed on action taken to implement the present resolution, in particular to submit as soon as possible a report to the Council containing recommendations for establishment of Somali police forces and thereafter to report no later than every ninety days on the progress achieved in accomplishing the objectives set out in the present resolution;

19. *Decides* to conduct a formal review of the progress towards accomplishing the purposes of the present resolution no later than 31 October 1993;

20. *Decides* to remain actively seized of the matter.

## RESOLUTION 837 (1993)

### ADOPTED BY THE SECURITY COUNCIL AT ITS 3229TH MEETING, ON 6 JUNE 1993

The Security Council,

*Reaffirming* its resolutions 733 (1992) of 23 January 1992, 746 (1992) of 17 March 1992, 751 (1992) of 24 April 1992, 767 (1992) of 27 July 1992, 775 (1992) of 28 August 1992, 794 (1992) of 3 December 1992 and 814 (1993) of 26 March 1993,

*Bearing in mind* General Assembly resolution 47/167 of 18 December 1992,

*Gravely alarmed* at the premeditated armed attacks launched by forces apparently belonging to the United Somali Congress (USC/SNA) against the personnel of the United Nations Operation in Somalia (UNOSOM II) on 5 June 1993,

*Strongly condemning* such actions, which directly undermine international efforts aimed at the restoration of peace and normalcy in Somalia,

*Expressing* outrage at the loss of life as a result of these criminal attacks,

*Reaffirming* its commitment to assist the people of Somalia in re-establishing conditions of normal life,

*Stressing* that the international community is involved in Somalia in order to help the people of Somalia who have suffered untold miseries due to years of civil strife in that country,

*Acknowledging* the fundamental importance of completing the comprehensive and effective programme for disarming all Somali parties, including movements and factions,

*Convinced* that the restoration of law and order throughout Somalia would contribute to humanitarian relief operations, reconciliation and political settlement, as well as to the rehabilitation of Somalia's political institutions and economy,

*Condemning strongly* the use of radio broadcasts, in particular by the USC/SNA, to incite attacks against United Nations personnel,

*Recalling* the statement made by its President on 31 March 1993 (S/25493) concerning the safety of United Nations forces and personnel deployed in conditions of strife and committed to consider promptly measures appropriate to the particular circumstances to ensure that persons responsible for attacks and other acts of violence against United Nations forces and personnel are held to account for their actions,

*Taking note* of the information provided to the Council by the Secretary-General on 6 June 1993,

*Determining* that the situation in Somalia continues to threaten peace and security in the region,

*Acting* under Chapter VII of the Charter of the United Nations,

1. *Strongly condemns* the unprovoked armed attacks against the personnel of UNOSOM II on 5 June 1993, which appear to have been part of a calculated and premeditated series of cease-fire violations to prevent by intimidation UNOSOM II from carrying out its mandate as provided for in resolution 814 (1993);

2. *Expresses* its condolences to the Government and people of Pakistan and the families of the UNOSOM II personnel who have lost their lives;

3. *Re-emphasizes* the crucial importance of the early implementation of the disarmament of all Somali parties, including movements and factions, in accordance with paragraphs 56–69 of the report of the Secretary-General of 3 March 1993, and of neutralizing radio broadcasting systems that contribute to the violence and attacks directed against UNOSOM II;

4. *Demands once again* that all Somali parties, including movements and factions, comply fully with the commitments they have undertaken in the agreements they concluded at the informal Preparatory Meeting on Somali Political Reconciliation in Addis Ababa, and in particular with their Agreement on Implementing the Cease-Fire and on Modalities of Disarmament (S/25168, Annex III);

5. *Reaffirms* that the Secretary-General is authorized under resolution 814 (1993) to take all necessary measures against all those responsible for the armed attacks referred to in paragraph 1 above, including against those responsible for publicly inciting such attacks, to establish the effective authority of UNOSOM II throughout Somalia, including to secure the investigation of their actions and their arrest and detention for prosecution, trial and punishment;

6. *Requests* the Secretary-General urgently to enquire into the incident, with particular emphasis on the role of those factional leaders involved;

7. *Encourages* the rapid and accelerated deployment of all UNOSOM II contingents to meet the full requirements of 28,000 men, all ranks, as well as equipment, as indicated in the Secretary-General's report of 3 March 1993 (S/25354);

8. *Urges* Member States to contribute, on an emergency basis, military support and transportation, including armoured personnel carriers, tanks and attack helicopters, to provide UNOSOM II the capability appropriately to confront

and deter armed attacks directed against it in the accomplishment of its mandate;

9. *Further requests* the Secretary-General to submit a report to the Council on the implementation of the present resolution, if possible within seven days from the date of its adoption;

10. *Decides* to remain actively seized of the matter.

# REPORT OF THE SECRETARY-GENERAL ON THE IMPLEMENTATION OF SECURITY COUNCIL RESOLUTION 837 (1993)

## INTRODUCTION

1. The present report is submitted in pursuance of paragraph 9 of Security Council resolution 837 (1993) on 6 June 1993. In that resolution, the Security Council, acting under Chapter VII of the Charter of the United Nations:

'1. *Strongly condemns* the unprovoked armed attacks against the personnel of UNOSOM II on 5 June 1993, which appear to have been part of a calculated and premeditated series of cease-fire violations to prevent by intimidation UNOSOM II from carrying out its mandate as provided for in resolution 814 (1993);

2. *Expresses* its condolences to the Government and people of Pakistan and the families of the UNOSOM II personnel who have lost their lives;

3. *Re-emphasizes* the crucial importance of the early implementation of the disarmament of all Somali parties, including movements and factions, in accordance with paragraphs 56 to 69 of the report of the Secretary-General of 3 March 1993 (S/25354), and of neutralizing radio broadcasting systems that contribute to the violence and attacks directed against UNOSOM II;

4. *Demands once again* that all Somali parties, including movements and factions, comply fully with the commitments they have undertaken in the agreements they concluded at the informal preparatory meeting on Somali political reconciliation in Addis Ababa, and in particular with their Agreement on implementing the cease-fire and on modalities of disarmament (S/25168, annex III);

5. *Reaffirms* that the Secretary-General is authorized under resolution 814 (1993) to take all necessary measures against all those responsible for the armed attacks referred to in paragraph 1 above, including against those responsible for publicly inciting such attacks, to establish the effective authority of UNOSOM II throughout Somalia, including to secure the investigation of their actions and their arrest and detention for prosecution, trial and punishment;

6. *Requests* the Secretary-General urgently to inquire into the incident, with particular emphasis on the role of those factional leaders involved;

7. *Encourages* the rapid and accelerated deployment of all UNOSOM II contingents to meet the full requirements of 28,000 men, all ranks,

as well as equipment, as indicated in the Secretary-General's report of 3 March 1993 (S/25354);

8. *Urges* Member States to contribute, on an emergency basis, military support and transportation, including armoured personnel carriers, tanks and attack helicopters, to provide UNOSOM II the capability appropriately to confront and deter armed attacks directed against it in the accomplishment of its mandate;

9. *Further requests* the Secretary-General to submit a report to the Council on the implementation of the present resolution, if possible within seven days from the date of its adoption.

2. In paragraph 57 of his report of 3 March 1993 (S/25354), which is referred to in section B, paragraph 5, of Security Council resolution 814 (1993) and paragraph 3 of Security Council resolution 837 (1993), the Secretary-General listed the military tasks included in UNOSOM II's mandate.

3. The present report is divided into five sections, of which the first three are based on the interim reports submitted to the members of the Security Council and the UNOSOM II troop-contributing countries on 6, 14 and 18 June 1993. Section I provides a brief account of the events leading up to the ambush of UNOSOM II troops in Mogadishu on 5 June 1993 and to the adoption of Security Council resolution 837 (1993). Section II covers the first phase of the implementation of the UNOSOM II programme, pursuant to resolution 837 (1993), to disarm South Mogadishu and neutralize broadcasting systems there that were inciting violence against UNOSOM II. Section III covers UNOSOM II's coordinated ground and air operation, launched on 17 June, to search and disarm the headquarters area in South Mogadishu of General Aidid (Chairman of the United Somali Congress/Somali National Alliance (USC/SNA) ). Section IV deals with the effect of the recent events on UNOSOM II humanitarian activities. Section V contains my observations on the events set out in the preceding four sections.

### I. ATTACKS ON UNOSOM II TROOPS ON 5 JUNE 1993

4. I wish to mention that, during the course of the events described in the present report, I remained in constant touch with my Special Representative in Somalia.

5. The events of 5 June 1993 in Mogadishu were triggered by a scheduled inventory by UNOSOM II of five militia weapon-storage sites, one of which was co-located with the radio transmission relay facility north of the city, with another at the radio broadcast studio in the city itself. Prior written notice of the inspection had been given to the staff of General Aidid, Chairman of USC/SNA. However, while the inspection was in progress, several apparently organized demonstrations, roadblocks, ambushes and armed attacks began throughout Mogadishu South, all of them directed against UNOSOM II troops,

including Pakistani troops guarding a feeding point for Somali civilians. Ostensibly these events were in protest against an alleged action by UNOSOM II, announced by General Aidid, to "seize" Radio Mogadishu (Aidid). No such seizure had taken place, nor was it intended. While General Aidid and USC/SNA denied it, the attacks that occurred on 5 June 1993 appeared to be a calculated, premeditated series of major cease-fire violations meant to challenge and intimidate UNOSOM II. The sequence of events is described in the following paragraphs.

6. At 4 p.m. on 4 June 1993, UNOSOM II sent letters to the USC/SNA faction in Mogadishu informing the latter of its plan to conduct, on the following day, weapons verification inspections of the authorized weapons storage sites in four locations in South Mogadishu and one site in Afgoy. The last inspections had been conducted by the Unified Task Force (UNITAF) in January and February 1993.

7. On the morning of 5 June 1993, the inspections began. Those at the Afgoy site and two of the four sites in Mogadishu were conducted without incident. The inspection at Site 5 – "Mogadishu Radio (Aidid)" location – went smoothly until it was near completion. At that time several agitators arrived on scene and began to incite the crowd that had gathered. At Site 4, a major storage site located at the Aidid radio retransmission facility, the inspection team met some verbal resistance but was allowed to enter and conduct the inspection. At this site, the team was subjected to sniper fire throughout the day. It was at Site 3 that a large number of weapons were found, including 62 tow missiles, 2 Milan missiles and 1 SA-7, which were later removed. Thirteen technical vehicles and a number of machine-guns previously in storage were no longer present.

8. At about 10 a.m. in other areas in South Mogadishu, demonstrations began and the UNOSOM II Force Command headquarters was fired on. Pakistani and Turkish soldiers returned fire. Later, Pakistani units returning from incidents elsewhere in Mogadishu transited 21 October Road, where they encountered a large, carefully prepared three-sided ambush that resulted in extensive casualties. The quick reaction force was deployed in the afternoon to relieve the Pakistani forces pinned down in a facility known as the "cigarette factory" on 21 October Road. At feeding station No. 20, a Pakistani unit helping with food distribution was attacked by a carefully coordinated group of gunmen who used a crowd of women and children as a shield to overwhelm United Nations soldiers who refused to fire at the crowd. Several soldiers were murdered, others were wounded and the remainder were captured.

9. During these attacks, militia forces employed automatic weapons, RPGs and hand grenades. Serious disturbances continued throughout the day, including attacks on UNOSOM II civilian headquarters (where two hand grenades were thrown into its compound but did not explode), isolation of and attacks on Pakistani forces at checkpoints, random sniper attacks and armed roadblocks. As a result of the various attacks, in particular the large ambush on 21 October Road and the attack on feeding station No. 20, 25 Pakistani soldiers were killed,

10 listed as missing and 57 wounded (54 Pakistani, 3 United States). Casualties on the Somali side are believed to have been high but their numbers are not yet known.

10. Contact with USC/SNA was difficult to establish during the morning because of the intensity of the disturbances around UNOSOM II headquarters. The first contact was made through a UNOSOM II national officer at 1300 hours. This was followed by an afternoon meeting between a UNOSOM II official and two USC/SNA senior officials at USC/SNA headquarters, during which USC/SNA attempted to disassociate itself from the incidents, asserting that the disturbances were spontaneous outbursts by an angry public. In the light of the organized nature of the attacks, the several Aidid radio broadcasts accusing UNOSOM II of wrongly shooting women and children without provocation, the USC/SNA disclaimer is difficult to accept. At an early evening meeting, even as USC/SNA emissaries were assuring UNOSOM II officials of their good intentions and desire for the restoration of peace, Aidid radio and vehicle-mounted loudspeakers were continuing to agitate the public to attack UNOSOM II.

11. From the incidents of 5 June, it was clear that numerous weapons still remain with the public at large in Mogadishu. It was also clear that this would have to be factored into the UNOSOM II follow-up to the incidents, if security was to be maintained. Although investigations were not complete, the attacks constituted a gross violation of the cease-fire agreement and a blatant attack on United Nations troops.

12. Early on 6 June, General Aidid's broadcast over Radio Mogadishu fell far short of calming the situation as his emissaries had indicated was his intention. Instead, he articulated more anti-UNOSOM II rhetoric, urged calm if UNOSOM II acquiesced to his demands and violence if it did not. At this juncture, it would appear that the General was seeking a confrontation with UNOSOM II in order to take control of the political reconciliation and of the efforts to reactivate the Somali judicial system.

13. UNOSOM II sent a written message to General Aidid advising him of the United Nations and international community's outrage and urging him to desist from the disastrous course he had set for himself and his followers. It was pointed out to General Aidid that that was the last opportunity for him to become part of the peace process.

14. In order better to protect the civilian staff of UNOSOM II and international agency and non-governmental organization (NGO) personnel after the 5 June attacks, the Special Representative decided to consolidate the staff of the operation into several secure and logistically supportable locations. From these sites UNOSOM II would continue to accomplish all essential work. Meanwhile, the Force Command was strengthening its posture and preparing for possible contingencies.

15. I have placed on record my appreciation and admiration for the courageous and disciplined manner in which the Pakistani and other UNOSOM II troops conducted themselves in very difficult circumstances while they were attempting to carry out their duties under the UNOSOM II mandate.

16. I have kept the Council fully informed of further developments relating to the situation in Mogadishu. On 6 June 1993 the Security Council, after considering the Secretary-General's report on the incidents in Mogadishu on 5 June, adopted resolution 837 (1993).

## II. ACTION TAKEN BY UNOSOM II: FIRST PHASE
### (12–14 JUNE 1993)

17. Preparations for the implementation of Security Council resolution 837 (1993) were undertaken by UNOSOM II immediately following the adoption of that resolution. The object of the subsequent UNOSOM II actions was to restore security and law and order in Mogadishu by implementing a comprehensive programme for disarmament in the capital, neutralizing broadcasting systems and other propaganda mechanisms used to incite violence and preventing further violations of the cease-fire. This would make it possible to resume the delivery of humanitarian assistance to the civilian population, facilitate economic rehabilitation and reconstruction and promote political reconciliation for all Somalis. At the same time UNOSOM II instituted a thorough investigation of the incidents of 5 June with a view to taking the measures indicated in paragraph 5 of resolution 837 (1993). UNOSOM II meanwhile remained open to dialogue, to ascertain if there was a way to carry out the resolution cooperatively. Regrettably, General Aidid and USC/SNA, by their actions, demonstrated that they did not desire a cooperative solution.

18. On 8 June 1993 a letter was addressed by the Special Representative of the Secretary-General to General Aidid, Chairman of USC/SNA, reminding him, inter alia, of the prohibition against the display of weapons and the requirement to cooperate fully in the disarmament programme in Mogadishu. However, efforts to deliver the letter to General Aidid personally were not successful until several days later. In a letter of the same date to the Chairmen of the 11 non-SNA Somali political factions, the Special Representative of the Secretary-General cautioned that no group or individual should seek to take advantage of the current tension in Mogadishu, and solicited the cooperation of all factions and movements towards the political and physical reconstruction of Somalia.

19. At 4 a.m. on 12 June, UNOSOM II began the implementation of the first phase of a programme pursuant to Security Council resolutions 814 (1993) and 837 (1993) to disarm Mogadishu South. This was an essential step in the light of the fact that the city was saturated with a vast arsenal of hidden illegal weapons, some of which had been used during the premeditated attacks of 5 June. In a series of carefully planned precision air and ground military actions, UNOSOM II disabled or destroyed ordnance, weapons and equipment located in three previously authorized weapons storage sites, and a related clandestine

military facility used for the ambush on 5 June. These and subsequent strikes were conducted utilizing tactics that would minimize casualties as well as collateral damage to nearby areas. Where possible, ammunition not already destroyed was safely detonated by trained explosive ordnance personnel. The relay transmitter site for Radio Mogadishu was occupied and ammunition removed. Elements of the Pakistani, French, United States, Moroccan and Italian contingents participated in the first day's actions.

20. Another major objective of the coordinated military action called for by the Security Council in paragraph 3 of resolution 837 (1993) was the neutralization of Radio Mogadishu, the former Somali State radio, which had been taken over by USC/SNA and was being used to encourage violence against UNOSOM II. Two main targets associated with the radio system were the broadcast studio in downtown Mogadishu and a radio relay transmitter facility in one of the major authorized weapons storage sites. The broadcast facility was disabled by precision air attack in the early morning when minimally occupied. This timing avoided the military and civilian casualties that would have resulted from a ground assault to seize the facility. The radio relay transmitter facility, on the other hand, was taken by integrated air and ground action, and held for the first day of operations. The site has since been evacuated and reusable equipment stored in a safe place. This equipment will be returned to the people of Somalia as soon as feasible. UNOSOM II intends to locate and take similar action in relation to Radio "Voice of the Somali Masses", which, since it started broadcasting recently, has issued inflammatory propaganda.

21. On 13 and 14 June UNOSOM II forces conducted additional precision air strikes on two clandestine weapons/ammunition storage sites within the SNA/Aidid Mogadishu stronghold area. One was a heavily guarded weapons, ammunition and vehicle storage area that held approximately 30 heavy weapons carrier "technical" vehicles in various states of repair. The site also served as a vehicle repair facility where "technicals" were assembled. In addition, the site was reported to contain large numbers of small arms and crew-served weapons, as well as an ammunition cache that included significant quantities of large-calibre automatic-weapons ordnance. The other site held technical vehicles, small arms and ammunition, plus heavy engineering equipment used to construct barricades. On the morning of 15 June, aerial reconnaissance observed and destroyed a 122-mm BM21-1 mobile rocket launcher in the stronghold area near the USC/SNA headquarters. This weapon is an indiscriminate 36-tube area weapon with a range of 500 metres to 20 kilometres, capable of striking anywhere in Mogadishu.

22. The actions of 12 to 14 June formed part of a continuing effort as called for by Security Council resolutions 814 (1993) and 837 (1993) effectively to initiate the disarmament process and neutralize all heavy weapons. This includes known USC/SNA weapons and ammunition storage sites and caches in and around Mogadishu, and any other which immediately threatened the city. UNOSOM II facilities were used to call on citizens of Mogadishu to turn in their arms peacefully and to help in the identification of clandestine arms

caches. Getting arms under control is fundamental to the restoration of law and order and public safety.

23. Preliminary reports indicate that civilian crowds, including women and children, were used by General Aidid and his supporters as human shields to screen attacks on UNOSOM II fixed guard posts or strong points. Similar tactics resulted in the deaths of 25 United Nations soldiers as a result of the attacks of 5 June and an undetermined number of Somali civilian deaths at KM-4 on 13 June 1993. Evidence in hand shows that a violent demonstration was staged by SNA elements in which the crowd was encouraged by agitators to attack Pakistani soldiers at a strong point. Shots were fired from the crowd at United Nations soldiers on the ground, and automatic weapons fire was directed at them from an adjacent building. A United Nations rooftop covering position returned fire on those shooting at the UNOSOM II soldiers on the ground. Witnesses have stated that armed Somalis nearby fired into the crowd, confirming that that was a carefully staged incident calculated to create casualties before the world press and try to weaken the United Nations forces' effectiveness in dealing with organized mobs in the future. UNOSOM II's Force Command is developing revised tactics and additional riot control equipment has been introduced as a means of maintaining control of similar crowds. A UNOSOM II investigation of the 13 June incident at KM-4 has been initiated, and every effort will be made to ascertain the facts and take whatever preventive action may be required to avoid any further civilian casualties.

24. Although the investigation was not complete at this stage, it was already apparent that there was a conspiracy to commit premeditated acts of violence and that agitation by various means was used in an attempt to stir public anger. Those responsible had not yet been identified but it was apparent that elements of USC/SNA conducted the attacks.

### III. ACTION TAKEN BY UNOSOM II: SECOND PHASE (17–25 JUNE 1993)

25. At 1.30 a.m. on 17 June, UNOSOM II forces undertook a coordinated ground and air operation whose purpose was to search, clear and disarm the Aidid headquarters area in South Mogadishu known to be a USC/SNA stronghold. Several clandestine arms storage sites in this area had already been neutralized on 13 and 14 June.

26. This operation was carried out in a manner designed to minimize Somali casualties and to allow those in the stronghold to depart. Its objectives were successfully accomplished by mid-afternoon. Mines, hand grenades, weapons and numerous documents were evacuated from the enclave. Pakistani units operated inside the stronghold, while Moroccan, Italian and French forces formed a mechanized cordon around it, sealing the area. Outside and on the periphery of the cordon, the SNA militia initiated a series of attacks and ambushes from military strongpoints, coordinated in many instances with ostensibly unarmed groups of civilians. In at least one case, the "unarmed" civilians

unleashed hand grenades at Moroccan troops who were holding their fire. Sim-ultaneously, armed gunmen opened fire from a different direction. In the ensu-ing engagement, the outnumbered Moroccan troops fought valiantly, but suf-fered a large number of casualties, including their battalion commander who, although seriously wounded, continued to direct the defence of his besieged unit until his death. I wish on this occasion to pay a special tribute to the Moroc-can soldiers for their great courage and devotion.

27. Subsequent coordinated UNOSOM II operations drove the militia from a number of their strong points, including the Digfer Hospital, which yielded a large number of militia prisoners from the hospital facility. The SNA militia used the hospital not only as a base for military operations but also as an ambush and defensive strong point with rifle and machine-gun positions firing against United Nations troops. Operations have continued to the present to attempt to locate additional clandestine weapons storage sites and to locate and disarm remaining elements of the SNA militia in Mogadishu.

28. The skill and courage with which United Nations coalition forces executed the cordon and the search, clear and disarm operation against the USC/SNA enclave and their professional response to the series of subsequent SNA attacks were impressive. By any measure, both the planned operation and the counter-action to SNA militia attacks represented significant successes. The position of SNA and of General Aidid have been eroded, in terms of attrition of forces, disruption of command/control/communications and loss of clandestine wea-pons and ammunition. Concurrently, in the Belet Weyne region, Italian forces secured and destroyed two extensive SNA weapons inventories, which included large numbers of tanks, artillery pieces, mortars, machine-guns, anti-aircraft guns, mines and ammunition. Although some of the heavier equipment was unserviceable, much was still usable. In addition, over 30 artillery pieces located about 6 kilometres north of Mogadishu were destroyed by the quick reaction force. Although still a threat to stability, it is expected that the SNA militia in Mogadishu will now be less of an impediment to disarmament, political rec-onciliation and rehabilitation. Humanitarian assistance has already been stepped up in most sections of Mogadishu and should be back to normal soon.

29. UNOSOM II has continued to face the use of civilian crowds with women and children in front, screening armed attacks on United Nations troops. Such tactics require adequate crowd control measures and equipment. Although more capability is now on hand, additional crowd control equipment (e.g. tear gas/CS) is being acquired on an urgent basis.

30. As reported previously, UNOSOM II will continue its initial disarmament effort until satisfied it has neutralized all known USC/SNA weapons and ammu-nition storage sites and caches in and around Mogadishu and any others that threaten the city. After this is complete, UNOSOM II will undertake an orderly sector-by-sector disarmament of the city. However, the emphasis will shift to cooperative efforts involving Somalis and UNOSOM II as soon as feasible. UNOSOM II is regularly appealing to the citizens of Mogadishu to turn in

their arms peacefully and to help in the location of clandestine arms caches. Disarmament is fundamental to the restoration of law and order and public safety, as well as to unimpeded progress in political reconciliation and national rehabilitation.

31. The United Nations investigation of the recent events has continued to progress, with evidence mounting in support of the premise that there was an SNA conspiracy to commit premeditated acts of violence against UNOSOM II on 5 June; that violations of international humanitarian law have been committed by SNA militia; and that agitation to stir public antagonism is also still being generated.

32. For the reasons set out above, the Special Representative of the Secretary-General for Somalia publicly called for the arrest and detention of General Mohamed Aidid on 17 June 1993. The arrest and detention of General Aidid would be carried out under UNOSOM II's existing mandate which, inter alia, authorizes such forceful action as may be required to neutralize armed elements that attack United Nations personnel. Moreover, and as reaffirmed in paragraph 5 of Security Council resolution 837 (1993) ". . . the Secretary-General is authorized . . . to take all necessary measures against all those responsible for the armed attacks . . . including to secure the investigation of their actions and their arrest and detention for prosecution, trial and punishment." General Aidid's militia continues to attack United Nations personnel with sniping, premeditated confrontations violating international humanitarian law, and provocative rhetoric. Moreover, there is increasing evidence that General Aidid deliberately and personally directed the use of women and children for attacks on UNOSOM II soldiers; and that he directed his militia to shoot into the crowd on 13 June in order to create casualties and embarrass the Pakistani forces and UNOSOM II before the assembled mission was being marginalized as a result of military actions in the past two weeks.

38. It is essential that the impartiality and neutrality of humanitarian assistance continue to be respected and that adequate resources be made available to speed up the implementation of the relief and rehabilitation programmes in all parts of the country. In this context, it is important that the pledges made at the humanitarian meeting in Addis Ababa in March 1993 are converted into actual disbursements and that additional commitments are made. UNOSOM II will, for its part, continue with efforts to facilitate a positive environment for the successful implementation of the humanitarian programmes.

### V. OBSERVATIONS

39. The unfolding of events in Mogadishu since 5 June 1993 must be seen against the background of the conditions that the United Nations Operation in Somalia was designed to remedy. It is the chaos, civil war, immense suffering and famine afflicting the Somali people that brought the international community and the United Nations to Somalia. The primary objectives of the mandate entrusted to UNOSOM II are to put an end to the plight of the Somali

people, set them firmly on the path to economic rehabilitation and political reconciliation and promote the rebuilding of Somali society and political institutions. This requires the restoration of peaceful conditions throughout Somalia and the effective implementation of the process of disarmament. All the Somali factions committed themselves to such goals under the Addis Ababa agreements, and the Security Council assigned them to UNOSOM II as a priority task.

40. I consider that the UNOSOM II actions set out in the present report have been successful in making it possible to return to the pursuit of the main objectives of the United Nations in Somalia. UNOSOM II military enforcement actions have largely neutralized heavy weapons and the command and control facilities of the factions responsible for the large-scale violations of the cease-fire in Mogadishu. These actions have also made it clear that deliberate attempts to disrupt United Nations and NGO humanitarian relief supplies cannot be tolerated. Already, various elements of Somali society have shown not only an interest in restraint and reconciliation, but also in voluntary disarmament. The tragic price paid by United Nations personnel as well as Somalis in the recent series of events should never be forgotten. However, by demonstrating that it was willing to pay, and exact, the cost of peacemaking, the United Nations may well have saved many more lives and accelerated the disarmament, reconciliation and rehabilitation process.

41. Following the military operations conducted between 12 and 18 June, it is hoped that, barring any unforeseen developments, UNOSOM II will now be able to revert to the peaceful disarmament of all factions and militias throughout the country. It had never been the intention of UNOSOM II to oppose any of the factions, as long as they refrained from violations of the cease-fire, acted with due regard to their own commitments to the Addis Ababa agreements and cooperated in the implementation of the mandate entrusted by the Security Council to this humanitarian operation. In fact UNOSOM II intends to continue to work with all the factions, in an effort to foster conditions for the implementation of the United Nations mandate.

42. The attacks on United Nations peace-keepers were tragic and disturbing incidents, but they will not divert the United Nations from its commitment to Somalia. All they prove is that, in the unique situation prevailing in that country, there are elements that continue to believe, and wrongly so, that their interests are best served by perpetuating chaos, destruction and death. These elements apparently consider that their political prospects would be diminished if conditions in Somalia were normalized and peace restored.

43. I now urge all Somali factions to join UNOSOM II in its mission of peace, disarmament and reconciliation as defined by the Security Council and agreed upon by the faction leaders at Addis Ababa. For my part, I am determined to pursue all necessary efforts to implement Security Council resolutions 814 (1993) and 837 (1993).

44. What the recent incidents in Mogadishu also demonstrated was the devotion of the soldiers of UNOSOM II, who on several occasions sustained death or severe injury while defending themselves and attempting to minimize civilian casualties.

45. I regret and mourn the loss of 29 United Nations soldiers from Pakistan and Morocco, killed in the performance of their peace-keeping duties, and the wounding of 88 soldiers from Morocco, Pakistan and the United States of America. I also deeply regret the casualties suffered by Somali civilians who were caught up in the incidents or were used deliberately to screen military attacks against UNOSOM II troops. In concluding this report, I wish to pay a tribute to my Special Representative, Admiral Jonathan Howe, the Force Commander, Lieutenant-General Cevik Bir, and to all the soldiers and civilian staff of UNOSOM II, as well as the staff of the United Nations agencies and of the NGOs, including Somali employees, for the dedication, courage and commitment they have shown in the performance of their complex and dangerous mission. I would also like to express my appreciation to those Member States which have contributed to the success of this Operation.

## RESOLUTION 954 (1994)

### ADOPTED BY THE SECURITY COUNCIL AT ITS 3447TH MEETING, ON 4 NOVEMBER 1994

The Security Council,

*Recalling* its resolution 733 (1992) of 23 January 1992 and all other relevant resolutions,

*Noting with appreciation* the work of the Security Council's mission in transmitting directly to Somalia's political parties the views of the Council on the situation in Somalia and on the future of the United Nations in that country,

*Having considered* the reports of the Secretary-General dated 17 September 1994 (S/1994/1068) and 14 October 1994 (S/1994/1166), and the oral report of the Security Council's mission to Somalia given on 31 October 1994,

*Paying tribute* to the thousands of personnel of the United Nations Operation in Somalia (UNOSOM), and to the Unified Task Force (UNITAF) as well as humanitarian relief personnel who have served in Somalia, and *honouring*, in particular, those who have sacrificed their lives in this service,

*Noting* that hundreds of thousands of human lives have been rescued from famine in Somalia through the efforts of the United Nations and the international community,

*Commending* the efforts of the special representatives of the Secretary-General to bring Somali factions together in national reconciliation,

*Reaffirming* that the people of Somalia bear the ultimate responsibility for achieving national reconciliation and bringing peace to Somalia,

*Convinced* that only a genuinely inclusive approach to political reconciliation would provide for a lasting political settlement and re-emergence of a civil society in Somalia,

*Recalling* that the date already foreseen for termination of the current United Nations Operation in Somalia (UNOSOM II) is the end of March 1995,

*Recognizing* that the lack of progress in the Somali peace process and in national reconciliation, in particular the lack of sufficient cooperation from the Somali parties over security issues, has fundamentally undermined the United Nations objectives in Somalia and, in these circumstances, continuation of UNOSOM II beyond March 1995 cannot be justified,

*Recognizing further* that termination of the mandate of UNOSOM II by the end of March 1995 implies a secure and orderly phasing out of its military component in advance of that date,

*Noting* the assurances of cooperation and non-interference with such withdrawal received from all Somali parties during the Council's mission to Somalia,

*Re-emphasizing* the importance the Council attaches to the safety and security of United Nations and other personnel engaged in humanitarian relief and peace-keeping in Somalia,

*Underlining particularly*, in this context, the overriding need for all possible measures and precautions to be taken to ensure that UNOSOM II does not suffer any casualties in the process of withdrawal,

*Emphasizing* its willingness to encourage the Secretary-General to sustain a facilitating or mediating political role for Somalia beyond March 1995 if that is what the Somalis want and if the Somali parties are willing to cooperate with the United Nations,

*Concerned* that the United Nations should continue to work with regional organizations, in particular the Organization of African Unity (OAU), the League of Arab States, and the Organization of the Islamic Conference (OIC), and with the Governments of neighbouring countries to promote reconciliation in Somalia and the re-emergence of a civil society there,

*Recognizing* also the impact that the situation in Somalia has had on neighbouring countries including, in particular, flows of refugees,

*Noting also* that the United Nations will do its best to sustain humanitarian activities in Somalia and to encourage non-governmental organizations to do likewise, but that their ability to do so will depend almost entirely on the degree of cooperation and security offered by Somali parties,

*Confident* of the willingness of the United Nations to remain ready to provide through its various agencies rehabilitation and reconstruction assistance, including assistance to the police and judiciary to the extent that the situation in Somalia develops in such a way as to make that practicable,

*Noting further* the interest of humanitarian agencies and non-governmental organizations in cooperating with the United Nations after the withdrawal of UNOSOM II in transitional arrangements for mutual assistance,

*Determining* that the situation in Somalia continues to threaten peace and security, and having regard to the exceptional circumstances including, in particular, the absence of a government in Somalia, acting under Chapter VII of the Charter of the United Nations,

1. *Decides* to extend the mandate of UNOSOM II for a final period until 31 March 1995;

2. *Affirms* that the primary purpose of UNOSOM II until its termination is to facilitate political reconciliation in Somalia;

3. *Welcomes* the intention of the Secretary-General, expressed in paragraph 23 of his report dated 14 October 1994, to continue throughout the period of the mandate of UNOSOM II, and even afterwards, the efforts of his special representative to help the Somali parties achieve national reconciliation;

4. *Urges* all Somali factions to negotiate as soon as possible an effective cease-fire and the formation of a transitional government of national unity;

5. *Decides* that every effort should be made to withdraw all UNOSOM II military forces and assets from Somalia in a secure and orderly manner as soon as possible, as described in the Secretary-General's report dated 14 October 1994, before the expiry date of the current mandate of UNOSOM II and without compromising on the paramount need of ensuring the safety of UNOSOM II personnel;

6. *Authorizes* UNOSOM II military forces to take those actions necessary to protect the UNOSOM II mission and the withdrawal of UNOSOM II personnel and assets, and, to the extent that the Force Commander deems it practicable and consistent, in the context of withdrawal, to protect personnel of relief organizations;

7. *Emphasizes* the responsibility of the Somali parties for the security and safety of UNOSOM II and other personnel engaged in humanitarian activities and in this context strongly demands that all parties in Somalia refrain from any acts of intimidation or violence against such personnel;

8. *Requests* Member States to provide assistance in the withdrawal of all UNOSOM II military forces and assets, including vehicles, weapons, and other equipment;

9. *Requests* that the Secretary-General keep the Council informed about the progress of the withdrawal process;

10. *Invites* the Organization of African Unity, the League of Arab States and the Organization of the Islamic Conference to continue their efforts in cooperation with the United Nations in the search for lasting peace in Somalia;

11. *Calls upon* all Member States, in particular the neighbouring States, to continue to provide support for all Somali efforts towards genuine peace and national reconciliation and to refrain from any action capable of exacerbating the conflict situation in Somalia;

12. *Reiterates* the need for the observance and strict monitoring of the general and complete embargo on all deliveries of weapons and military equipment to Somalia, as decided in paragraph 5 of resolution 733 (1992) and in this regard requests the Committee established by resolution 751 (1992) of 24 April 1992 to fulfil its mandate as described in paragraph 11 of that resolution, in particular to seek the cooperation of neighbouring States for the effective implementation of this embargo;

13. *Further requests* the Secretary-General to continue to monitor the situation in Somalia and to the extent possible to keep the Security Council informed in particular about developments affecting the humanitarian situation, the security situation for humanitarian personnel in Somalia, repatriation of refugees and impacts on neighbouring countries; and to report to the Security Council before 31 March 1995 on the situation in Somalia and to submit suggestions concerning the role that the United Nations could play in Somalia beyond that date;

14. *Decides* to remain actively seized of the matter.

## Appendix D
# The General Framework Agreement for Peace in Bosnia and Herzegovina

## Section A

In Paris on 14 December 1995, the presidents of the Republic of Bosnia and Herzegovina, the Republic of Croatia, and the Federal Republic of Yugoslavia signed the General Framework Agreement for Peace in Bosnia and Herzegovina, also known as the Dayton Agreement. This agreement, comprising 11 articles (for text, see Section B below), set out the principles for the maintenance of a unitary and sovereign Republic of Bosnia and Herzegovina, consisting of two Entities: Republika Srpska and the Federation of Bosnia and Herzegovina. The latter was to control 51 per cent of the territory of the republic. The agreement also set out a series of constitutional provisions relating to the bicameral legislature of the unitary state, the election of a three man presidency, the role and responsibilities of central government and the general relationship between the two Entities and the central government.

As a corollary to the seeming willingness of the Balkan parties to seal a peace deal after over three years of fighting in Bosnia, the Dayton Agreement also set out the responsibilities of the organs and institutions of the international community to ensure that the peace would be a lasting one. Included in these provisions were: the definition of the role to be played by the OSCE in the areas of confidence-building, monitoring elections, and arms control; the continuing operation of the International War Crimes Tribunal; the creation of a Commission of Human Rights to be monitored by both the OSCE and the Council of Europe; the creation of a UN International Police Task Force; and the nomination of a High Representative to monitor and oversee all civilian aspects of the peace plan. The most important provision relating to the work of the international community in ensuring the success of the peace plan was the direct military involvement of NATO through the Implementation Force, (IFOR). This was a major new development in the international mechanisms involved in attempting to bring peace to this war-torn area: UNPROFOR was to be relieved of its responsibilities in Bosnia and replaced by IFOR, which was to be an implementation and not a peacekeeping force, led by a US general and consisting of some 60,000 NATO troops including a US contingent of some 20,000 troops.

This peace accord had been approached by a long and arduous route. In the public eye it had only been achieved because of the indefatigable work of the US envoy, Richard Holbrooke. In reality, however, events on the ground in

Bosnia and its environs throughout 1995 had favoured this outcome. The increasing diplomatic involvement of the United States made a significant difference to the warring parties' perceptions of how much they stood to gain or lose by pursuing conflict, and a series of events in 1995 drew the United States further and further into the Bosnian mire and resulted in the transformation of the UN peacekeeping and humanitarian mission into a peace implementation mission. All the Bosnian parties to the dispute were brought to accept this, although often with great reluctance. Those involved from outside, including President Milosevic, the EU and the UN, breathed a sigh of relief.

The move away from a UN-dominated peacekeeping operation began in February 1995, when NATO issued a strong ultimatum to the Bosnian Serbs, in the wake of the explosion of a mortar shell in Sarajevo market on 5 February which resulted in 68 deaths and nearly 200 wounded. Even though this was the last of a sequence of NATO-issued threats, which in the past the Bosnian Serbs had scorned, the increasing US diplomatic manoeuvring behind the scenes paradoxically lent 'diplomatic muscle' to the existing military potential. This was manifested at the beginning of March by the creation of a Muslim–Croat Federation, heavily brokered, if not forced upon the parties, by the United States, which indicated that the balance of diplomatic and military forces arrayed against the Serbs was growing stronger and more coherent.

The shifting balance of power within the regional context, and the heightened role of NATO, forced the Bosnian Serb leadership into a series of rash retaliatory measures which were to have enormous repercussions. In late May, the Serbs abducted and held hostage dozens of UN peacekeepers and observers from remote positions in an attempt to intimidate NATO into withdrawing its threat to use force against Serb positions if the latters' heavy artillery and other weaponry were not removed from certain key positions, (primarily around Sarajevo). In itself, this move was not considered out of character for the Bosnian Serbs, though it was portrayed in some quarters as a sign of the increasing desperation of the Bosnian Serb forces and leadership in the face of mounting military and diplomatic pressure. Nevertheless, it did trigger a Western response beyond the normal diplomatic negotiations aimed at releasing the hostages, in that Britain and France decided to deploy a newly styled Rapid Reaction Force in Bosnia. This force, consisting of national troops outside UN jurisdiction, was intended to protect the British and French troops operating in Bosnia under the UN flag and mandate. It was a bizarre arrangement, yet one which indicated that the thankless task of the UNPROFOR operation in Bosnia was constantly evolving into an operation in which other regional organisations such as NATO and individual states such as Britain and France were taking the lead. What emerged in the summer of 1995 was a gradual shift of emphasis away from the peacekeeping role of UNPROFOR to a more proactive policy of enforcement, which would later lead to the implementation force agreed at Dayton, Ohio, and signed in Paris.

Two major events in late July and early August 1995 damaged the image of the UN as a viable organisation for dealing with conflicts such as that in Bosnia and the utility and success of peacekeeping operations. These events also dramatically altered the military and territorial scenario on the ground in the Balkans. Their ramifications had two important consequences.

The first involved the collapse of the UN-designated and -protected 'safe areas' of Zepa and Srebrenica to Bosnian Serb attacks and the ensuing allegations of mass murders committed by the Bosnian Serbs against the Muslim men of Srebrenica. This discredited the UN and highlighted the impotence of UNPROFOR as the international community had repeatedly stated that the safe areas would be defended from Serb aggression. It was swiftly followed in early August by the stunning success of the Croatian armed forces in overrunning the Krajina and driving out the local Serbs. This too undermined the authority of UN, which had commenced its involvement in the wars of the former Yugoslavia by deploying UNPROFOR as a traditional peacekeeping force to keep Croats and Serbs apart in the Krajina while a diplomatic solution was negotiated. Internationally, the UN was discredited and UNPROFOR shown to be an inadequate mechanism through which to attempt to provide an acceptable and lasting peace for Bosnia and other parts of former Yugoslavia.

The second consequence involved the development of the military and territorial situation on the ground, as a result both of Croat successes in the Krajina and the increasingly emboldened attitude of the Bosnian government army in its military operations against the Bosnian Serbs. Throughout August the war in Bosnia flared up with renewed vigour and the Bosnian Serbs were on the receiving end of Croat and Muslim attacks along the whole of their front lines – a precursor to the major offensive to be conducted by the Croats and Muslims, in tandem, in September and October. The Bosnian Serbs were also under political and military pressure from other sources since Milosevic steered well clear of providing them with any overt diplomatic support, insisting that they should sue for peace, while NATO with strong American insistence came into the military picture more emphatically.

Toward the end of August, NATO aircraft, and the previously deployed Anglo-French Rapid Reaction Force, pounded Serbian positions around Sarajevo, and targeted and destroyed a range of Serb military, logistics, and command and control installations throughout the Serb-controlled territory. This provided a clear signal of the intent and determination of the international community to pursue a solution to the Bosnian conflict through the use of force if necessary. It also eventually caused enough disruption and dislocation to the Bosnian Serb military machine to allow the Croat and Muslim forces to prosecute their military offensive with great territorial success. Paradoxically, the Bosnian Serb escalation of attacks on UN positions, and the overrunning of the safe areas, helped the UN, as it forced a concentration and relocation of peacekeeping forces to make them less vulnerable to counter-attack in the wake of NATO air strikes.

As the many internationally brokered attempts at negotiating peace had for the most part foundered on the inability of the local warring parties to agree to the demarcation of frontiers on the maps, the NATO bombardment paved the way for a significant redressing in the balance of power on the ground that was fundamental to the final agreement in Dayton. Now on the receiving end of a formidable array of diplomatic and military muscle, the Bosnian Serbs were dragged back to the negotiating table in Geneva in an attempt to thrash out a ceasefire and the basic principles of a peace settlement, including the demarcation of frontiers. This the Bosnian Serbs did with great reluctance, but the mounting pressure placed on them by the United States and Milosevic (who could no longer rely on the support of Serbs at large after the disastrous loss of the Krajina and who hence was ready to sign a peace deal to retain his position in power) meant that they had few alternatives.

The final incentive for the Bosnian Serbs was provided by the great territorial gains made by the Croats and Muslims through their renewed, and to date most successful, military campaigns in Bosnia throughout September and early October. While negotiations orchestrated by Holbrooke continued, the Bosnian Serbs were being pushed back in all parts of Bosnia to the extent that even the vital city of Banja Luka came under threat. More importantly, the Bosnian Serb retreat meant that the frontiers in Bosnia were forced back toward the 51–49 per cent Croat–Muslim/Serb split which was the agreed benchmark for any short term settlement. What had not been achieved since 1992 through international diplomacy and the threat of the use of force was rapidly coming about through the successes of the Croat–Muslim military machine to which the broader international community turned a blind eye under pressure from Washington. A basic set of principles for a peace deal was agreed in Geneva on 9 September, and while war still raged, a ceasefire was set for 12 October, after which intensive negotiations would take place for a final settlement.

The role of the United States in forcing all the parties into signing the General Framework Agreement for Peace in Bosnia and Herzegovina was vital in both military and political terms. The United States lent its weight militarily, through increased participation in NATO operations, and finally indicated its willingness to send troops to the region to police a peace deal. Diplomatically, the United States persuaded Milosevic that the time had come for a settlement by making obvious the long-term consequences of war, but also by throwing its weight behind the Croat and Muslim causes by tacitly agreeing to the military campaigns in Krajina and Bosnia; this finally forced the Bosnian Serbs to accept the Dayton accords. What became obvious throughout 1995 was that even though diplomacy could play a leading role in reaching peace it was the changing military situation on the ground, and the evolving balance of power, which would provide the final catalyst for a settlement. And while the UNPROFOR mission would be disbanded and replaced by the Implementation Force with a different role, the UN's peace-keeping mission had played a significant role in maintaining the Bosnian war on the international agenda. UNPROFOR had neither the necessary military instruments nor political direction to bring peace to Bosnia, but it certainly provided a framework both politically and militarily.

The Dayton Agreement, in many ways, was a reworking of previous plans proposed by the UN and the EU and not a novel departure. By the time of the conference, not only did the participants have the lessons of more than three years of abortive peacekeeping to draw on, there was also a range of Security Council resolutions already in place. These provided the essential context for the final negotiation of the peace. During the course of its involvement, the UN had also pioneered new forms of proactive conflict management, making any retreat to traditional and more passive peacekeeping in the future unlikely. The experience of UNPROFOR was therefore by no means wholly negative. Nonetheless, in many ways the peace settlement indicated that the use of force still pays. While we may laud the onset of peace in Bosnia, what we are left with is a country split in two by force of arms – a unitary sovereign state with two *Entities*.

Section B

# GENERAL FRAMEWORK AGREEMENT FOR PEACE IN BOSNIA AND HERZEGOVINA

The Republic of Bosnia and Herzegovina, the Republic of Croatia and the Federal Republic of Yugoslavia (the "Parties"),

*Recognizing* the need for a comprehensive settlement to bring an end to the tragic conflict in the region,

*Desiring* to contribute toward that end and to promote an enduring peace and stability,

*Affirming* their commitment to the Agreed Basic Principles issued on September 8, 1995, the Further Agreed Basic Principles issued on September 26, 1995, and the cease-fire agreements of September 14 and October 5, 1995,

*Noting* the agreement of August 29, 1995, which authorized the delegation of the Federal Republic of Yugoslavia to sign, on behalf of the Republika Srpska, the parts of the peace plan concerning it, with the obligation to implement the agreement that is reached strictly and consequently,

Have agreed as follows:

### ARTICLE I

The Parties shall conduct their relations in accordance with the principles set forth in the United Nations Charter, as well as the Helsinki Final Act and other documents of the Organization for Security and Cooperation in Europe. In particular, the Parties shall fully respect the sovereign equality of one another, shall settle disputes by peaceful means, and shall refrain from any action, by threat or use of force or otherwise, against the territorial integrity or political independence of Bosnia and Herzegovina or any other State.

### ARTICLE II

The Parties welcome and endorse the arrangements that have been made concerning the military aspects of the peace settlement and aspects of regional stabilization, as set forth in the Agreements at Annex 1-A and Annex 1-B. The Parties shall fully respect and promote fulfillment of the commitments made in Annex 1-A, and shall comply fully with their commitments as set forth in Annex 1-B.

### ARTICLE III

The Parties welcome and endorse the arrangements that have been made concerning the boundary demarcation between the two Entities, the Federation of Bosnia and Herzegovina and Republika Srpska, as set forth in the Agreement at Annex 2. The Parties shall fully respect and promote fulfillment of the commitments made therein.

### ARTICLE IV

The Parties welcome and endorse the elections program for Bosnia and Herzegovina as set forth in Annex 3. The Parties shall fully respect and promote fulfillment of that program.

## ARTICLE V

The Parties welcome and endorse the arrangements that have been made concerning the Constitution of Bosnia and Herzegovina, as set forth in Annex 4. The Parties shall fully respect and promote fulfillment of the commitments made therein.

## ARTICLE VI

The Parties welcome and endorse the arrangements that have been made concerning the establishment of an arbitration tribunal, a Commission on Human Rights, a Commission on Refugees and Displaced Persons, a Commission to Preserve National Monuments, and Bosnia and Herzegovina Public Corporations, as set forth in the Agreements at Annexes 5–9. The Parties shall fully respect and promote fulfillment of the commitments made therein.

## ARTICLE VII

Recognizing that the observance of human rights and the protection of refugees and displaced persons are of vital importance in achieving a lasting peace, the Parties agree to and shall comply fully with the provisions concerning human rights set forth in Chapter One of the Agreement at Annex 6, as well as the provisions concerning refugees and displaced persons set forth in Chapter One of the Agreement at Annex 7.

## ARTICLE VIII

The Parties welcome and endorse the arrangements that have been made concerning the implementation of this peace settlement, including in particular those pertaining to the civilian (non-military) implementation, as set forth in the Agreement at Annex 10, and the international police task force, as set forth in the Agreement at Annex 11. The Parties shall fully respect and promote fulfillment of the commitments made therein.

## ARTICLE IX

The Parties shall cooperate fully with all entities involved in implementation of this peace settlement, as described in the Annexes to this Agreement, or which are otherwise authorized by the United Nations Security Council, pursuant to the obligation of all Parties to cooperate in the investigation and prosecution of war crimes and other violations of international humanitarian law.

## ARTICLE X

The Federal Republic of Yugoslavia and the Republic of Bosnia and Herzegovina recognize each other as sovereign independent States within their international borders. Further aspects of their mutual recognition will be subject to subsequent discussions.

## ARTICLE XI

This Agreement shall enter into force upon signature.

DONE at Paris, this fourteenth day of December, 1995, in the Bosnian, Croatian, English and Serbian languages, each text being equally authentic.

ANNEXES*

| | |
|---|---|
| Annex 1-A | Agreement on Military Aspects of the Peace Settlement |
| Annex 1-B | Agreement on Regional Stabilization |
| Annex 2 | Agreement on Inter-Entity Boundary Line and Related Issues |
| Annex 3 | Agreement on Elections |
| Annex 4 | Constitution |
| Annex 5 | Agreement on Arbitration |
| Annex 6 | Agreement on Human Rights |
| Annex 7 | Agreement on Refugees and Displaced Persons |
| Annex 8 | Agreement on the Commission to Preserve National Monuments |
| Annex 9 | Agreement on Bosnia and Herzegovina Public Corporations |
| Annex 10 | Agreement on Civilian Implementation |
| Annex 11 | Agreement on International Police Task Force |

* Not included here.

# Index

# LSE MONOGRAPHS IN INTERNATIONAL STUDIES